Diction for Singers

Introduction

About this book

The following chapters will guide you to pronounce the sounds of English, Italian, Latin, French, German, and Spanish. This book does not presume to be an exhaustive account of the phonology of these languages. Rather it is intended as a concise reference for singers who need to pronounce these languages in their libretti or song texts. It is especially suited for use as an undergraduate text in diction classes and offers a solid foundation in pronouncing these languages, as well as future use as a standard reference.

Rules of pronunciation are important to learn—to know when to pronounce closed *e* and open *e*, for instance—because they will expedite your recognizing patterns in the languages. But the rules themselves are not the *most* important thing to emphasize. It is much more important to hear the speech patterns of each language and articulate them precisely, to learn to hear your own speech and the speech of others, and, finally, to refine your awareness of the delicate movements of your articulators and their effect on your speech sounds and singing tone.

Keep in mind that language is dynamic: within a language, even within a single native speaker, there are variations of pronunciation. The pronunciations are sometimes so irregular that even dictionaries disagree on them. The rules should not be considered as rigid truths for pronunciation in all cases, all the time: they are best considered merely as *tools* for recognizing recurring patterns in pronunciation.

How to use this book

Each chapter contains three sections. The first section is an "at-a-glance" chart of sounds. This chart is most helpful as a reminder of a particular pronunciation, or as a comparison of the sounds of one language to the next. For example, the letters *ai* appear in every language, each with a different pronunciation. In French, *mais* is pronounced [mɛ]; in German, *mai* is pronounced [mɑɪ]; in Latin *laicus* is pronounced ['lɑ i kus]. These different pronunciations of *ai* are easy to see on these charts. Of course, the chart will not by itself provide all that you need in order to pronounce the language: it is a reference best used after you have studied the language.

The middle section explains the *general tools* you need to pronounce that language. There are concise rules for how to divide a word into syllables, how to determine the stressing, and how to handle the special features of that language. These tools are condensed, streamlined, and organized to facilitate your learning them, to have them easily at hand to pry apart a spelling and extract its pronunciation. For instance, in the chapter on Spanish diction, under the special feature "Assimilation of *n*," you will learn when to pronounce *n* as *m*. Or, in the chapter on Italian diction, under the special feature "Consecutive Vowels," you will learn how to sing triphthongs when the composer has given you only one note for all three vowel sounds.

The third section is a detailed description of each vowel and consonant (and significant groupings of vowels and consonants) for that language. This section serves as a special resource, almost like a concise encyclopedia of letters and their corresponding sounds. For example, under The letter *e* in Italian, you will find a full discussion that includes how to handle the final *e*'s, when and where to pronounce *e* as *open* [ɛ] or *closed* [e] and the exceptions to those rules, and word examples to practice. Use this section as a special reference, a classroom drill, a source for more detailed information of each letter.

The International Phonetic Alphabet and Articulating Sounds

Successfully pronouncing a language will ultimately require skillful and flexible — sometimes subtle, almost imperceptible — adjustments of your lips, tongue, jaw, soft palate, and cheeks in order to produce a particular sound. You will discover that each sound is affected by *even the smallest movements of your articulators.*

All of the pronunciation rules and tips for pronouncing the various sounds of a language will have little meaning if you cannot produce a desired sound by skillful and subtle adjustments of your articulators. The companion book to this volume, International Phonetic Alphabet for Singers, will lead you through drills and exercises so that you can acquire the requisite use of your articulators. Those drills will help you learn to skillfully shape isolated sounds, make subtle adjustments, tune your ear and produce sounds with the expanded, refined discrimination you need as a singer. You will find that these skills will aid you considerably in mastering the pronunciation of each different language.

On the next two pages, you will find charts of the IPA symbols used throughout this text. Notice that there is a chart for vowels and another for consonants. These charts not only represent the individual sounds you must distinguish, but also describe a meaningful relationship between the sounds and how they are produced. The impact of this relationship on singing and diction is fully explored in the International Phonetic Alphabet for Singers.

Read through the following excerpts taken from the IPA for Singers to orient you to the charts.

Vowels

The sound you identify as a vowel sound is the result of the acoustical properties of your vocal tract (mouth, throat, and nose). Each vowel sound has a specific harmonic structure, governed by the position of your lips, jaw, tongue, and velum — articulators that change the size and shape of your vocal tract.

A diphthong may include a pure vowel and a glide, as in the word use [juz].

A vowel is called a pure vowel when its sound can be sustained without movement of the articulators or any change in the quality of sound until the air flow ceases. A diphthong is made up of two vowel sounds that have an acoustic result perceived as a single distinguishable unit. In English there are sixteen pure vowel sounds and six diphthongs.

The Vowel Diagram, created by Daniel Jones of University College, London, illustrates the relationship of vowels to each other. It was developed by taking X-ray images of the position of the tongue when articulating various vowels.

You will meet terms such as open e, *or* closed e, *which refer to the relative space between the tongue and the roof of the mouth when pronouncing a vowel. The space is more open for* open e *than* closed e, *for instance.*

On the diagram, the terms *forward, central,* and *back* refer to whether the high point of the tongue is forward, central or back in the mouth. *Closed, mid,* and *open* refer to the width of the space between the tongue and the roof of the mouth. The closer the tongue to the roof, the more closed the vowel. The more open the space and more dropped the jaw, the more open the vowel. The terms *rounding* and *unrounding* refer to the position of the lips. Most back vowels use rounded lips, while forward vowels are produced with unrounded lips.

The phrase a more rounded sound *generally refers to the sound made when the lips are more rounded. You will hear the French* schwa *described as a more round* schwa *than English, for instance.*

Adjoining vowels on the Vowel Diagram are very similar in their physical production. For example, the two vowels [i] and [ɪ], which are next to each other, are produced with minimal differences in the position of the tongue and jaw.

Introduction

4

In your vocal studies, you will investigate pure vowel production for good diction and you will also encounter vowel modification to govern tonal quality and vocal freedom. Vowel modification is the deliberate altering of a vowel sound by slightly opening or closing your mouth, rounding or unrounding your lips, or moving the body of your tongue more forward or back in your mouth. Learning to use modified vowels is an important and necessary part of your training that takes place in the vocal studio.

Explore the articulation of the two forward vowels [i] and [ɪ] by sustaining an [i] sound and then sliding slowly to [ɪ]. Feel the gradual and tiny movements of your tongue and jaw. The skill to discern when the [i] has finally opened enough to become [ɪ] is typical of the skills required to successfully learn diction.

Do the same exploration from [e] to [ɛ], or [æ] to [a]. Then feel the movements of your lips and jaw as you slide on the back vowels from [u] to [ʊ], or [o] to [ɔ]. Continue to slip around from vowel to vowel to experience the feeling and sounds of the adjoining vowels on the Vowel Diagram.

Vowel Diagram

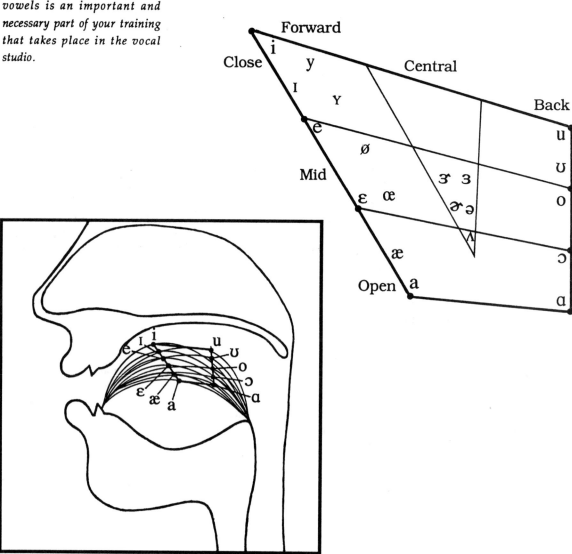

Consonants

A consonant is a speech sound that is formed when the articulators interrupt the flow of air through the vocal tract. Consonants are classified according to the place of articulation, the manner of articulation, and the voicing of the consonant.

The *place of articulation* refers to the place in the vocal tract where the interruption of the air flow occurs. The points of the vocal tract where breath interruption occurs are: the lips, teeth, tongue, alveolar ridge, hard palate, velum, and glottis. For example, the place of articulation for [p] is at the lips, because the flow of breath is interrupted at the lips.

The *manner of articulation* refers to the method of interruption of the breath flow, whether by a complete interruption or by a partial interruption in the flow of air. For example, the manner of articulation for [p] is that the air flow is stopped completely before being released suddenly.

There are six different manners of articulation.

1. Stop-plosive — the air flow is completely prevented from passing through the mouth or the nose and then is released suddenly. The stop-plosive consonants are [p b t d k g]. These consonants are sometimes referred to simply as *stop consonants*.

2. Fricative — the air flow is partially interrupted, thus producing a noisy sound. The fricative consonants in English are [f v], [θ ð], [ʃ ʒ], [s z], and [h].

3. Nasal — the vocal tract is blocked at some point within the oral cavity, but the dropped velum allows air to travel through the nasal passageway. There are only three nasal consonants in English: [m], [n], and *ng* [ŋ].

4. Lateral — the tongue tip lifts to touch the teeth and alveolar ridge and the breath flows past one or both sides of the tongue. There is only one lateral consonant in English: [l].

5. Glide — the sound is characterized by a movement of the articulators from one position to another. The glides in English are [r], the *y* sound [j], and [w].

6. Affricative — the sound is produced by a stop followed by a fricative consonant forming a single sound. The two affricate (or combination) consonants in English are *ch* [ʧ] as in *cheek* and *dg* [ʤ] as in *fudge*.

The classification of *voicing* indicates whether the consonant is produced with vocal fold vibration (voiced) or without vocal fold vibration (unvoiced). In English, there are several pairs of consonants (called cognates) that have the same place and manner of articulation. Cognates are differentiated only by the voicing. An example of cognates would be [p] and [b], or [f] and [v].

Consonant Chart

	Place of Articulation													
	Both Lips		Upper Teeth and Lower Lips		Tongue and Upper Teeth		Tongue and Teeth Ridge		Tongue and Hard Palate		Tongue and Soft Palate		Glottis	
	unv.	v.	unv.	v.	unv.	v.	unv.	v.	unv.	v.	unv.	v.	unv.	v.
Fricative		β	f	v	θ	ð	s	z	ʃ ç	ʒ	x	ɣ	h	
Stop-Plosive	p	b					t	d			k	g		
Nasal		m						n	ɲ			ŋ		
Lateral									l ʎ					
Glide	hw	ɥ w							r j					

Note: Additional symbols used in this text are the [ɾ], which represents the tongue tip flipped r, and [r̄], which represents trilled r.

English Diction

Phonology is the science of speech sounds.

As a speaker of American English, you have already acquired a large body of information (mostly unconscious) concerning the individual sounds and sound patterns of English. Bearing this in mind, you will not need to learn the phonological system of American English in detail. Rather, you will need to learn the specific issues that will enhance the musical and artistic expressiveness of your singing.

In the following sections you will read aloud many sample words that will help you become aware of your articulation habits in speech. You will find that these habits transfer into your singing. With an increased sensitivity to your own articulation, you can sing with clear diction, avoid typical problems of singing in English, and gain a new appreciation of how precise articulation results in effective singing diction — all of which helps lead to beautiful singing.

The chapter begins by describing the difference between *misarticulation* and *mispronunciation,* a helpful distinction when studying the other languages as well. Then, three basic guidelines that describe "good diction" are presented. Again, these guidelines apply to all languages. The third section will describe the typical problems that interfere with achieving good diction. It will include exercises to focus on each sound and bring into your awareness the problems associated with that sound. The rest of the chapter deals with the special topics relevant to singing in English.

Language Diction

Language diction is the study of two aspects of language, *articulation* and *pronunciation*. Keeping these two aspects in mind as you study diction will help direct your attention to understand and resolve diction problems.

Articulation is the process of forming or shaping the individual sounds of a language by the movements of the articulators.

Pronunciation is the selection of sounds and syllabic stress. For example, ea in English can be pronounced in a variety of ways, as in <u>ea</u>t, h<u>ea</u>d, pr<u>ea</u>mble. Selecting the sound to match the spelling is pronunciation.

While studying this text, we will present articulation rules, which will tell you how to produce a particular sound, and pronunciation rules, which will tell you which sounds to choose when you look at a spelling.

Misarticulations are errors in shaping specific speech sounds. These errors tend to generalize within a person's speech—that is, the same speech sound is often misarticulated in other words. For example, if you hear someone say [tɪn] instead of [tɛn] for the word *ten*, that person is misarticulating the phoneme [ɛ]. The tongue is arched too high and forward for [ɛ]. It is likely that that person will make this same articulation error in similar words (where the letter *e* is followed by a nasal consonant) and, for instance, will substitute [ɪ] for [ɛ] in these words: *tempt, when, pen, meant,* and *many.* As another example, you may hear someone say *d* in the word *these* (deez); that person is misarticulating the *th* [ð]. Again, this error would tend to generalize in that person's speech.

Mispronunciations, on the other hand, are errors in selecting the sounds to pronounce a word. These errors can typically be corrected simply by consulting a dictionary. They are not habits connected with producing a specific sound. A few common mispronunciations (mis-selections of sounds) are:

	incorrect	correct
prescription	[pɚskrɪpʃən]	[prəskrɪpʃən]
athletic	[æthə'lɛtɪk]	[æθ'lɛtɪk]
walk	[wɔlk]	[wɔk]

Since you already generally know (unconsciously) how to pronounce the spellings you see in English, this chapter is more concerned with articulation than with pronunciation. The other chapters of this book, however, are more concerned with pronunciation and how to select the appropriate sounds when you look at a word's spelling.

What is Good Diction?

It is possible to confuse good English diction with affected speech, because, in the beginning, clear articulate speech may sound artificial to you. However, since non-standard speech patterns or habits can distract the audience and divert their attention away from the tone and lyrics being sung, clear articulation is important for the artistry of your music. Precise diction, rather than being artificial, actually forms the springboard from which you can project your artistry outward to your audience.

You can evaluate singing diction by three characteristics: 1) whether the words are understandable, 2) whether the articulation and pronunciation is appropriate for the music and the occasion, and 3) whether or not the diction calls attention to itself.

Understandable Words:
How many times have you heard American opera singers singing in English and thought they were singing in a foreign language? Consider how much of their artistry was lost, how much of the libretto's impact was diluted. Consider why — even though these singers were pronouncing their own language — their words were not understandable. How were they using their articulators — their lips, tongue, jaw, soft palate, velum — to obscure the intelligibility of the words and the meaning of the language?

Achieving understandable words in a song is invaluable and requires special attention. To sing understandable words, keep in mind the following considerations.

— *articulate the sounds of the language—the vowels and the consonants—with precision, clarity, and good projective energy.* Phonetically, words and sentences are nothing more than a stream of consonants and vowels. In casual speech, you *think* a whole sentence and automatically produce a stream of vowels and consonants—however, any unconscious habits, deletions, and errors automatically stream out as well. In singing, you need to break down the sentence into each individual consonant and vowel, and shape the articulation of them with precision and energy. They should not be unconsciously slurred over. Like a loomsmith examining each thread before weaving it into a tapestry, consider the articulation of each sound as essential to the overall impact of your singing.

— *be sure the vowels and consonants that you are singing are actually the ones written in the words.* The number of people who unknowingly misarticulate sounds in our language is surprising. They will habitually substitute such sounds as *aw* [ɔ] for *ah* [ɑ] (saying [hɔrt] instead of [hɑrt] for the word *heart*) or substitute [d] for [t] (saying *priddy* for *pretty*). Listen to the sounds you are articulating and learn to cut through your habits and use your articulators with finesse.

— *stay aware of the vowels you are singing, even when you are modifying a vowel to achieve a more resonant tone.* You need to distinguish between when you are modifying a vowel because of artistic choice and when you are modifying a vowel because of misarticulation. You may have heard singers who over-modify all of their vowels. Their diction becomes muddy,

It is not pretentious or artificial to speak distinctly, although it may be unfamiliar at first. Language is music when all the sounds of a word are clearly said. Arthur Lessac likened the individual consonants to different instruments in an orchestra, each one punctuating the stream of vowel sounds with its particular timbre. The analogy is fine — learn to "play" consonants, to sing them artistically, with sensitivity, with expressiveness, with color.

IPA for Singers *is the companion articulation workbook that will guide you in acquiring these skills with precision.*

Sometimes the muddiness of a singer's diction—where the vowels all sound alike and the consonants seem all but absent— is due to a well-intended effort to achieve an even tone, a continuous ring in the voice, which is an issue of resonance. However, an even resonance can be maintained while you sing a wide range of clear, distinct vowel sounds, and rich, vibrant consonant sounds. As you iron out the wrinkles in your resonance, be careful not to iron out the dist-inctiveness of the vowels and the richness of the consonants.

This text reflects General American Speech. Kenyon and Knott's A Pronouncing Dictionary of American English will also distinguish General American Speech pronunciations from regional dialect pronunciations for you.

unexpressive, indistinct: instead of teeming with rich, clear, distinct sounds, the words all tend to sound alike.

— *articulate the consonants precisely enough for the audience to discern where the words begin and end.* As a soloist in operas, art song recitals, and in concerts with symphony orchestras, you will sing in large halls, and, for your words to be heard and understood in these large performance spaces, you must learn to fully articulate consonants. Well-resonated vowels will give your voice its carrying power and loudness, but it is your skillful articulation of consonants that gives projection to your words, defines when and where your words begin and end, and delivers the intelligibility of the poem or libretto.

— *connect the words together in a way that follows the natural flow of the language and includes meaningful stressing.* Much of a sentence's intelligibility is communicated by the pattern of stressing among the words, the give and take of emphasis, the rhythm. Avoid over-separating words, over-stressing syllables or words, and giving equally heavy stress to each syllable or word, and learn to allow meaningful, dynamic stressing and unstressing within a group of words.

Appropriate Articulation and Pronunciation:

It is important that your diction be appropriate to your music and your audience. You will need to discriminate among your diction choices to know the difference between when you are singing with repetitive speech habits and when you are making artistic diction choices, and to know the difference between General American Speech and non-standard speech.

When singing art songs and opera, use stage diction, or General American Speech, the most accepted prestige dialect in the United States. In concert performances, General American speech artistically supports the content of the music. Your diction would be inappropriate and would not serve your music if you used a non-standard pronunciation or dialect while singing this literature.

When singing a wide variety of styles of music, you may need to vary your diction. In some songs by Charles Ives, for example, you may need to sing with non-standard dialects. Broadway, pop, folk, or jazz singing will all demand their own diction. Your articulation and pronunciation should match the style and content of the music and occasion, otherwise it will interfere with the music.

Non-obtrusive Articulation and Pronunciation:

Singing diction is effective when it does not distract the listeners by calling attention to itself. It should unobtrusively support and enhance the music. Diction habits that call attention to themselves include over-articulation, muffled or slurred articulation, mispronunciations, regionalisms, and other typical diction problems that you will find discussed later in this chapter.

Typical Diction Problems

In this section we will describe the typical diction problems that prevent singing with good diction as defined above and will offer exercises and solutions to clarify them. When in casual speech, these problems (unless you are listening for them) may hardly seem noticeable and may just seem part of the speakers "personality." In singing, however, these problems become glaring and can be quite distracting. These typical problems fall under specific classifications: muffledness, substitution, addition and omission of sounds, and mis-stressing. Perhaps the most prominent problem is *muffledness*.

Muffledness

The speech problem called *muffledness* results from sluggish articulation of consonants. There are three types of muffledness: *incomplete closure* for the stop-plosive consonants, *incomplete friction* for the fricative consonants, and *insufficient nasality* for the nasal consonants. We will examine each of these separately.

Muffledness due to incomplete closure

Incomplete closure means that the articulators are not closed enough to completely stop the air flow for the stop-plosive consonants [p b t d k g]. The following exercises focus on these stop plosives individually.

The stop-plosive consonants [p] and [b]

To say the consonants [p] and [b], your lips should be firmly pressed together. Most people articulate initial [p] and [b] reasonably well, yet use incomplete closure in the medial and final positions.

Notice your own articulation habits as you read the words below. Are you completely closing your lips? Can you feel the difference between complete and incomplete closure?

Read aloud.

Initial [p]	[b]
peg	beg
post	boast

Once you begin to experience clean, precise diction, you may be amazed to notice how many people speak and sing with muffledness.

A stop-plosive consonant is one in which the air flow is completely prevented from passing through the mouth or the nose and then is released suddenly. For full discussion of stop-plosive consonants, refer to page 5.

A consonant is a speech sound produced by stopping or restricting the air flow. The tongue and the lips work together to restrict the air flow. There is little leeway for these articulators to be mis-placed.

Medial [p]	[b]
happy	abbey
puppy	bubble
rumple	rumble
helpful	probably
Final [p]	[b]
rope	robe
cap	cab

The stop-plosive consonants [t] and [d]

The consonants [t] and [d] appear frequently in English words. Sing the word *pretty* (select any pitch) and then sing the common misarticulation *preddy*. Feel the difference between the articulation of the unvoiced [t] and voiced [d].

Notice how firm your closure is for each of the words listed below. Can you feel the tip of your tongue press firmly against the alveolar ridge for each [t] and [d], particularly in the medial and final positions?

Throughout this book, read the examples to bring the point of the exercise into your awareness. Then sing a few of the words. Pick any pitch, any rhythm, and carry the focus of the exercise into a melodic line.

Read aloud.

Initial [t]	[d]
tie	die
ton	don

Medial [t]	[d]
plotting	plodding
matter	madder
latter	ladder
patted	padded
shutter	shudder
pretty	(not *preddy*)
city	(not *cidy*)
little	(not *liddle*)

Final [t]	[d]
wrote	road
tight	tide

These paired words will help you articulate a well-formed [t].

Read aloud.

bit her	bitter
bet her	better
but her	butter
sit he	city
let her	letter
it he	pretty

lit her	little
it his	it is easy
hit him	hit a ball
what he	what is that
thought high	thought I would

Notice that when the final letter *d* follows a voiced consonant, it is pronounced as voiced [d]. However, when *d* follows an unvoiced consonant, it is pronounced [t].

Read aloud.

[t]	[d]
clipped	hummed
kicked	sunned

The stop-plosive consonants [k] and [g]

For [k] and [g], the back of the tongue must be firmly pressed against the soft palate. As you read aloud these words, notice whether you can feel the back of your tongue touch the soft palate and completely close as you say [k] and [g].

Read aloud.

Initial [k]	[g]
kit	give
cane	gain

Medial [k]	[g]
racket	ragged
wicks	wigs

Final [k]	[g]
luck	lug
tack	tag

These words end with [sk], [skt], or [sks]. Be sure to use firm closure on the [k] sound. Do not omit it!

Read aloud.

asked	basks	desks	risk
whisk	disc	husks	tasks

The sound [k] in these common words must be fully stopped. Feel your articulation.

Read aloud.

acceptable	chicken
aching	accede
talkative	working
succulent	lucky
backing	

You have probably heard people fail to completely stop the [g] in words when it should have full closure. How do you say the [g] in these words? Feel the closure for [g].

Read aloud.

ignition   cognition
recognize

Note: The letter *g* is silent in these words.

Read aloud.

diaphragm   phlegm
sign   designer
resign

Note: The letter *g* is pronounced in these words; compare with the preceding list.

Read aloud.

signal   phlegmatic
signify   malignant
resignation

The combination consonant *x* [ks] or [gz]

The letter *x* in English, [ks] or [gz], is a combination consonant that has two pronunciations, both of which include a stop-plosive sound. Be sure to give the stop-plosive consonants [k] and [g] full closure in these two sounds.

When the letter *x* precedes a consonant sound, including a pronounced *h*, use [ks].

extra   expect
exhale   expense
excite   expel
excel   experiment
exclaim

When the letter *x* is final, pronounce it as [ks].

fox   box
ax

When the letter *x* is followed by a vowel and the primary stress falls on the initial *ex*, pronounce it as [ks].

exit   exodus
exercise   exorable

These rules describe how the letter x's pronunciation is dependent upon its position in the word and its neighboring letters. You will meet similar rules later in the book as you study other languages. You will see them written in this pattern: "When this letter is in this position, pronounce it this way; when in that position, pronounce it that way". Each language will have similarities and differences for individual letters and their position in the word. The chart of sounds at the beginning of each chapter will help you keep the languages straight.

When the letter *x* is followed by a vowel or silent *h*, pronounce it as [gz].

exalt	exotic
exist	example
examination	exactly
exhaust	exhilarate
exhume	

Muffledness due to incomplete friction

A singer's diction can be muffled because of incomplete friction in the formation of the fricative consonants [f v θ ð s z ʃ ʒ h]. To produce these consonants, your mouth cavity should be narrowed so that the air flow is restricted, except for *h*, where the restriction is at the glottis. If the mouth cavity is not narrowed enough or if the sound is not maintained for enough duration, the consonant sounds will become indistinct, or will almost sound like a stop consonant.

Read through the following exercises and explore the sounds of these fricative consonants. Learn to savor them, enrich them, draw out the special sound qualities inherent in each: they can add tremendous vibrancy and expressiveness to your diction.

Fricatives are also called continuants because they can be sustained or continued.

The fricative consonants [f] and [v]

Read aloud, sustaining each consonant sound for four slow counts.

```
        1   2   3   4
[f]_____
[v]_____
```

Be sure that you give sufficient duration to the [f] and [v] sounds, particularly when they are in the final position of a word. You will know whether you have sufficient duration when the consonant is truly fricative and not a stop. Feel a gentle, buzzy vibration on your lower lip. You will feel a stronger vibration as you articulate the voiced [v] than the unvoiced [f]. Feel and listen for the vibration.

Read aloud.

Initial [f]	[v]
fail	vail
fat	vat
Medial [f]	**[v]**
refer	reveal
leafer	lever
coffer	cover
muffler	gravestone
after	everyone
graphmaker	driveway

Final [f]	[v]
half	have
proof	prove
safe	save

The fricative consonants [θ] and [ð]

The name of the symbol [θ] is theta; [ð] is ethe or crossed d.

Pay attention to your articulation of unvoiced *th* [θ] and voiced *th* [ð]. Be sure to pronounce these fricative consonants with sufficient duration. Slip the rim of the tongue between the upper and lower front teeth. Neither force the breath nor bite down on the tongue. On the voiced [ð], as in the word *these*, feel a tingling vibration on the tip of your tongue outside of the teeth.

Read aloud sustaining each consonant sound for four slow counts.

```
              1    2    3    4
unvoiced  [θ_____]
(as in thing)
voiced    [ð_____]
(as in these)
```

What are your articulation habits with [θ] and [ð]? Do you use sufficient friction? Be sure to give [ð] longer duration.

Read aloud.

Initial [θ]	[ð]
thin	them
third	these

Medial [θ]	[ð]
faithful	clothes (not *close*)
method	weather
ethics	rather
ethereal	loathsome
birthday	breathe deeply
pathway	bathe daily
north wind	smooths
worth it	worthy

Final [θ]	[ð]
loath	loathe
forsooth	soothe
sheath	sheathe

The fricative [ð] must not sound like a stop consonant. Definitely do not substitute a [d] for [ð], as you hear occasionally in dialects. To avoid saying [d] be sure the tip of your tongue slips between the teeth.

Read aloud.

[d]	[ð]
dare	there
day	they
dine	thine
dough	though

If your tongue feels thick and awkward as you pronounce the fricative [ð], it is probably because this articulation is unfamiliar. Give yourself time and repetition to get the tongue to move smoothly and fluidly.

Be sure to give fricative duration to a *th* after a consonant.

Read aloud.

Just think.
Fast thinking.
Pick the winner!
Can this be so!
(Feel the gentle movement of the tip of the tongue as it glides from behind the upper teeth for the [n] in *can* to the [ð] of *this* in the sentence: "Can this be so!")

Be sure that [ð] is fully voiced and has good duration. Enjoy the long, buzzy sound of [ð].

Pronounce the *th* in consonant clusters.

Read aloud.

[θ]	[ð]
earth's	soothes
anthem	clothed
fifth	truths
youth's	breathes
anesthetic	mouthed
width	rhythm

The fricative consonants [s] and [z]

To avoid muffled diction, articulate the consonants [s] and [z] cleanly and clearly. Compare and contrast unvoiced [s] and voiced [z] as you complete the following exercises.

Read aloud, sustaining each sound for four slow counts.

	1	2	3	4
unvoiced	[s_____]			
voiced	[z_____]			

Some people misarticulate s and z by mis-placement of the tongue. The result is called a lisp. Additional attention must be given to these sounds if you have a lisp.

Initial [s]	[z]
sip	zip
sink	zinc
Medial [s]	[z]
lacy	lazy
misty	music
pencil	puzzle
Final [s]	[z]
bets	beds
a piece	appease
this	these

There are two combination consonants that include both a stop and a fricative consonant: *ts*[ts] and *dz*[dz]. Read these words, carefully articulating these two sounds.

Read aloud using *ts* [ts].

bets	thefts
cats	artists
limits	

Read aloud using *dz* [dz].

bends	beads
holds	scalds
demands	

The fricative consonants [ʃ] and [ʒ]

To avoid muffled diction, articulate [ʃ] as in *she* and [ʒ] as in *azure* or *vision* with sufficient friction and duration.

Read aloud, sustaining each sound for four slow counts.

	1	2	3	4	
unvoiced	[ʃ_____]
voiced	[ʒ_____]

There is no initial [ʒ] in English.

Read aloud.

Initial [ʃ]	
sure	
sheep	
Medial [ʃ]	[ʒ]
assure	visual
ocean	delusion
Final [ʃ]	[ʒ]
cash	beige
mash	mirage

The fricative consonant [h]

The consonant *h* is an aspirate sound in English. It needs to be heard, but not over-aspirated. Be sure that you use suitable friction.

Read aloud.
Initial [h]
half   hold
head   heat

Be careful to pronounce *h* clearly in each of these phrases.

Read aloud.
That's his job.
We forgave her.
How could he do it?
I told him.

Medial *h* is sometimes pronounced, sometimes silent.

Pronounce *h* in these words.

Read aloud.
exhale   prohibit
unholy   mishap
inhuman

Do not pronounce the *h* in these words. It is silent.

Read aloud.
prohibition   exhaust
exhibit   exhilarate

Muffledness due to insufficient nasalization

There are three nasal consonants in English: [m], [n], and *ng* [ŋ]. When you sing with a well articulated nasal consonant, your diction will become more understandable and expressive, and your vocalization will improve. Without sufficient duration or nasalization of the three nasal consonants, your diction and vocalization will suffer. You will sound as though you've got a cold in your head—very muffled.

A special feature of English is that when a nasal consonant is located in a word before another consonant or before a silence (before a pause at the end of a phrase, for instance), it is pronounced with a longer duration than when it is before a vowel.

Nasal consonants are defined as those produced with air flowing through the nasal passages. They are also called continuants, because they can be sustained, or continued. Singers usually hum on an [m] sound, but they can hum successfully on any of the three nasal consonants.

Singers can also hum on enya [ɲ], a nasal consonant in Italian and French.

The letter *m*

In the following words, each *m* is positioned before a consonant or silence. Take the opportunity to say the long nasal consonants. Feel as though you are humming the [m] as you speak these words. Let the [m] sound sing-out in your speech and in your singing.

Read aloud, letting each underlined *m* vibrate fully.

limber	named	amplify	rumble
farmed	comfort	thimble	hamster
some	deem	him	home
slam	ham	hem	sum

Read aloud this sentence, giving long duration to the underlined *m*'s.

Sometimes it causes me to tremble, tremble, tremble...("Were You There," a spiritual)

The word *tremmmmmmble* sung with a long *m* has quite a different rhythm than *treeeeeeemble* sung with a long vowel. You may notice how the lengthening of the consonant sound [m] results in a shorter vowel duration. Observing this element of duration in singing is important for effective diction.

The letter n

Notice how you articulate the consonant [n]. Does the tip of your tongue lightly touch the boundary between the alveolar ridge and the teeth? It should: if it doesn't, put it there. Make a gentle humming sound and feel the vibration at the tip of the tongue.

In English, just like [m], the sound of [n] has longer duration before a consonant or a silence than before a vowel. Bring this sound into your awareness by vibrating each [n] fully.

Read aloud.

concave	infantile	confuse	unprovoked
consent	mention	canyon	unrestrained
incident	conflict	clean	when
cone	win	spin	plan

Notice the natural rhythm of these words in which *n* is followed by a vowel. The duration of the sound of [n] will be shorter than in the words above.

Read aloud.

honey	money	many	penny
any	bunny	not	net
sunny	tunnel	winner	loner

The sound of *ng* [ŋ]

Pronounce the sound of *ng* [ŋ] as in *sing*. Be sure to use a firm closure between the back of your tongue and the velum. Notice that these words end with the sound [ŋ] and they do not include a [g] sound. *Hang* is [hæŋ] not [hæŋg].

Allow the final [ŋ] to vibrate with good duration.

Read aloud.

sing	thing	throng	fling
gong	stung	hung	long
cling	song	ring	king
tongue	rang	young	swing

Be sure that you do not add a [g] sound after the [ŋ] (say *banging* [bæŋɪŋ], not [bæŋgɪŋ]).

Read aloud.

banging	singing	flinging
springing	clinging	longing
hangar	wronging	wringing

Be sure that you do not substitute [n] for [ŋ] in the *-ing* suffix. For instance, do not say *cookin'* for *cooking*.

Read aloud.

baking	parking	aching
looking	working	talking

Some speakers incorrectly use what may be called an "ng click;" that is, they put a [g] or [k] sound at word boundaries. Listen carefully to your articulation as you read these words aloud. Use firm closure for [ŋ] and move cleanly to the next sound without an "ng click".

Read aloud.

a long way
hang it up
the thing is
the song is

These words are correctly pronounced with a [k] sound after [ŋ].

Read aloud.

bank	banker
Lincoln	drunk
wrinkle	drunkard
think	ankle

These words are correctly pronounced with a [g] sound after [ŋ].

Read aloud.

finger	stronger
language	angle
single	England

Omission of Sounds

A singer may occasionally omit sounds that should be pronounced in standard speech. Often these omissions are simply mispronunciations that can be corrected by consulting a dictionary, such as Kenyon and Knott's <u>A</u> <u>Pronouncing</u> <u>Dictionary</u> <u>of</u> <u>American</u> <u>English</u>.

At other times, however, the omitted sounds are habitual misarticulations, which tend to follow common patterns.

Read aloud these words. Do you tend to omit any of the indicated sounds?

1. Pronounce the [k] sound in these words using firm closure.

ask (not *ax*)	asked (not *axed*)
disc (not *diss*)	discs
task	tasks
basked	adjective
act	contact
reject	liked

2. Pronounce the [t] and [ts] sounds in these words using firm closure.

kept (not *kep'*)	tourists (not *touriss*)
tact (not *tac'*)	tests
texts	last

3. What about these final consonants? Pronounce them clearly.

   clasp (not *class*)
   bulb
   bland

4. The *th* sounds, [θ] and [ð], are often omitted by American speakers. What do you do in your speech?

myths (not *miss*)	earth's
youth's	breathes
writhes	soothes
clothed	breathed
bathed	anthem
rhythm	fifths
sixths	depths

5. And what about these sentences? Do you say all the sounds?

I'm going to (not *Ah'm gonna* nor *Ah'muh nuh*)
Give me (not *Gimme*)
Help me (not *Hep me*)

Addition of Sounds

Some singers add sounds that should not be there. The following lists include examples. Listen carefully to your speech. Do you add any of these sounds?

1. In some dialects, an [r] is added to a vowel that occurs at the end of a syllable, or even within a word.

   Read aloud.

wash	not	*warsh*
idea	not	*idear*
Linda	not	*Lindar*
piano	not	*pianer*
banana	not	*bananer*

   Louisiana and Arkansas
              not *Lousianar* and *Arkansas*

2. How do you say the important word, *accompanist*?

   Do you say *ac-com-pa-nist* or *ac-com-pani-ist*, adding the extra vowel *i* in the third syllable?

3. Some speakers add schwa [ə] preceding an [r] or [l].

   Read aloud.

fierce	[fɪrs]	not	[fɪərs]
wheel	[whil]	not	[whiəl]
meal	[mil]	not	[miəl]
sail	[seɪl]	not	[seɪəl]

4. In these words the letter *l* is silent. Be careful not to add [l].

   Read aloud.

walk	[wɔk]	not	[wɔlk]
talk	[tɔk]	not	[tɔlk]
calm	[kɑm]	not	[kɑlm]
psalm	[sɑm]	not	[sɑlm]

5. Do you inadvertently add a [j] between words that end and begin with a vowel?

   Read aloud.

I am	not	*I yam*

Substitution of Sounds

Sometimes misarticulations are classified as *substitutions of sounds*, which simply means that when you expect to hear one sound, you hear another.

Substitutions are caused by an habitual mis-use of one or more of the articulators. For example, if a singer's tongue is habitually too far forward in the mouth for an [ɛ] when it is before [n], *pen* will sound like *pin, hen* like *hin, den* like *din*. However, that same singer may have little or no difficulty articulating [ɛ] before [d] or [t], as in *bed* or *bet*.

Substitutions can be either isolated in a specific speech sound or be part of regional dialects: New Englanders typically substitute [a] for [ɑ] and say pahk the cah *for* park the car; *and New Yorkers typically substitute* Earl *for* oil, *for example.*

Any sequence of sounds may trigger an habitual mis-use of one or more of the articulators resulting in substitutions. A few common patterns are listed below.

Lips

[ʊ] is substituted for [u] when the lips are too lax and unrounded.
>   *wooed* sounds like *would*

[ɝ] is substituted for [ɔɪ] when the lips are too unrounded.
>   *oil* sounds like *Earl*
>   *foil* sounds like *furl*
>   *boil* sounds like *beryl*

The vowel [ʊ], as in look, good, book, *and* took *is commonly misarticulated by singers. Learn to zero-in precisely on this vowel.*

[ɑ] is substituted for [ɔ] also when the lips are too unrounded.
>   *caught* sounds like *cot*

[ɔ] is substituted for [ɑ] when the lips are too rounded.
>   *star* sounds like *stawr*
>   *lard* sounds like *lord*
>   *ardor* sounds like *order*

[o] is substituted for [ɔ] also when the lips are too rounded.
>   *bought* sounds like *boat*
>   *off* sounds like *oaf*

Jaw

[ʊ] is substituted for [ʌ] when the jaw fails to drop and the mouth is too closed.
>   *love* [lʌv] will sound like [lʊv]

Tongue

[e] is substituted for [ɛ] when the tongue is brought too high and forward.
>   *egg* [ɛg] will sound like [eg]
>   *leg* [lɛg] will sound like [leg]
>   *treasure* ['trɛ ʒɚ] will sound like ['tre ʒɚ]

[ɪ] is substituted for [ɛ] also when the tongue is brought too high and forward.
>   *tent* sounds like *tint*
>   *tempt* sounds like *timpt*
>   *men* sounds like *min*

[ɪ] or [ɛ] is substituted for [ʌ] when the tongue is too high and too forward.

> *just a minute* sounds like *jist a minute* or *jest a minute*

[æ] is substituted for [ɛ] when the tongue is too far down and back.

> *guess* sounds like *gas*

[a] is substituted for [aɪ] when the tongue is too lax.

> *fight* [faɪt] sounds like [fat]
> *height* [haɪt] sounds like *hot* [hat]

[s] is substituted for [θ] when the tip of the tongue is too far back.

> *thick* sounds like *sick*

[d] is substituted for [ð] when the tongue is too far back.

> *them* sounds like *dem*

Velum

Nasal [ẽɪ] is substituted for [eɪ] when the velum is lazy and dropped.

> *main* [meɪn] sounds like [mẽɪn]

Voicing and unvoicing

[p] is substituted for [b] when there is inadequate voicing.

> *cab* sounds like *cap*

[k] is substituted for [g] also when there is inadequate voicing.

> *tag* sounds like *tak*

All speech sounds can have substitutions. Those listed above are just a few of them. Notice that they all relate to habits of using the articulators. You will want to keep your articulators flexible, capable of refined movements, and not locked into habitual patterns. To become a masterful singer, you will want to acquire exquisite control of moving your tongue, lips, cheeks, jaw, and velum—and move them independently of each other.

However, because substitutions generally occur out of awareness, you will need to listen to your own speech with special attention. A substitution will feel and sound normal to you—after all, it will be a familiar habit—so you will need to discriminate carefully among the sounds you think you hear and the sounds you are actually producing.

The workbook <u>International</u> <u>Phonetic</u> <u>Alphabet</u> <u>for</u> <u>Singers</u> is a special resource that will help you clarify each of the speech sounds in English. Detailed descriptions of each sound, lists of sample words that compare and contrast sounds, singing exercises and numerous articulation drills are laid out so that you can learn to discriminate, isolate, and produce specific sounds with skill.

A tongue habitually carried too far down and back in the mouth might result in substitutions with the entire series of forward vowels.

The articulation habit of using a too high and forward position of the tongue results in a thin vocal quality.

The articulation habit of using a retracted tongue results in a throaty, muffled, dark vocal quality.

Nasalization of vowels tends to occur before nasal consonants.

Mis-Placed Stress

In any language, the manner of handling stress within a word or a phrase is an element of diction that is critical for correct pronunciation and understandable words.

Stressing in English is accomplished by patterns of strong-weak emphasis that occur at fairly regular intervals. English uses a secondary stress to maintain a similar time length between strong stresses. (Other languages, by contrast, permit only one primary stress in a phrase followed by several weak stresses.) English also has the phenomenon of unstressing. Unstressing means, as the name suggests, pronouncing syllables with weak intensity and short duration. In unstressed syllables, American speakers actually change the normal vowel sound to an indistinct, brief *uh* [ə] or *ih* [ɪ]. For example, in the word *demon* ['di mən] the unstressed second syllable uses the weak [ə] and not the stressed vowel sound of *o* [o].

In singing, you must be careful to pronounce the unstressed vowels properly—otherwise the words will sound pretentious and will become more difficult to understand.

> In the following words, notice the underlined unstressed vowels. Do you pronounce these syllables with [ə] or [ɪ]?
>
> Read aloud.
>
> | pall<u>i</u>d | ['pæ lɪd] | lett<u>u</u>ce | ['lɛ təs] |
> | breakf<u>a</u>st | ['brɛk fəst] | el<u>e</u>ment | ['ɛ lə mənt] |
> | <u>a</u>nal<u>y</u>s<u>i</u>s | [ə 'næ lə səs] | or [ə 'næ lɪ sɪs] | |
> | beaut<u>i</u>ful | ['bju tə fəl] | or ['bju tɪ fəl] | |

The difference in stressing among various languages is one of the major elements that creates the unique nationalistic flavors in songs from different cultures. Language and its pattern of stress has enormous impact on phrasing and the shape of the melodic line. This is one of the reasons why translations of the lyrics are not often very successful.

As a singer, you are challenged with the task of maintaining the naturalness of language even when the stresses of the music seem to contradict the normal stresses of the words. By keeping the play of the stresses as you sing the melodic line, the meaning and expression in the words have a chance to spring out. Sadly, you will hear singers — too focused on tonal quality, perhaps — who neglect the normal stress and rhythm of the words, who over-articulate with equal, heavy stress on every syllable. As a result, their diction becomes obtrusive, their words difficult to understand, the meaning of the text snuffed out. Instead of the poetry and music fusing together, the pretentious sounding quality that emerges is, on occasion, almost comical and causes the singers to lose dramatic and artistic believability.

A simple, yet effective method for carrying the stress and rhythm of the words into the melodic line is to read the poem aloud as a dramatic reading, which will establish the meaning of the poem and the individual phrases in order to find the natural stressing. Immediately after the reading, sing the phrases so that you can transfer the pattern of meaningful stress from speech into song. Or, as an interim step between speaking and singing, you might speak the text with exaggerated inflection (talk-sing), and approximate the outline of your melodic line immediately after the dramatic reading.

Other Special Diction Considerations in English

We have defined good diction as when the words are intelligible and appropriate for the music and occasion, and the diction does not call attention to itself. Then we described the typical problems that interfere with achieving it—muffledness, omission and addition of sounds, substitution of sounds, mis-placed stress. There are, however, other special considerations that need attention when singing in English.

Diphthongs

A diphthong is a vowel unit made up of two pure vowels with the acoustic result being perceived as a single unit. There are four diphthongs in English:

> [aɪ] as in *high, I, my, lie*
> [aʊ] as in *house, bounce, brow, cow*
> [ɔɪ] as in *boy, toy, boil, poise*
> [ju] as in *use, huge, music, cube*

For the diphthongs [aɪ], [aʊ], and [ɔɪ] sing the first vowel with a long duration and then glide to the second vowel just as you release the note.

Sing these words containing diphthongs:

[aɪ] *height:* [ha - - ɪt]
[aʊ] *house:* [hɑ - - ʊs]
[ɔɪ] *boy:* [bɔ - - ɪ]

Sing the diphthong [ju] differently. Glide quickly past the first sound of [j] and then sing the second vowel for a longer duration.

Sing these words.

[ju] *use:* [ju - - z]
[ju] *huge:* [hju - - ʤ]
[ju] *cube:* [kju - - b]

Singing without natural stressing is particularly unsuccessful in popular music, where it is appropriate to use more informal speech.

The sound [ju] is sometimes classified as a glide instead of a diphthong.

The Retroflex r

The English consonant *r* does not exist in other languages. It is called a *retroflex r* because the tip of the tongue is curled up and backwards. The tip of the tongue does not make contact with any part of the roof of the mouth as it would in other languages where the *r* is flipped or trilled.

When *r* occurs initially in a word or syllable, it is a brief, gliding consonant sound. You will sing it just like you speak it.

> Read aloud these words with *retroflex r*.
> Initial [r]: rose, red, write, rich
> Initial consonant plus [r]: bring, brought, shrewd, shrill
> Medial [r], beginning a syllable: very, weary, direct, arrive

The R-colored Vowels [ɝ] and [ɚ]
and the R-Less Vowels [ɜ] and [ə]

When the letter *r* follows a vowel in the same syllable, the *r* often loses its consonant quality and blends with the preceding vowel to become an r-colored vowel.

The r-colored vowel sound is produced with the tip of the tongue retracted and suspended in the center of the mouth. Many people are unaware that this vowel sound exists in our language.

The IPA symbol [ɝ] represents the r-colored vowel sound in stressed syllables and the IPA symbol [ɚ] represents the r-colored vowel in unstressed syllables. [ɝ] and [ɚ] are actually the same sound: they are used to indicate difference in stressing.

Stressed ur [ɝ] *is also called* r-colored vowel *or* hooked reverse epsilon.

Instressed ur [ɚ] *is also called* hooked schwa.

> Read aloud the following words that contain [ɝ] in stressed syllables.
> > fur, burr, her, sir, learn, mercy, dirty, purple, earth

> Read aloud the following words that contain [ɚ] in unstressed syllables.
> > ever, scepter, sugar, dollar, mirror, humor, measure, pleasure

The r-colored vowels offer a challenge in singing. The suspension of the tip of the tongue in the center of the mouth results in a tense vocal production and a tonal quality that is unpleasant on long, sustained notes.

Fortunately, there is a simple, two-step solution.

Step One: Simply drop the r-color. Sing the r-less vowel [ɜ] in stressed syllables and r-less *schwa* [ə] in unstressed syllables. Again, these two symbols represent the same sound and are used only to indicate the difference in stressing.

You can find the sound of dropping the *r* by saying the following words using a southern or British accent. Just pretend you are Scarlett O'Hara or Rhett Butler in "Gone With the Wind."

Read aloud using [ɜ] in stressed syllables. Be sure to drop the "*r*".

girl, hurt, lurk, earth, curb

Read aloud using [ə] in unstressed syllables. Be sure to drop the "*r*".

summer, brother, mother, actor, dollar, humor

Step Two: Add a soft gliding [r] after the vowel, just as you release the sound.

The result of these two steps is easy vocalization and good, clear diction. Your audience will be unaware of your articulation adjustments. And they will easily understand your words.

Sing these words with stressed [ɜ] followed by a soft [r].

bird	[bɜ -	(r)d]
earth	[ɜ -	(r)θ]
fur	[fɜ- -	(r)]

Sing these words with unstressed [ə] followed by a soft [r].

dollar	['dɑ -	lə(r)]
ever	['ɛ -	və(r)]
mirror	['mɪ -	rə(r)]

Timing Your Articulation in Singing

Timing your articulation with the music is an expressive and important element of diction. Words have their own unique rhythm in speech which must be also observed in singing. To prevent your words from dragging behind the beat, you must put the vowel directly on the beat — which, of course, means that the previous consonant must anticipate the beat.

Stressed r-less ur *is also called* reversed epsilon.

You might notice that singing on [ʌ] *with slightly rounded lips produces the sound of* [ɜ]. *But you must round your lips: otherwise bird* [bɜrd], *for instance, will sound like bud* [bʌd].

You may notice that the sound of [ɜ] *is similar to the sound of umlauted ö* [œ] *in German. However, the lips are more rounded for* [œ] *less than for* [ɜ].

As an exercise, sing only the vowels in the line taken from from the Christmas carol "Hark! The Herald Angels Sing." Feel a clear pulse on the underlined vowels.

Hark	the	herald	angels	sing
[ɑ̠	ə	ɛ ə	e̠ɪ ə	ɹ]

Now add the consonants, but keep the underlined vowels on the beat. Repeat this exercise with your own songs.

Sounds in Connected Speech

The previous sections have been concerned with individual sounds. This section will focus on groups of sounds and the way that words or phrases link or blend together. You will find that certain sounds can be modified by the surrounding sounds when they are linked together.

Under several common circumstances, a sound in a word may appropriately disappear. This phenomena is called *elision*.

1. In normal conversation speech, an unstressed vowel followed by *l* or *n* disappears and the result is a *syllabic* [l̩] or [n̩]. When a syllable containing a *syllabic* [l̩] or [n̩] occurs under a note in the music, you will need to reinstate the unstressed vowel sound of schwa [ə].

sudden	sing	sud	-	den
[ˈsʌ dn̩]		[ˈsʌ		dən]
fiddle	sing	fid	-	dle
[ˈfɪ dl̩]		[ˈfɪ		dəl]
little	sing	lit	-	tle
[ˈlɪ tl̩]		[ˈlɪ		təl]

2. Within words, the alveolar consonants *t* and *d* are often elided in speech. They may be either elided or pronounced in singing, depending upon the tempo of the music, the size of the hall and the need for projection.

Read aloud, pronouncing the *t* and *d*.

grandmother	sandwich
postman	sandpaper

3. At word boundaries, a final stop consonant (mostly *t* or *d*) may be elided when surrounded by other consonants, particularly when the following consonant is a stop as in *first‿day*.

In singing, these final stop consonants may be either pronounced or elided depending upon several considerations: the particular consonant combination, the expressive needs of the words and music, the tempo, the size of the hall and the need for projection. However, you must be careful that your choices do not result in heavy, over-articulation.

first day	had to see	quick game
Bob pushed	not dense	the snake glides
didn't call	deep basket	last kiss

The following paired words contain consonant combinations that you must consider individually by using the above criteria. Some combinations might be elided while others are pronounced.

Sing these words aloud, once in a fast tempo, then in a slow tempo with maximum projection. What are your personal choices?

cast them	not thin	Ned scolded

4. In rapid informal speech, the pronouns *he, him, his, her,* and *them* often lose their initial consonant sounds. This should not occur in singing.
Read aloud.
   Give it to him not *Give it to 'im.*
   Does he know?
   I saw her yesterday.

5. When *have* is used as an auxiliary verb, it is often pronounced as [əv]. Pronounce the *h* in singing.
Read aloud.
   I could have gone.
   We should have told her.

6. The word *to* in an unstressed position in a sentence is often reduced to schwa [tə] or [tʊ], particularly before a vowel. This should not occur in concert literature.
Read aloud.

to me		tried to wait
has to go		to Ann
ought to	not	*oughta*
want to	not	*wanta*
going to	not	*goin'tuh*

7. When the word *of* forms part of a prepositional phrase it is often pronounced [ə]. This should not occur in formal singing.
Read aloud.

cup of coffee not   *cuppa coffee*
lots of time   not   *lots a time.*

In other instances, a sound is altered under the influence of a neighboring sound. This modification process is referred to as *assimilation*. The following words are correctly spoken and sung with assimilation.

When *t* and *u* combine they produce [ʧu] as in *picture:*
['pɪk ʧʊr] or['pɪk ʧɚ] — not ['pɪk tʊr].

Read aloud.

literature   mature
situation   virtue
fortune   statue

When *d* and *u* combine they produce [ʤu] as in *education*
[ˌɛʤu 'keɪ ʃən] or [ˌɛʤə 'keɪ ʃən] —not [ˌɛdju 'keɪ ʃən].

Read aloud.

graduation   gradual
individual   residual

When *s* and *u* combine they produce [ʃu] as in *tissue*
[tɪ ʃʊ] — not [tɪ sju].

Read aloud.

issue   fissure

Although the above assimilation are appropriate, the following assimilation at word boundaries is considered sloppy and inappropriate when singing English. The consonants that are most easily influenced by neighboring sounds are *t*, *d*, *s*, *z*, and *n*. Instances such as the following should be avoided.

When *t* and *y* combine they produce [tj] as in *last year*
[læst jɪr] — not [læs ʧɪr] (last cheer).

Read aloud.

don't you
that you

When *d* and *y* combine they produce [dj] as in *would_you*
[wʊd ju] — not [wʊd ʧu] (would chu).

> could_you
> behind_you

When *s* and *y* combine they produce [sj] as in *miss_you*
[mɪs ju] — not [mɪ ʃu] (miss shoe).

Still another characteristic of connected speech is related to final word sounds that carry over to the next syllable of the following word. This linking feature is, far from being unacceptable, is recommended.

1. Link final consonants to initial vowels of the next word.
   Read aloud.
   > lifts_it   cold_and wet   that_is_easy
   > punched_it   use_imagination

   Do not link words if the meaning is obscured.

   Tim ate it should not sound like *Tim mated*.

2. Blend repeated consonants across word boundaries. In this case, the doubled consonant is slightly lengthened.
   Read aloud.
   > keep_pace   ten_notes
   > make_candy   good_deal
   > this_smile   that_time
   > big_girl   Bob_build
   > small_lie

Sounds Unique to English

English, like every language, has sounds and sound patterns that set it apart from the other languages mentioned in succeeding chapters. Awareness of these sounds and patterns will help keep you from pronouncing them when you sing in other languages.

Simple Vowels

1. The most frequently occurring vowel in English is the *schwa* [ə]. It occurs in unstressed syllables and its cousin *uh* [ʌ], in stressed syllables. These central vowels do not exist at all in the phonological systems of some of the other languages described in the later chapters of this book.

   Read aloud.
   > [ʌ]   [ə]
   > bud   simmer
   > hut   actor

2. Several other English vowels are not found in other languages: [æ], [ʊ], [ɝ], [ɜ], [ɚ].

Read aloud.

hat	[hæt]
look	[lʊk]
learn	[lɝn] or [lɜrn]
simmer	['sɪ mɚ]

Finding Correct Pronunciations

Sadly, (for our lives would be easier if the opposite were true), English spelling generally does not reflect English pronunciation. You cannot determine preferred, standard pronunciation by just looking at a word. In order to decide if you have incorrect or non-standard pronunciations, you must listen to educated speakers or consult a dictionary. The following are a few commonly mispronounced words.

	Correct		Incorrect
strength	[strɛŋkθ]	not	[strɛnθ]
length	[lɛŋkθ]	not	[lɛnθ]
absurd	[əb 'sɝd]	not	[ˌæb 'sɝd]
chasm	['kæ zəm]	not	['tʃæ zəm]
mischievous	['mɪs tʃɪ vəs]	not	[mɪs 'tʃi vɪəs]

Final Note

While studying English diction, errors that are rather subtle, such as singing [luk] instead of [lʊk] for the word *look,* are relatively easy to hear because we know the language. As we listen to foreigners wrestle with pronouncing our language, their errors also leap out at us: we hear their articulation habits and stressing that are carried over from their native tongue, creating a distinct accent. In the next chapters the shoe will be on the other foot, and you will, like the foreigner, be singing sounds without benefit of growing up with the sounds of the language. And you have the added task of singing all of the languages like the natives—without an English accent.

However, unlike a foreigner, you will have the set of guidelines presented in this book to train yourself to articulate the sounds properly. As you learn these guidelines, keep in mind how specific and subtle the differences in sounds can be in English, from [strɛnθ] to[strɛŋkθ], for example, and tune your ears and articulators to that degree of subtlety, and you will acquire fine singing diction in the other languages.

Italian Diction

The dialect of Tuscany, particularly that of Florence, is considered the national standard for Italian diction for stage and singing. The following rules reflect the pronunciations of top level singers.

Italian is often considered a "phonetic" language because the orthographic letters of the alphabet are pronounced with a single sound or with few variations. This concept is so widespread that Italian-English dictionaries do not even include the pronunciation of words. They only indicate stressed *e* and *o* and voiced or unvoiced *s* and *z*. And presently there are no Italian dictionaries that use the International Phonetic Alphabet.

Yet, it is only partially true that Italian is a "phonetic" language. Although many letters of the alphabet are pronounced with a single sound, some vowels and consonants can be pronounced in a variety of ways. For instance, you can pronounce vowels (other than *a*) as open, closed, or as glides. To choose the correct option, you will need to know the stressing of the syllable, the position of the vowel in the word, and the specific letter that adjoins it. Two and three consecutive vowels also have options and you will need to know whether to pronounce them as diphthongs, glides, triphthongs or as two syllables.

Some consonants, prominently *c*, *g*, *s* and *z*, also may be pronounced in different ways. Again, your choice will depend upon the position of the consonant in the word and the adjoining letters.

Since the dictionaries will not tell you these variations, you will need some general rules to clarify your pronounciation choices. The material in "Special Features of Italian" will give you a complete description of how to pronounce the letters you see with the appropriate sound. You will learn where to divide words, when to pronounce consecutive vowels as diphthongs, glides, triphthongs, or as two syllables. You will also learn special articulation and pronunciation features of the language, beginning with how to determine the stressing of syllables. Then, *as a special resource*, you will find each letter and frequently used combinations of letters listed alphabetically and discussed individually in the "Italian Vowels in Detail" and "Italian Consonants in Detail".

36

Chart of Italian Sounds

The following chart lists the sounds of the Italian language in alphabetic order. Refer to this chart to quickly check the sound of a spelling. There are some special circumstances and exceptions to the sounds that cannot be presented easily in a simple chart. Detail is included in the discussion of the individual sounds.

Italian Letter & Position in Word		IPA	Example & IPA		Page
a	a	[ɑ]	amare	[ɑ 'mɑ re]	56
	ae (two syllables)	[ɑː ɛ]	aere	['ɑː ɛ re]	57
	ai (diphthong)	[ɑːi]	mai	[mɑːi]	57
	ao (two syllables)	[ɑː ɔ]	Paolo	['pɑː ɔ lo]	57
	au (diphthong)	[ɑːu]	lauda	['lɑːu da]	57
b	b	[b]	batti	['bɑtː ti]	77
	bb	[b]	labbro	['lɑbː bro]	77
c	c before *a, o, u*	[k]	canta	['kɑn ta]	77
	cc before *a, o, u*	[kː k]	ecco	['ɛkː ko]	78
	c before *e* or *i*	[ʧ]	certo	['ʧɛr to]	78
	cc before *e* or *i*	[tː ʧ]	Puccini	[putː 'ʧi ni]	78
	c before a *consonant*	[k]	classico	['klɑ si ko]	79
	ch	[k]	chiama	['kjɑ ma]	79
	cch	[kː k]	occhi	['ɔkː ki]	79
	cqu	[kː k]	acqua	['ɑkː kwa]	80
d	d	[d]	diva	['di va]	80
	dd	[dː d]	addio	[ɑdː 'diː o]	80
e	e unstressed	[e]	legale	[le 'gɑ le]	60
	e unstressed before *l,m,n,r* plus another *consonant*	[ɛ]	beltà	[bɛl 'tɑ]	60
	e ending a syllable	[e]	pena	['pe na]	61
	e ending a stressed antepenult	[ɛ]	gelida	['ʤe li da]	61
	e before *s* plus another *consonant*	[ɛ]	funesto	[fu 'nɛ sto]	61
	e after *i* or *u*	[ɛ]	cielo	['ʧɛ lo]	62
	e before *vowel*	[ɛ]	sei	[sɛːi]	62
	è or é final	[e]	chè, ché	[ke]	63
	e before a *consonant* in same syllable	[ɛ]	sempre	['sɛm pre]	62
	e before a double *consonant*	[e]	stella	['stelː la]	62
		or [ɛ]	bella	['bɛlː la]	
	e in suffixes and diminutives*	[e]	Musetta	[mu 'zetː ta]	63
	ea (two syllables)	[ɛː ɑ]	idea	[i 'dɛː a]	64
	ei (diphthong)	[ɛːi]	lei	[lɛːi]	64
	eo (two syllables)	[ɛː ɔ]	Orfeo	[ɔr 'fɛː ɔ]	64
	eu (diphthong)	[ɛːu]	euro	['ɛːu ro]	65

* Can be open [ɛ] or closed [e]. Check a dictionary.

Italian Letter & Position in Word		IPA	Example & IPA		Page
f	f	[f]	fato	['fɑ to]	81
	ff	[fː f]	affani	[ɑfː 'fɑ ni]	81
g	g before *a, o, u* or a *consonant*	[g]	gala	['gɑ lɑ]	81
	gg before *a, o, u* or a *consonant*	[gː g]	bugga	['bugː gɑ]	82
	g before *e* or *i*	[ʤ]	giorni	['ʤor ni]	81
	gg before *e* or *i*	[dː ʤ]	raggio	[rɑd: ʤo]	82
	gh	[g]	ghetta	['getː tɑ]	82
	gli	[ʎ]	foglia	['fɔ ʎɑ]	83
	gl before *a, o,* or *u*	[gl]	glauca	['glɑːu kɑ]	83
	gn in the same syllable	[ɲ]	ogni	['o ɲi]	83
	gu	[gw]	guardare	['gwɑr 'dɑ re]	83
h	h	*silent*	ho, chi	[ɔ] [ki]	83
i	i final or before a *consonant*	[i]	finiti	[fi 'ni ti]	65
	i after a *vowel*	[i]	poi	[pɔːi]	65
	i after *c, g, sc* and before *vowel*	*silent*	giusto	['ʤu sto]	66
	ia (glide)	[jɑ]	fiamma	['fjɑmː mɑ]	66
	ia (two syllables)	[iː ɑ]	Maria	[mɑ 'riː ɑ]	67
	ie (glide)	[jɛ]	vieni	['vjɛ ni]	67
	ie (two syllables)	[iː e]	follie	[folː 'liː e]	68
	iei (triphthong)	[jɛːi]	miei	[mjɛːi]	68
	io (glide)	[jɔ]	fiocco	['fjɔkː ko]	68
	io (two syllables)	[iː o]	mio	['miː o]	68
	iu (glide)	[ju]	liuto	['lju to]	69
j	j used only in older spellings	[j]	gajo	['gɑː jo]	84
k	k used only in foreign words				84
l	l	[l]	libertà	[li bɛr 'tɑ]	84
	ll	[lːl]	bello	['bɛlː lo]	84
m	m	[m]	mano	['mɑ no]	85
	mm	[mː m]	gemma	[ʤɛmː mɑ]	85
n	n	[n]	numero	['nu me ro]	85
	nn	[nː n]	donna	['dɔnː nɑ]	85
	n before *k* or *g*	[ŋ]	bianco	['bjɑŋ ko]	85
			sangue	['sɑŋ gwe]	

Italian Letter & Position in Word		IPA	Example & IPA		Page
o	o unstressed	[o]	sospiro	[so 'spi ro]	70
	o unstressed, before *r* plus another *consonant*	[ɔ]	tornare	[tɔr 'nɑ re]	70
	o ending a syllable	[o]	sola	['so lɑ]	70
	o ending a stressed antepenult	[ɔ]	opera	['ɔ pe rɑ]	71
	o after *i* or *u*	[ɔ]	piove	['pjɔ ve]	71
	o final and accented	[ɔ]	farò	[fɑ 'rɔ]	71
	o before *gli*	[ɔ]	foglia	['fɔ ʎɑ]	71
	o before a *consonant* and a *glide*	[ɔ]	gloria	['glɔ rjɑ]	72
	o before a *consonant* in same syllable	[ɔ]	forza	['fɔr tsɑ]	72
	o before *l* followed by *c,f,g,m,p,*or *t*	[o]	dolce	['dol tʃe]	72
	o before *mb, mm, mp*	[o]	ombra	['om brɑ]	72
	o before single *n* in same syllable	[o]	donde	['don de]	73
	o before double *consonant*	[o]	bocca	['bokː kɑ]	73
		[ɔ]	lotto	['lɔtː to]	
	oa (two syllables)	[ɔː ɑ]	balboa	[bɑl 'bɔː ɑ]	73
	oe (two syllables)	[ɔː ɛ]	poesia	[pɔ ɛ 'ziː ɑ]	73
	oi (diphthong)	[ɔːi]	poi	[pɔːi]	73
	oia, oja (two syllables)	[ɔː jɑ]	gioia	[dʒɔː jɑ]	73
p	p	[p]	porto	['pɔr to]	86
	pp	[pː p]	drappo	['drɑpː po]	86
q	qu	[kw]	qui	[kwi]	86
r	r flipped or trilled	[r]	rado	['rɑ do]	86
	rr	[rː r]	terra	['tɛrː rɑ]	87
s	s initial in word before a *vowel*	[s]	sento	[sɛn to]	87
	s initial in word before *unvoiced consonant*	[s]	sforzando	[sfɔr 'tsɑn do]	88
	s initial in syllable, after a *consonant,* and before a *vowel*	[s]	pensare	[pɛn 'sɑ re]	88
	s final	[s]	Radamès	[rɑ dɑ 'mɛs]	88
	ss	[sː s]	vissi	['visː si]	89
	s between two *vowels*	[z]	tesoro	[te 'zɔ ro]	88
	s *voiced consonant*	[z]	smanie	['zmɑ nje]	89
	sc before *a, o,* or *u*	[sk]	scolta	['skol tɑ]	89
	sc before *e* or *i*	[ʃ]	scena	['ʃe nɑ]	89
	sch	[sk]	scherzo	['skɛr tso]	90

Italian Letter & Position in Word			IPA	Example & IPA		Page
t	t		[t]	tanto	['tɑn to]	90
	tt		[tː t]	batti	['bɑtː ti]	90
u	u	before a *consonant*	[u]	fugare	[fu 'gɑ re]	74
	u	after a *vowel*	[u]	liuto	['lju to]	74
	ua	(glide)	[wɑ]	quanto	['kwɑn to]	74
	ua	(two syllables)	[uː ɑ]	tua	[tuː ɑ]	74
	ue	(glide)	[wɛ]	guerra	[gwɛrː rɑ]	75
	ue	(two syllables)	[uː e]	tue	[tuː e]	75
	ui	(glide)	[wi]	languire	[lɑŋ 'gwi re]	75
	ui	(two syllables)	[uː i]	lui	[luː i]	75
	uo	(glide)	[wɔ]	vuole	['vwɔ le]	75
	uo	(two syllables)	[uː o]	tuo	[tuː o]	76
	uai	(triphthong)	[wɑːi]	buai	[bwɑːi]	76
	uie	(triphthong)	[wjɛ]	quiete	['kwjɛ te]	76
	uio	(two syllables)	[uː jɔ]	buio	[buː jɔ]	76
	uoi	(triphthong)	[wɔːi]	tuoi	[twɔːi]	76
v	v		[v]	voce	['vo tʃe]	90
	vv		[vː v]	avverso	[avː 'vɛr so]	91
w	w, x, y, used only in foreign words					91
z	z	unvoiced	[ts]	zio	[tsiː o]	91
	z	voiced	[dz]	bronzo	['brɔn dzo]	92
	zz	unvoiced	[tː ts]	nozze	['nɔtː tse]	92
	zz	voiced	[dː dz]	bizzaro	[bidː 'dza ro]	92

Special Features of Italian

Syllabification

You will need to divide a word into syllables before you can determine the pronunciation of the letters in a word. The following rules will tell you how to divide a word into syllables. First notice whether there is a single consonant, two consonants, three consonants, or two or more consecutive vowels in the word. Then, depending upon what you see, follow the rules below.

Single Consonant

When a syllable ends with a vowel, it is called an open *syllable.*

When there is a single consonant between two vowels, put the consonant with the second vowel.

no-me	['no me]	a-mo-re	[a 'mo re]
fa-re	['fa re]	fi-ni-ti	[fi 'ni ti]

Two Consonants

When a syllable ends with a consonant, it is called a closed *syllable.*

When a consonant is doubled, separate the two consonants.

don-na	['dɔnː na]	bab-bo	['babː bo]
tut-ti	['tutː ti]	col-la	['kolː la]

When there are two consonants with the same sound (doubled phonetic consonants), separate the two consonants.

c-q:	ac-qua	['akː kwa]
g-gh:	ag-ghin-da-re	[agː gin 'da re]
c-ch:	oc-chi	['ɔkː ki]

When *l, m, n,* or *r* precede another *consonant*, separate the two consonants:

vol-to	['vɔl to]	tem-po	['tɛm po]
ven-to	['vɛn to]	par-ma	['par ma]

Note: You can remember this rule by referring to it as the "Lemoner plus another consonant" rule, because the consonants *l, m, n,* and *r* are used in the word "Lemoner".

A digraph is a combination of two or more letters that represent a single sound.

Otherwise, put two consonants, including the digraphs *ch* [k], *gli* [ʎ], and *gn* [ɲ], with the syllable that follows.

fi-glio	['fi ʎo]	la-scia	['la ʃa]
so-gno	['so ɲo]	ci-fra	['tʃi fra]
mi-sto	['mi sto]	ve-nu-sta	[ve 'nu sta]
re-cla-ma	[re 'kla ma]	du-ches-sa	[du 'kesː sa]

Three Consonants

In a cluster of three consonants, separate the first consonant from
the other two unless the first consonant is an *s*.

men-tre	['men tre]	bar-chet-ta	[bɑr 'ketː ta]
al-tro	['ɑl tro]	sem-pre	['sɛm pre]

If the first consonant is an *s*, cluster all three consonants in the
same syllable.

e-stre-mo	[e 'stre mo]	ma-sche-ra	['ma ske rɑ]
mo-stra	['mo strɑ]	di-scre-zio-ne	[di skre 'tsjɔ ne]

Consecutive Vowels:

When two or three vowels are consecutive, they usually form
diphthongs, glides, or triphthongs. Put them into a single syllable.

Diphthongs

mai	[mɑːi]
sei	[sɛːi]
poi	[pɔːi]
dei	[dɛːi]

Glides

chio-ma	['kjɔ mɑ]
fie-rez-za	[fje 'rɛtː tsa]
qua	[kwɑ]
suo-no	['swɔ no]

Triphthongs

suoi	[swɔːi]
tuoi	[twɔːi]
miei	[mjɛːi]
lan-guia-te	[laŋ 'gwjɑ te]

*The [ː] after a vowel indicates
that the vowel should be given
greater duration. It does not
indicate the end of a syllable.*

In Italian, the vowels *a*, *o*, and *e* are considered strong vowels.
When two strong vowels are consecutive, they form two
syllables.

ide-a	[i 'dɛː a]	po-eta	[pɔ 'ɛ tɑ]

When a stressed *i* or *u* precedes a final vowel without an accent
mark, the two vowels will form two syllables.

mio	['miː o]	tuo	['tuː o]
polizi-a	[po li 'tsiː a]	agoni-a	[ɑ go 'niː ɑ]

*The rules that indicate whether
consecutive vowels are to be
pronounced as glides,
diphthongs, or two syllables
are found on page 50.*

Stressing

In Italian, you will usually pronounce the next-to-last syllable with the primary stress, but you will find that any syllable may be stressed.

An accent mark over a final vowel will tell you to stress the last syllable.

| perchè | [pɛr ˈke] |
| libertà | [li bɛr ˈtɑ] |

There are no consistent rules to tell you when to stress the third-to-last or the fourth-to-last syllable. This situation presents a challenge to you. You will need to listen to the musical stress of the melodic line and let it guide you into pronouncing the words with the appropriate stress. You may need to refer to a dictionary. Also, to help you with the words in this book that receive the primary stress on the third- or fourth-to-last syllable, we have underlined the stressed vowel.

| opera | [ˈɔ pe rɑ] | Sabato | [ˈsɑ bɑ to] |

In all IPA transcriptions, primary stress is indicated by placing a diacritical mark [ˈ] above and before the stressed syllable.

Rules for Stressing

In most Italian words, give the primary stress to the next-to-last syllable.

| Ro-ma | [ˈro ma] | vac-ca | [ˈvakː ka] |
| mes-sa | [ˈmesː sa] | con-ten-to | [kon ˈtɛn to] |

When there is a accent mark over the final syllable, give primary stress to the last syllable.

| mor-rò | [morː ˈrɔ] | ser-vi-tù | [sɛr vi ˈtu] |
| sal-te-rà | [sɑl te ˈrɑ] | per-chè | [pɛr ˈke] |

In some Italian words, the third-to-last syllable will receive primary stress.

| ge-li-da | [ˈʤɛ li dɑ] | ec-co-la | [ˈɛkː ko lɑ] |
| pal-pi-to | [ˈpɑl pi to] | po-ve-ro | [ˈpɔ ve ro] |

In a few words, it is the fourth-to-last syllable that receives the primary stress. Again, when you see a vowel underlined, stress that syllable.

fabbricano [ˈfɑbː bri kɑ no]

Additional Comments about Stressing

Be careful to pronounce words with appropriate stressing. By changing the stress pattern of a polysyllabic word you may also change the meaning of the word.

perdono	['pɛr do no] means *they lose*
perdono	[pɛr 'do no] means *pardon*
meta	['mɛ tɑ] means *goal*
metà	[me 'tɑ] means *half*

Accent marks in a monosyllable often indicate a change in the meaning of the word. Accent marks do not indicate a change in pronounciation (as they would in French).

With grave accent		Without grave accent	
è	[ɛ] means *he, is*	e	[e] means *and*
chè	[ke] means *because*	che	[ke] means *that, who*
sì	[si] means *yes*	si	[si] means *himself*
dà	[dɑ] means *he gives*	da	[dɑ] means *from*

Double Consonants

In Italian, double consonants add a special quality to expression of the words. Speak or sing double consonants with a more prolonged *duration* than a single consonant. You can hear the prolonged sound of doubled consonant in English when one word ends with the same consonant that begins the next word, as in *tall⏑lasses, even⏑now, hog⏑games,* and *life⏑force.* Notice how you linger on the consonants when saying these words.

Read the following pairs of Italian words aloud to contrast the pronunciation of single and double consonants. Notice how changing the duration of the consonants affects the meanings of the words.

[m]	m'ama	['ma ma]	means *loves me*
[mːm]	mamma	['mamː ma]	means *mother*
[l]	bela	['bɛ la]	means *it bleats*
[lː l]	bella	['bɛlː la]	means *beautiful*
[n]	ano	['a no]	means *anus*
[nː n]	anno	['anː no]	means *year*
[t]	note	['nɔ te]	means *notes*
[tː t]	notte	['nɔtː te]	means *night*
[k]	eco	['ɛ ko]	means *echo*
[kː k]	ecco	['ɛkː ko]	means *here*
[t]	face	['fa tʃe]	means *torch*
[tː t]	facce	['fatː tʃe]	means *faces*

There are three accent marks in Italian: the acute accent [´], the grave accent [`], and the circumflex [ˆ]. You will see the grave accent more frequently than the other two.

The different pronunciations of single and double consonants often indicates different meanings of words and creates a special rhythm for the Italian language.

In IPA transcriptions, a colon [ː] after a consonant indicates that the sound should be prolonged. To emphasize further the importance of the long sound of a doubled consonant, you will see the consonant symbol written a second time. For example, you will see bello transcribed as ['bɛː lo].

However, when pronouncing a double consonant, do not repeat the consonant sound, merely lengthen it.

Special Doubling

When a monosyllablic word ends with a vowel and is followed by a word that begins with a consonant, pronounce the initial consonant in the second word as a double consonant.

a Roma   [ɑrː 'ro mɑ]   è bene [ɛbː 'bɛ ne]
chi sa   [kisː 'sɑ]

Long and Short Vowels

In Italian, vowels in stressed syllables are pronounced with either a long or short duration. Give longer duration to a vowel that is before a single consonant than to a vowel that is before two or more consonants.

Read aloud the following words. Prolong the vowels indicated by (¯), and shorten the vowels indicated by (˘).

Lengthening the vowel may help you avoid pronouncing single consonants as double consonants.

Long Vowels		Short Vowels	
fāme	['fɑ me]	fătto	['fɑtː to]
cāra	['kɑ rɑ]	căccia	['kɑtː tʃɑ]
vēro	['ve ro]	vĕste	['vɛ ste]
prēga	['pre gɑ]	piăzza	[pjɑtː tsɑ]
sōle	['so le]	sŏmma	['sɔmː mɑ]
rōsa	['rɔ zɑ]	rŏtta	['rotː tɑ]
vōce	['vo tʃe]	vŏlgo	['vol go]
pūma	['pu mɑ]	pŭnto	['pun to]
tūta	['tu tɑ]	tŭtta	['tutː tɑ]

Note: The duration of a vowel does not always correlate to its open or closed pronunciation. For example, the closed [o] can be pronounced long or short.

vōce   ['vo ʧe]   vŏlgo ['vol go]

The Consonant l

Italians always pronounce the consonant *l* as a clear, dental sound, with the tip of the tongue touching the back of the upper front teeth. You can find a clear *l* in the English words *leap, lit, let, lot, late*. The English language more often, however, uses a dark *l* with the tip of the tongue touching the alveolar ridge as in the words *full, help, wall, fell, truly*. Be sure to always use the clear *l* in Italian, as in these words: *diletto* [di 'lɛtː to], *lieto* ['lje to], *idolo* ['i do lo], *sol* [sol], *gloria* ['glɔ rjɑ].

The Consonants d, t, and n

In Italian the consonants *d*, *t*, and *n* are dental consonants. That is, they are articulated with the tip of the tongue touching the back of the upper front teeth.

By contrast, English speakers form the consonants *d*, *t*, and *n* with the tip of the tongue touching the alveolar ridge as in *dungeon, total, not*. Learn to articulate *d, t* and *n* dentally in Italian words such as *dunque* ['dun kwe], *tema* ['tɛ mɑ], *natale* [nɑ 'tɑ le].

The Stop-Plosive Consonants

In English, you pronounce the stop-plosive consonants (*b, p, d, t, g,* and *k*) by stopping the flow of air through your mouth and nose and then releasing the air plosively. Pronounce the English words *tote* and *team* and notice your articulation of the stop-plosive consonant [t]. The tip of your tongue lifts to touch the alveolar ridge to stop the flow of air through the mouth. Feel the air pressure build up and then explosively release with an aspirate or fricative sound.

In Italian, the stop-plosive consonants are articulated with less aspiration than in English. We call these Italian consonants "dry" consonants to describe the reduction of aspiration.

Return to your articulation of [t]. This time pronounce [t] as an Italian dental, dry stop-plosive consonant. Put the tip of your tongue at the back of the upper front teeth instead of the alveolar ridge. During the stop portion of the articulation, give less build up of air pressure. Then release the sound with minimal aspiration.

Repeat the sound of [t] several times:

[t], [t], [t], [t], [t]

Then read aloud these words using a dental, dry [t]:

totale	[to 'tɑ le]
tira	['ti rɑ]
attento	[ɑtː 'tɛn to]
attico	['ɑtː ti ko]

In Italian, remember to articulate all the the stop-plosive consonants in this manner, with minimal plosiveness and aspiration.

The Italian Vowel a

In Italian, the vowel *a* is a sound that is similar to the *ah* in *father*. However, you will find that different authors use different IPA transcriptions for this sound. Some use the bright [a], as Bostoners say *pahk the cahr*, and others use dark [ɑ] as in *father*.

In his <u>Descriptive</u> <u>Italian</u> <u>Grammar</u>, the Italian grammarian Robert A. Hall writes: "The low vowel *a* is indifferent as to front or back tongue-position," which indicates that the orthographic letter *a* can be pronounced either as [a] or [ɑ].

This book transcribes the letter *a* as [ɑ]. We suggest that you think of *a* as being located between [ɑ] and [a] on the vowel diagram.

There are two major cautions for American singers concerning the orthographic *a*. First you must be careful not to substitute the neutral sounds of *schwa* [ə] as in *about* and *uh* [ʌ] in *bud* for the pronounciation of *a*. These sounds do not exist in the Italian language. Never use [ə] in the following words:

bella	['bɛlː lɑ]	is not	['bɛlː lə]
pizza	['pitː tsɑ]	is not	['pitː tsə]
Amarilli	[ɑ mɑ 'rilː li]	is not	[ɑ mə 'rilː li]
tessitura	[tesː si 'tu rɑ]	is not	[tesː si 'tu rə]

Secondly, in some American dialects, the sounds of *ah* [ɑ] and *aw* [ɔ] are poorly distinguished. You must be careful to keep the sound of Italian *ah* [ɑ] clear and bright, not rounded toward the vowel *aw* [ɔ].

The Italian Vowels *e* and *o*

In Italian the closed pronunciation of the vowels *e* [e], as in *chaotic*, and *o* [o], as in *obey*, are pure vowels and must never be pronounced with the English diphthongal [eɪ], as in *bait*, and [oʊ], as in *boat*. Amercian singers must master the pure, closed sounds of these vowels to avoid singing with a heavy English accent. The <u>International</u> <u>Phonetic</u> <u>Alphabet</u> <u>for</u> <u>Singers</u>, a manual that teaches the sounds and symbols of the IPA, offers the following exercises to bring these diphthongs [eɪ] and [oʊ] into your awareness.

> "Speak the word *aim* aloud in slow motion while noticing what your tongue does. Just before the *m* of *aim*, you should be able to feel the front part of your tongue move forward and up from [e] to [ɪ]. Listen to the vowel change. This gliding tongue movement produces the diphthong.

Vowel Diagram

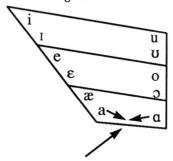

You may find it useful to think of the Italian a as though formed between bright ah *and* dark ah. *This, however, is a subtle point.*

"To isolate the pure [e] sound, try speaking the word *hay* aloud in slow motion without moving the tongue to [ɪ]. The word will sound incomplete, strange, and unfamiliar to most Americans. If you do not make a gliding movement with the tongue, you will be producing a pure [e].

"Speak the word *hoe* aloud in slow motion to notice the movement of your lips and tongue. You should be able to tell that your lips become more rounded as the sound progresses from [o] to [ʊ]. The back of the tongue also moves upward from [o]. You may be less conscious of this movement, because it is so slight. It is easily seen in x-ray images.

"To isolate the pure [o] sound try speaking the word *hoe* in slow motion *without* moving the lips or tongue. The words will sound incomplete and strange to an American. Without the gliding movement, you will produce a pure [o]."

Both of the vowels *e* and *o* have closed and open pronunciations. The orthographic *e* will be pronounced as pure, closed [e] or open [ɛ], as in *bed*. The orthographic *o* will be pronounced as pure, closed [o] or open [ɔ], as in *bought*. The rules for when to use closed and open vowels in the pronunciation of words will be presented in the listings for The letter e and The letter o.

A closed vowel is one that has a smaller space between the high point of the tongue and the roof of the mouth. An open vowel is one that has a larger space than the closed vowel.

Flipped and Trilled r

The Italian *r* is either a flipped or trilled tongue point *r*; it is never the retroflex *r* of English.

When Italians say the flipped *r*, it sounds very much like a Britisher saying an *r* in words like *very* (*ved-dy*) or *merry* (*med-dy*). Practicing the flipped *r* will help you achieve a trilled *r*, which is so essential for good Italian diction.

Speak the following words using a British accent for the flipped *r* column. Notice that the tip of the tongue quickly flips against the alveolar ridge.

In this text the tongue point Italian r is represented by the IPA symbol [r]. The IPA symbol for the flipped r is [ɾ], and [ř] for the trilled r, however, for simplicity, this chapter will use the symbol [r] to indicate both flipped and trilled r. Rules for flipped and trilled r are presented on pages 86 and 87.

Flipped *r* (between vowels)	Trilled *r*
caro ['kɑ ro] meaning *dear*	carro ['kɑrː ro] meaning *cart*
furore [fu 'ro re] meaning *rage*	ferro ['fɛrː ro] meaning *iron*
Figaro ['fi gɑ ro]	Ferrando [fɛrː 'rɑn do]

The Two Italian Glides: [j] and [w]

The glides [j] and [w] are already familiar to you as an English speaking singer. The symbol [j], named *yot* [jɔt], represents the sound of *y* in *you*. Produce it by moving the tongue to a position for *ee* [i] as in *beet*, then quickly shifting to the vowel that follows: as in *yes* [jɛs] or *yet* [jɛt].

The symbol [w] represents the sound of *w* in *went*, *wine*, or *wear*. Produce it by rounding your lips as if to say *oo* [u] in *boot*, then quickly shifting to the vowel that follows, as in *we* [wi].

Enya [ɲ] and Elya [ʎ]

As an English speaking singer, you have two new sounds to learn in Italian: the consonants *enya* [ɲ] and *elya* [ʎ].

Enya [ɲ], as in the Italian word *ogni* ['o ɲi], does not exist in English, but a similar sound can be found in the *ni* of the word *onion* ['ʌnjən]. Notice that to pronounce the [nj] in *onion*, two articulatory actions are required: the tip of the tongue must lift to touch to the teeth ridge for [n], then must lower to touch the back of the bottom front teeth for [j]. To pronounce the *enya* [ɲ], by contrast, only one articulatory action is required.

The teeth ridge is also called the alveolar ridge.

Make the sound of *enya* [ɲ] by slightly parting your lips, putting the tip of the tongue behind the bottom front teeth and arching your tongue upward so that the high arch of the tongue touches the boundary between the teeth ridge and the hard palate. Add voice and you will hear the nasal, palatal consonant sound *enya* [ɲ]. Although the enya sounds something like [n], it is made with the blade of your tongue touching the palate rather than the tip of your tongue touching the teeth ridge.

Elya [ʎ], as found in *foglia* ['fɔ ʎa], is another sound that does not exist in English. However, a similar sound can be found in *million* ['mɪ ljən]. Notice again how two articulatory actions of the tongue are needed to say [lj]. Place the tip of the tongue on the teeth ridge for the consonant [l] and then move it to the back of the bottom front teeth for the glide [j]. By contrast, to say *elya* [ʎ] only a single tongue action is needed.

Produce the sound of *elya* [ʎ] by slightly parting your lips, putting the tip of your tongue behind the bottom front teeth, and arching your tongue so that the arch of the tongue touches the front of the hard palate. Add voice and let the air exit over the sides of the tongue. You will hear a sound something like an [l], only it is made with the blade of the tongue, not the tip, against the boundary between the teeth ridge and the hard palate.

Apocopation

You will find that, except for a few monosyllables, most Italian words end with a vowel. Therefore, when a word ends in a consonant, immediately consider that it has been apocopated...that is, the word has been shortened by dropping the final vowel or syllable. An apostrophe is only used when an entire syllable has been apocopated.

sole becomes *sol*	*cantare* becomes *cantar*
siamo becomes *siam*	*partiamo* becomes *partiam*
fatale becomes *fatal*	*viene* becomes *vien*
poco becomes *po'*	*guarda* becomes *gua'*

Notice that in an apocopated word a closed syllable is created where there had been an open syllable. Although this affects the syllabification of the word, it does not change the original open or closed pronunciation of the vowel.

potere	[po 'te re]	becomes	*poter*	[po 'ter]
piacere	[pja 'tʃe re]	becomes	*piacer*	[pja 'tʃer]
padrone	[pa 'dro ne]	becomes	*padron*	[pa 'dron]
core	['kɔ re]	becomes	*cor*	[kɔr]
(from *cuore* ['kwɔ re])				

Elision

To link words together smoothly, you may hear an Italian speaker drop the final vowel of a word before an initial vowel of the next word. This linking process is called *elision*. The elided vowel is indicated by an apostrophe between the words.

quelle aria	becomes	*quell'aria*	[kwelː 'la rja]
bello uomo	becomes	*bell'uomo*	[bɛlː 'lwɔ mo]
una altra parte	becomes	*un'altra parte*	[u 'nal tra 'par te]
mi amate	becomes	*m'amate*	[ma 'ma te]
lo amico	becomes	*l'amico*	[la 'mi ko]
vi aspetto	becomes	*v'aspetto*	[va 'spɛtː to]
dove è Ernesto	becomes	*dov'è Ernesto*	['do vɛ ɛr 'nɛ sto]

Rules for Pronouncing Consecutive Vowels

Consecutive vowels will form either a diphthong, a glide, a triphthong, or two syllables.

Diphthongs

A *diphthong* is composed of two consecutive vowels uttered in a single impulse of breath to form one syllable. Each Italian diphthong will include one strong vowel (*a, e,* or *o*) followed by one weak vowel (*i* or *u*), which make Italian diphthongs easy to recognize.

In the IPA transcriptions, the colon [ː] after the vowel indicates the lengthening of the vowel sound. The symbol [ː] can be used within a syllable or between syllables.

When pronouncing and transcribing the weak vowels i and u as the second vowel, you must be careful never to use ih [ɪ] (as in bit) or oo [ʊ] (as in book). These two vowels do not exist in Italian.

You can find diphthongs in English in such words as *my* [maɪ], *boy* [bɔɪ] or *gown* [gaʊn]. Notice that as you pronounce these words, you will prolong the first vowel longer than the second vowel.

The same timing holds true in Italian diphthongs; that is, you will pronounce the first vowel longer and the second one shorter. Pronounce the Italian words *mai* [maːi], *poi* [pɔːi], or *gaudio* ['gaːu djo] and notice the similarities to the diphthongs in *my, boy,* and *gown.* Unlike English diphthongs, however, pronounce the second weak vowel of Italian diphthongs with a pure, distinct quality of [i] or [u]. The second weak vowel should not resemble a glide, nor open to [ɪ] or [ʊ].

Read aloud these words to become familiar with the sounds of the diphthongs.

Diphthongs with *i* as the second vowel:

ai	[aːi]	mai	[maːi]
ei	[eːi]	pei	[peːi] (less frequent)
ei	[ɛːi]	sei	[sɛːi]
oi	[oːi]	voi	[voːi]
oi	[ɔːi]	poi	[pɔːi]

Diphthongs with *u* as the second vowel:

The *eu* and *au* diphthongs are used less frequently than other diphthongs.

eu	[eːu]	Euridice	[eːu ri 'tʃe]
eu	[ɛːu]	eu-ro	['ɛːu ro]
au	[aːu]	cau-to	['kaːu to]

Glides

The sound of [j], called jot [jɔt], is similar to a very brief ee [i] as in beet. And [w] is similar to a very brief oo [u] as in boot.

Like diphthongs, *glides* are composed of two consecutive vowels uttered in a single impulse of breath to form one syllable. A glide will include one weak vowel (*i* or *u*) followed by another vowel, as in *più* [pju] and *qui* [kwi]. Notice that the weak vowels *i* or *u* are pronounced as [j] or [w]. Glides can be heard in the words in the English words *pew* [pju] and *queen* [kwin].

Unlike a diphthong, the first vowel in a glide is short and the second vowel is long.

> Read aloud the following vowel combinations to become familiar with the sound of a glide.

Six glides with *i* [j] first.

ia	[jɑ]	chia-ma-re	[kjɑ 'mɑ re]
ie	[je]	ca-va-lie-re	[kɑ vɑ 'lje re] (less frequent)
ie	[jɛ]	vie-ni	['vjɛ ni]
io	[jo]	piom-bo	['pjom bo] (less frequent)
io	[jɔ]	chio-do	['kjɔ do]
iu	[ju]	fiu-me	['fju me]

Six glides with *u* [w] first:

ua	[wɑ]	quan-do	['kwɑn do]
ue	[we]	que-sto	['kwe sto] (less frequent)
ue	[wɛ]	guer-ra	['gwɛrː rɑ]
ui	[wi]	qui	[kwi]
uo	[wo]	quo-ta-li-zio	[kwo tɑ 'li ʧjo] (less frequent)
uo	[wɔ]	uo-mo	['wɔ mo]

Look for the combination of *i* or *u* followed by another vowel, which you will usually pronounce as a glide.

> Read aloud.

più	[pju]	può	[pwɔ]
Liù	[lju]	qua	[kwɑ]
odiò	[o 'djɔ]	segue	['se gwe]
aria	['ɑ rjɑ]	uomo	['wɔ mo]
chiuso	['kju zo]	dileguò	[di le 'gwɔ]

Three exceptions do not conform to this rule:

1. When *i* comes after *c*, *g*, or *sc*, and is followed by *a, o, u* or *e*, the *i* is silent. This is the only instance when a vowel is silent in Italian. (See <u>The letter i</u>)

ciò	[ʧɔ]	già	[ʤɑ]
cielo	['ʧɛ lo]	sciolto	['ʃɔl to]

2. When a *stressed i* is followed by another vowel that is final in the word and there is no accent mark, the result is two syllables. (See the following section, <u>Two Syllables</u>)

m<u>i</u>o	['miː o]	l<u>u</u>i	['luː i]
<u>i</u>o	['iː o]	s<u>u</u>e	['suː e]
mal<u>i</u>a	[mɑ 'liː ɑ]	poliz<u>i</u>a	[po li 'tsiː ɑ]

3. When a *stressed i* is followed by the third person plural verb ending *-ano*, the result is two syllables. (See the following section, <u>Two Syllables</u>.)

siano	['siː ɑ no]	fiano	['fiː ɑ no]

The term "glide" may be used to refer either to the specific speech sounds [j] *and* [w] *or to refer to the vowel combination which includes a* [j] *or* [w].

The glides [j] *and* [w] *are sometimes called semi-vowels or semi-consonants.*

This rule for silent i is an important one to keep in mind. Giovanni [ʤo 'vɑnː ni], *for instance, is never pronounced* [ʤio 'vɑnː ni].

Triphthongs

A *triphthong* is composed of three consecutive vowels uttered in a single impulse of breath to form one syllable as in *tuoi* [twɔːi] or *quieto* ['kwjɛ to].

1. A triphthong usually consists of a semi-vowel (either [j] or [w]) and a diphthong.

miei	[mjɛːi]	ri-nun-ziai	[ri nun 'tsjaːi]
suoi	[swɔːi]	tuoi	[twɔːi]

2. Sometimes a triphthong consists of two semi-vowels and one vowel.

quie-to	['kwjɛ to]	se-guia-te	[se 'gwja te]
lan-guia-te	[lɑn 'gwja te]	a-iuo-la	[ɑ 'jwɔ lɑ]

Two Syllables

Two consecutive strong vowels (*a, e,* or *o*) generally constitute two separate syllables. The first vowel is usually stressed, but not always. Also, in strong vowel combinations, the *e* and *o* are pronounced as open [ɛ] and open [ɔ].

Read aloud.

ae	[ɑɛ]	pa-esano	[pɑː ɛ 'zɑ no]-first vowel stressed
		ca-endo	[kɑ 'ɛn do]-second vowel stressed
ao	[ɑɔ]	Pa-olo	['pɑː ɔ lo]
ea	[ɛɑ]	ide-a	[i 'dɛː ɑ]
eo	[ɛɔ]	Orfe-o	[ɔr 'fɛː ɔ]
oa	[ɔɑ]	balbo-a	[bɑl 'bɔː ɑ]-first vowel stressed
		so-ave	[sɔ 'ɑ ve]-second vowel stressed
oe	[ɔɛ]	ero-e	[e 'rɔː ɛ]-first vowel stressed
		po-eta	[pɔ 'ɛ tɑ]-second vowel stressed

1. Small Two or Three Letter Words

In small two or three letter words, when an *i* or *u* is followed by a final vowel without an accent mark, the *i* or *u* become stressed and the two vowels constitute two separate syllables:

Pronounce these small words of two or three letters as two syllables.

mio	['miː o]	lui	['luː i]
io	['iː o]	tua	['tuː ɑ]
sia	['siː o]	due	['duː e]
zio	['tsiː o]	sue	['suː e]
zii	['tsiː i]	tuo	['tuː o]

Sing these words with a long first vowel and a short second vowel as you would a diphthong. However, the second vowel has more strength and may even be sung on a separate note when called for in the musical notation.

In the vowel combination ui, *pronounce the usually weak* u̲ *as a strong vowel to create two syllables, as in* lu̲i.

Flip through the pages of your Twenty-Four Italian Songs and Arias to see how often these small two syllable words occur. Notice how frequently the composer has provided two notes in the melody for the two vowels.

2. Polysyllabic Words

The only certain clue to pronouncing a weak vowel (*i* or *u*) followed by a final vowel in polysyllabic words is whether there is an accent mark over the final vowel. Then, pronounce the final vowels as a glide as in *dileguò* [di le 'gwɔ] or *odiò* [o 'djɔ]

If there is no accent mark, you must know which syllable is stressed before you can know the pronunciation. If the stress is on the weak vowel you will pronounce the vowels as two syllables, as in *sinfonia* [sin fo 'niː a] and *malia* [ma 'liː a]. If the stress is on a syllable that comes before the final vowels you will pronounce the final vowels as a glide, as in *statua* ['sta twa] and *Italia* [i 'ta lja].

To know when this irregular stressing has occured, you will need to be attentive to how the word is set metrically in the melody line, or you will need to refer to a dictionary.

Pronounce the final two vowels in these polysyllabic words as two syllables.

signoria	[si ɲo 'riː a]
polizia	[po li 'tsiː a]
poesia	[pɔ ɛ 'ziː a]
agonia	[a go 'niː a]
bramosia	[bra mo 'ziː a]
natio	[na 'tiː o]

Additional Comments About Consecutive Vowels

There is a difference of opinion among pedagogues about how to classify the normally weak *i* and *u* when they receive the primary stress of the word and are followed by a final vowel with no accent mark. Some pedagogues prefer to classify these consecutive vowels as two separate syllables, while others classify them as diphthongs.

However, the question of how to classify these consecutive vowels is of less consequence than how to sing them. According to Frederick Agard and Robert Di Pietro "It must be kept in mind that these observations of the vowels forming two syllables are made on the basis of modern spoken language. In poetry, opera librettos, and other artistic uses of the language, any sequence of two (or more) vowels may constitute a single syllable peak." This is important because you may see only one note given to the two-syllable more consecutive vowels. See below.

Singing Consecutive Vowels

In music, a glide or diphthong will usually be written under a single note. You must decide how to divide the timing of the two vowels.

When the first sound is a glide, you will have no difficulty with the timing. The quick, gliding movement of the semi-vowel guides the pronunciation so that the second vowel has the longer duration.

Musical Example of Glides

Example from *Danza, danza fanciulla gentile* - Durante

al suo - no
[swɔ_____]

When the vowel combination is a diphthong, however, you must prolong the first vowel and shorten the second vowel. The proportion of timing becomes significant. See the examples below to observe appropriate choices.

Musical Examples of Diphthongs

Example from *Il mio bel foco* - Marcello

che giam- mai s'e stin -gue - ra
[mɑː i]

Example from *Se tu m'ami* - Pergolesi

sei sog-get- to
[sɛː i]

Example from *O del mio dolce ardor*- von Gluck

L'au - ra che tu re -spi - ri
[lɑː u]
[lɑː u]

Musical Example of Triphthongs

Example from *Vergin, tutto amor* - Durante

♪ | ♩ ♪ ♪ ♪ ♪ | ♩ ♪

suo   duol   suoi   tri-sti   ac - cen-ti

♪♪♪

[swɔ i]

Musical Examples of Singing Consecutive Vowels that Constitute Two Syllables

Example from *Pur dicesti, o bocca bella* - Lotti

♪ | ♩ ♩ | ♩ ♩ |

di   sua   fa - cel - la

♪ ♪

[suː a]

Divide two syllables with a longer first vowel and shorter second vowel. Or divide the two syllables equally.

♪ | ♩. ♪ | ♩

il   mio   pia - cer

♩. ♪

[miː o]

Very often the composer will provide two separate notes for small two-syllable words; so you will not need to make a decision about how to divide them rhythmically.

Connecting Words in Italian

In singing, several vowels at word boundries are sometimes assigned to a single note. You will need to know the translation of the words in order to decide the appropriate timing for the vowel combinations. The meaning of the words will indicate which vowel or syllable to stress. For example, the vowels of nouns or verbs will receive stronger stress and longer duration than articles or prepositions. If there is a question about stress, simply divide the timing of the vowels equally.

Italian is a legato language. To avoid separation or glottal stops between words, the final vowel of one word is connected to the initial vowel of the next word. To maintain appropriate flow of speech these vowels must be joined smoothly, sung in one impulse of breath without separation.

Musical Examples

Example from *Amarilli* - Caccini

♪ ♪ | 𝅝 | 𝅝 |

è il   mio a - mo - re

♪♪ ♪♪♪

['e il   'miːo a]

Example from *Se tu m'ami* - Pergolesi

♪ ♪ ♪ ♪ ♪ | ♪ ♪ ♪ ♪ |

ma   de-gli uo-mi-ni il   con -si -glio

[ma de ʎwɔ mi nil   kon si ʎo]

Italian Vowels in Detail

There are only seven vowel sounds in Italian represented by five orthographic letters as indicated by the chart below.

a	[ɑ]
e	[e] or [ɛ]
i	[i]
o	[o] or [ɔ]
u	[u]

Note: The letters *a*, *e*, and *o* are strong vowels; *i* and *u* are weak vowels. The weak letters *i* and *u* in certain vowel combinations may be pronounced as glides [j] and [w]. (See "Consecutive Vowels: Glides" on page 50.)

The letter

In Italian, the letter *a* is always pronounced as [ɑ], never anything else. This is true when the letter is by itself in a syllable, or combined with a glide, diphthong, triphthong, or another strong vowel. Also, unlike the letters *e* and *o*, the pronunciation of *a* is unaffected by whether it occurs in a stressed or unstressed syllable.

Caution: When *a* is in an unstressed position, be careful to pronounce it as [ɑ] and not as *schwa* [ə], as you would in English.

Compare and contrast.

	English	Italian
papa	['pɑ pə]	['pɑ pɑ]
pizza	['piːt tsə]	['piːt tsɑ]
terracotta	[tɛ rə 'kɑ tə]	[terː rɑ 'kɔtː tɑ]
pasta	['pɑ stə]	['pɑ stɑ]

The single letter a

Pronounce the single letter *a* as [ɑ].

Read aloud.

stancare	[stɑn 'kɑ re]	amare	[a 'mɑ re]
Amarilli	[a mɑ 'rilː li]	affani	[afː 'fɑ ni]

The letter a in consecutive vowel groups

The letter

a

ae

Pronounce *ae* as two syllables [ɑː ɛ]. When the strong vowel *a* precedes the strong vowel *e*, pronounce the vowels as two syllables.

Read aloud.

paesano [pɑː ɛ 'zɑ no]
aere   ['ɑː ɛ re]

ai

Pronounce *ai* as the diphthong [ɑːi].

Read aloud.

mai	[mɑːi]	traino	['trɑːi no]
vedrai	[ve 'drɑːi]	l'amai	[lɑ 'mɑːi]
andrai	[an 'drɑːi]	dai	[dɑːi]

aiu

Pronounce *aiu* (*a* plus a diphthong) as [ɑ 'ju].

Note: Pronounce *a* as a separate syllable when followed by a glide, diphthong, or triphthong.

| aiuto | [ɑ 'ju to] | aiulo | [ɑ 'jwɔ lo] |
| guaio | ['gwɑː jɔ] | fumaiolo | [fu mɑ 'jɔ lo] |

ao

Pronounce *ao* as two syllables [ɑː ɔ]. When the strong vowel *a* precedes the strong vowel *o*, pronounce the vowels as two syllables.

Read aloud.

Paolo ['pɑː ɔlo]   pilao [pi 'lɑː ɔ]

au

Pronounce *au* as the diphthong [ɑːu].

Read aloud.

pausa	['pɑːu zɑ]	lauda	['lɑːu dɑ]
causa	['kɑːu zɑ]]	rauco	['rɑːu ko]
autore	[ɑːu 'to re]	audace	[ɑːu 'dɑ tʃe]

Note: The first vowel of the diphthong *au* is usually elongated. One common exception is in the word *pau̠ra* [pɑu: rɑ], where the second vowel is elongated.

The letter

The Italian letter *e* has two pronounciations: closed [e] as in *chaotic* and open [ɛ] as in *bet*. It is important to note that the Italian closed [e] is a pure vowel sound, never diphthongal [eɪ] as in the English word *bay* [beɪ]. Be especially careful to use pure [e] and not [eɪ].

In order to determine the pronunciation of the letter *e*, you must first decide whether it occurs in a stressed or unstressed syllable (see page 42 for how to determine stressed and unstressed syllables). The letter *e* in a stressed syllable is referred to as *stressed e*, in an unstressed syllable, *unstressed e*.

The letter *e* in stressed syllables

If you determine that the syllable is stressed, then you will need to make a choice between [e] or [ɛ]: stressed *e* will have no other pronunciations. Your choice is significant not only for correct pronunciation, but because sometimes the meaning of the word is dependant on it. Compare the list below.

venti	['ven ti]	means *twenty*
	['vɛn ti]	means *winds*
legge	['ledː dʒe]	means *law*
	['lɛdː dʒe]	means he *reads*
mezzo	['metː tso]	means *over-ripe*
	['mɛdː dzo]	means *medium* (mezzo-soprano)

The pronunciation rules for stressed *e* are listed below. They will provide reliable choices for when to sing open [ɛ] or closed [e]. However, because there are many words that are exceptions to rules in Italian, it is wise to keep a dictionary handy at all times.

> Note: In dictionaries, pronunciation of stressed *e* is indicated by an acute accent, *é*, for closed [e] and a grave accent, *è*, for open [ɛ].

The letter *e* in unstressed syllables

If you determine that the *e* is in an unstressed syllable, then the pronunciation of it should be closed [e], except when it comes before *l*, *m*, *n*, or *r* plus another *consonant*. However, whether you sing unstressed *e* as closed or open will not influence the meaning of the word, as it might for stressed *e*. Consider what phonetician Claude Wise writes: "The difference between [e] and [ɛ] is significant only in stressed syllables. Elsewhere, (in unstressed syllables) the vowel sound may vary over a continuous range from [e] to [ɛ], with a statistical predominance of the more open types before nasals, laterals, or trills."

Ultimately, whether to sing unstressed *e* as closed [e] or open [ɛ] will be a matter of your personal aesthetics and you will encounter varying opinions among vocal pedagogues. For many years, vocal pedagogues have directed singers to pronounce unstressed *e* as open [ɛ] in all syllables that follow the stressed syllable. They were perhaps motivated to avoid any of the following three problems of singing closed [e] in unstressed syllables:

American singers often have a tendency to sing a diphthonged [eɪ] rather than a pure [e]. With this diphthongized *e, dove, amore,* and *cantare* would sound like ['do veɪ], [ɑ 'mo reɪ], and [cɑn 'tɑ reɪ]. The resulting English accent is unpleasant, and is particularly noticable because so many Italian words end with unstressed *e*. To avoid this problem, pedagogues have instructed singers to sing unstressed *e* as open [ɛ], particularly at the end of words.

In English, unstressed *e* usually becomes the *schwa* [ə] sound and almost never a closed [e] sound. (The words *vacation* and *chaotic* are notable exceptions.) The closed [e] sound is usually found only in stressed syllables, so an American singer will have a tendency to over-stress the unstressed syllable in Italian when pronouncing it as closed [e]. *Dove, amore,* and *cantare* will tend to sound like [do 've], [ɑ mo 're], and [cɑn tɑ 're], which is incorrect pronunciation. To avoid this unpleasant stressed sound, pedagogues have also recommended [ɛ] for pronouncing unstressed *e*.

A third notion — that open [ɛ] will be more conducive to singing with a resonant tone — sometimes prompts the choice of [ɛ] for unstressed *e*.

My personal choice is to sing unstressed *e* as closed [e]. This sound follows spoken Italian, where unstressed *e* is always closed [e] except before *l, m, n,* or *r* plus another *consonant,* and singing closed [e] will add authenticity to the pronunciation. Many top pedagogues have become interested in matching the spoken language. In <u>Phonetic Readings of Songs and Arias,</u> for example, unstressed *e* is transcribed as closed [e]. It is certainly possible for American singers to overcome their own speech habits of diphthongizing and over-emphasizing the closed [e] sound. As for facilitating singing, the dynamics of vowel modification will include more choices than open [ɛ], so choosing open [ɛ] over closed [e] is not valuable as a general rule for unstressed *e*.

Use this discussion to make your personal choice whether to sing open [ɛ] or closed [e] for unstressed *e*. Then, become aware of your choice and keep it consistant throughout your work. It will make a difference.

the single letter e unstressed

The letter

e

In the following words, pronounce each unstressed *e* as closed [e].

Read aloud.

legale	[le 'ɑɑ le]	ferrare	[ferː 'rɑ re]
legato	[le 'ɑɑ to]	regale	[re 'ɑɑ le]
tenere	[te 'ne re]	venire	[ve 'ni re]
luce	['lu tʃe]	fosse	['fɔsː se]
mare	['mɑ re]	maschera	['mɑ ske rɑ]
amore	[ɑ 'mo re]	credere	['kre de re]
opera	['ɔ pe rɑ]	confondere	[kon 'fon de re]

Repeat the words a second time and pronounce each unstressed *e* that follows the stressed syllable as open [ɛ]. Listen and feel the difference. (See the discussion above in The letter *e*).

Read aloud to compare and contrast.

legale	[le 'ɑɑ lɛ]	ferrare	[ferː 'rɑ rɛ]
legato	[le 'ɑɑ to]	regale	[re 'ɑɑ lɛ]
tenere	[te 'ne rɛ]	venire	[ve 'ni rɛ]
luce	['lu tʃɛ]	fosse	['fɔsː sɛ]
mare	['mɑ rɛ]	maschera	['mɑ skɛ rɑ]
amore	[ɑ 'mo rɛ]	credere	['krɛ de rɛ]
opera	['ɔ pɛ rɑ]	confondere	[kon 'fon dɛ rɛ]

When unstressed *e* is followed by *l, m, n, r* and another *consonant,* pronounce it as [ɛ] .

Read aloud.

beltade	[bɛl 'tɑ de]	gentile	[dʒɛn 'ti le]
tempesta	[tɛm 'pɛ stɑ]	versare	[vɛr 'sɑ re]
entrare	[ɛn 'trɑ re]	mercè	[mɛr 'tʃe]

Note: For a memory "tickler," remember this rule as the *lemoner* rule (the consonants *l, m, n,* and *r* being used in this word): *Lemoner plus another consonant.*

When the letter *e* ends a stressed syllable, usually pronounce it as

The single letter e stressed

When the letter *e* ends a stressed syllable, usually pronounce it as [e].

Read aloud.

pe-na	['pe nɑ]	se-gno	['se ɲo]
pre-sa	['pre zɑ]	se-ra	['se rɑ]
stre-ga	['stre gɑ]	e-gli	['e ʎi]
che	[ke]	e	[e] (meaning *and*)

These common words do not follow the normal rule. Pronounce them with open [ɛ].

bene	['bɛ ne]	(means *good*)
breve	['brɛ ve]	(means *short*)
speme	['spɛ me]	(means *hope*)
prego	['prɛ go]	(means *I pray*)

Here are three important exceptions. See the following rules.

1. When *e* ends a stressed antepenult syllable, pronounce it as [ɛ].

Read aloud.

te-ne-ro	['tɛ ne ro]	me-di-co	['mɛ di ko]
ge-li-da	['dʒɛ li dɑ]	e-ti-co	['ɛ ti ko]

Note: Rely upon the metric stress of the melodic line to help you know when to irregularly give the primary stress to the third-to-last syllable.

2. When *stressed e* ends a syllable before an *s* plus another consonant, pronounce it as [ɛ].

Read aloud.

fu-ne-sto	[fu 'nɛ sto]	tem-pe-sta	[tɛm 'pɛ stɑ]
pre-sto	['prɛ sto]	fe-sta	['fɛ stɑ]

Exception: The common word *questo* ['kwe sto] is pronounced with a closed [e].

The letter

e

3. When *stressed e* ends a syllable after *i* or *u*, usually pronounce it as [ɛ].

Read aloud.

cie-lo	['tʃɛ lo]	que-ru-lo	['kwɛ ru lo]
pie-no	['pjɛ no]	guer-ra	['gwɛrː rɑ]

Note: The vowel *e*, after the glides [j] and [w], is usually pronounced as open [ɛ], but sometimes it is pronounced as closed [e]:

quelle   [kwelː le]

It is also closed [e] in final unstressed syllables:

smanie   ['zmɑ nje]   foglie   ['fɔ ʎe].

When stressed *e* is before a vowel (as in a diphthong or two syllables), pronounce it as [ɛ]. (See <u>The letter e</u>, "Consecutive Vowel Groups", page 64.)

Read aloud.

Diphthongs:	lei	[lɛːi]	sei	[sɛːi]
Two Syllables:	idea	[i 'dɛː ɑ]	reo	['rɛː o]

Note: See the musical examples that illustrate how to sing diphthongs, triphthongs, and two syllables on page 54.

When stressed *e* is followed by a consonant in the same syllable, usually pronounce it as [ɛ].

Read aloud.

sempre	['sɛm pre]	certo	['tʃɛr to]
verso	['vɛr so]	scherzo	['skɛr tso]
pendere	['pɛn de re]		
venti	['vɛn ti] (meaning *winds*)		

Exceptions: Pronounce these common words with closed [e].

verde	['ver de]	Verdi	['ver di]
venti	['ven ti] (meaning *twenty*)		

When stressed *e* is followed by a double consonant, check a dictionary. Sometimes it is pronounced as open [ɛ], sometimes closed [e].

Compare and contrast.

	closed:		open:
stella	['stelː lɑ]	ecco	['ɛkː ko]
ella	['elː lɑ]	presso	['prɛsː so]
secco	['sekː ko]	bella	['bɛlː lɑ]

When *é or è* is final, pronounce it as closed [e].

> Note: A grave or an acute accent over a final *e* will not affect its pronunciation.

Read aloud.

The letter

e

chè, ché   [ke] meaning *because, why*
perchè, perché   [pɛr 'ke] meaning *because, why*
mercè, mercé   [mɛr 'ʧe] *meaning thanks*
sè, sé   [se] meaning *him, himself*

Exception: Notice the difference in pronounciation and meaning in these two common words:

e [e] means *and*   è [ɛ] means *is*

e in suffixes and diminutives

In Italian, many words have endings that include a stressed *e*. These are sometimes pronounced [e] and sometimes [ɛ]. To determine the correct pronounciation, check a dictionary.

> Note: Since most Italian dictionaries do not use IPA transcriptions, you will need to rely upon other marks. Most dictionaries indicate closed and open pronounciations by an accent mark over the stressed vowel: acute accent (é) for closed [e] or a grave accent (è) for open [ɛ].

In these stressed endings, *e* is usually closed :
emmo, esco, essa, esti, evole, ezza, mente, etto, etta, etti, ette

> Note: The gender changes on the final vowels (such as *-etto* to *-etta*) will not affect the pronunciation of *e*.

Read aloud.

closed:			
	Musetta	[mu 'zetː tɑ]	*-etta*
	Violette	[vjɔ 'letː tɑ]	*-ette*
	contessa	[kon tesː sɑ]	*-essa*
	principessa	[prin ʧi 'pesː sɑ]	*-essa*
	monumento	[mo nu 'men to]	*-mento*
	vagamento	[vɑ gɑ 'men to]	*-mento*
	piacevole	[pja 'ʧe vo le]	*-evole*
	brezza	['brezː zɑ]	*-ezza*
	bellezza	[be lezː zɑ]	*-ezza*
	avemmo	[ɑ 'vemː mo]	*-emmo*
	promesso	[pro 'mesː sɑ]	*-esso*

The letter

e

Notice that in these words -etto is pronounced as open [ɛ]

aspetto	[a 'spɛtː to]	letto	['lɛtː to]
diletto	[di 'lɛtː to]	petto	['pɛtː to]
oggetto	[ogː 'gɛtː to]	rispetto	[ri 'spɛtː to]

In these stressed endings the e tends to be open [ɛ]:
ero, ello, and *ente*.

Read aloud.

open:	mistero	[mi 'stɛ rɔ] -ero
	altero	[al 'tɛ rɔ] -ero
	cappella	[kapː 'pɛlː la] -ella
	dolente	[do 'lɛn te] -ente

The letter e in consecutive vowel

See general rules for consecutive vowels on page 50.

ea

Pronounce *ea* as two syllables [ɛː a]. When the strong vowel *e* precedes the strong vowel *a*, pronounce them as two syllables.

Read aloud.

ide-a	[i 'dɛː a]	e-to-pe-a	[e to 'pɛː a]
stri-de-a	[stri 'dɛː a]	di-scio-glie-a	[di ʃo 'ʎɛː a]

Exceptions: Pronounce these common words with closed [e]:

tacea	[ta 'tʃeː a]	credea	[kre 'deː a]

ei

Pronounce *ei* as the diphthong [ɛːi].

Read aloud.

lei	[lɛːi]	sei	[sɛːi]
costei	[ko 'stɛːi]	bei	[bɛːi]
potrei	[po 'trɛːi]	vorrei	[vorː 'rɛːi]

Exception: Pronounce *pei* as [peːi], with a closed [e].

eo

Pronounce *eo* as two syllables [ɛː ɔ]. When the strong vowel *e* precedes the strong vowel *o*, pronounce them as two syllables.

Read aloud.

re-o	['rɛː ɔ]	Orfeo	[ɔr 'fɛː ɔ]
creola	['krɛː ɔ la]	leopardo	[lɛː ɔ 'par do]

eu

Pronounce *eu* as the diphthong [ɛːu]. This diphthong is used infrequently in Italian. Sometimes pronounce it as [ɛːu]; other times as [eːu]. If in doubt, pronounce it [ɛːu], in a stressed syllable and [eːu] in an unstressed syllable.

Compare and contrast.

euro	['ɛːu ro]	pseudo	['psɛːu do]
Euridice	[eːu ri 'di tʃe]	eufonia	[eːu 'fɔnja]

The letter

i

The letter *i* as a single vowel in a syllable is always pronounced as [i]. When *i* is combined with another vowel in a syllable, you will need to decide whether to pronounce it as [i] the glide [j] or whether it is silent. See the rules below.

Caution: In English, unstressed *i* will often be pronounced as [ɪ]. Do not carry this practice into Italian. The letter *i* is never pronounced as [ɪ].

Compare and contrast.

impero [im 'pe ro]   not [ɪm 'pe ro]

The single letter i

When *i* is final or before another consonant, pronounce it as [i].

Read aloud.

di	[di]	destino	[de 'sti no]	capiro	[ka 'pi ro]
il	[il]	finiti	[fi 'ni ti]	litigare	[li ti 'ga re]

When *i* is after a vowel, pronounce it as [i].

An *i* after a vowel forms a diphthong. Pronounce *i* as [i] giving it shorter duration than the preceding vowel.

Read aloud.

noi	[noːi]	pei	[pɛːi]	mai	[maːi]
voi	[voːi]	sei	[sɛːi]	sai	[saːi]
poi	[pɔːi]	lei	[lɛːi]	laida	['laːi da]

The letter

When *i* is after *c, g,* or *sc* and before *a, o, u* or *e* , it is silent.

> Note: The silent *i* acts like a diacritical mark to soften the pronounciations of *c, g,* and *sc.*

Read aloud.

baciare	[ba 'tʃa re]	sciala	['ʃa la]
cielo	['tʃɛ lo]	sciolto	['ʃol to]
ciò	[tʃɔ]	sciuppo	['ʃupː po]
fanciulla	[fan 'tʃulː la]	lascia	['la ʃa]
già	[dʒa]		
gioco	['dʒɔ ko]		
giusto	['dʒu sto]		
vagheggiar	[va ɡedː 'dʒar]		

Exception: In Italian, a final stressed syllable is usually indicated by an accent mark, as in *dileguò*. However, in a few words you will find a final stressed syllable without an accent mark. In this case, you will pronounce the *i* as [i], even though it would otherwise be silent.

Lucia   [lu 'tʃiː a]   nostalgia   [no stal 'dʒiː a]

There is no clear rule that determines whether a final syllable without an accent mark is stressed. You must rely on the metric stress of the melodic line or refer to a dictionary.

The letter i in consecutive vowels

See general rules for consecutive vowels on page 50.

ia

When *ia* is in the interior of a word, pronounce the *i* as a glide [ja].

Read aloud.

fiamma	['fjamː ma]	piaga	['pja ɡa]
piante	['pjan te]	sembiante	[sɛm 'bjan te]
bianca	['bjan ka]	schiava	['skja ra]
andiam	[an 'djam]		

When *ia* is unstressed and final in a word, pronounce the *i* as a glide [ja].

Read aloud.

gloria	['glɔ rja]	Italia	[i 'ta lja]
storia	['stɔ rja]	vittoria	[vitː 'tɔ rja]
aria	['a rja]	infamia	[in 'fa mja]
vicchia	['vikː kja]		

ia (cont.)

When *ia* is in small three letter words that have no accent mark, pronounce them as two syllables [iː ɑ].

> Read aloud.
>
> mia [miː ɑ]   pia ['piː ɑ]
> via ['viː ɑ]   fia ['fiː ɑ]

In polysyllabic words, when *i* is stressed and followed by final *a* and there is no accent mark, pronounce *ia* as two syllables.

> Read aloud.
>
> grafia [grɑ 'fiː ɑ]   Maria [mɑ 'riː ɑ]
> follia [folː 'liː ɑ]   gelosia [dʒe lo 'ziː ɑ]

Also pronounce *ia* as two syllables in words where stressed *i* precedes *-ano* in the third personal plural verb ending.

> Read aloud.
>
> siano   ['siː ɑ no]   fiano   [fiː ɑ no]

ie

Usually pronounce *ie* as a glide [jɛ] when it is in the interior of a word or when it is in a final stressed syllable with an accent mark.

> Read aloud.
>
> barbiere [bɑr 'bjɛ re]   pieno   ['pjɛ no]
> chiesa   ['kjɛ zɑ]   piè   ['pjɛ]
> chiedo   ['kjɛ do]   vieni   ['vjɛ ni]
> tiene   ['tjɛ ne]   obbediente [obː be 'djɛn te]

> Exceptions: Pronounce *ie* in these common words as closed [je].
>
> Read aloud.
>
> liete   ['lje te]   fiero   ['fje ro]
> insieme [in 'sje me]   pietà   [pje 'tɑ]
> siete   ['sje te]   pensiero [pɛn 'sje ro]

Pronounce *ie* as two syllables [iː e] when it is in small three letter words, without an accent.

> Read aloud.
>
> mie   [miː e]

The letter

i

The letter

i

ie (cont.)

Pronounce *ie* as two syllables when it is in polysyllabic words, when *i* is stressed and followed by final *e*, and when there is no accent mark. (See "Two Syllables" page 52.)

> Read aloud.
> follie [folː 'liː ɛ]

iei (triphthong)

Pronounce *iei* as a triphthong [jɛːi]. A triphthong is a sequence of three vowel sounds that occur in the same syllable, usually composed of a glide and a diphthong,

> Read aloud.
> miei [mjɛːi]

io

When *io* is in the interior of a word, usually pronounce it as [jɔ].

> Read aloud.
> chiodo [ˈkjɔ do]   fiocco [ˈfjɔkː ko]
> ansioso [an ˈsjɔ zo]   studio [ˈstu djɔ]
> viola [ˈvjɔ la]   violetta [ˈvjɔ ˈletː ta]

> Exception: Pronounce *io* in these common words as closed [jo].

> fiore [ˈfjo re]   passione [pasː ˈsjo ne]

When *io* is unstressed and final in a word, pronounce it as [jɔ].

> Read aloud.
> rimedio [ri ˈmɛ djɔ]   silenzio [si ˈlɛn tsjɔ]
> Canio [ˈka njɔ]   Vecchio [ˈvɛkː kjɔ]

Pronounce *io* as two syllables [iː o] when it is in small, two or three letter words without an accent mark.

> Read aloud.
> io [iː o]   mio [miː o]   dio [diː o]

Pronounce *io* as two syllables [iː o] when *i* is stressed and followed by final *o* without an accent mark.

> Read aloud.
> addio [adː ˈdiː o]   colpio [kol ˈpiː o]
> natio [na ˈtiː o]   desio [de ˈziː o]
> oblio [o ˈbliː o]

iu

When *iu* is in the interior of a word or in a final stressed syllable with an accent mark, pronounce it as a glide [ju].

Read aloud.

Liù	[lju]	piuma	['pju mɑ]
più	[pju]	schiuda	['skju dɑ]
liuto	['lju to]	piuttosto	[pjutː 'tɔ sto]

The letter

You will pronounce the Italian *o* in one of two ways: closed [o] as in the English word *obey*, and open [ɔ] as the *aw* sound in *awe*.

Caution: Be careful to sing pure [o] in Italian and never use diphthongal [oʊ] as you would in the English word *bone*.

In order to determine the pronunciation of the letter *o*, you must first determine whether it occurs in a stressed or unstressed syllable. The letter *o* in a stressed syllable is referred to as *stressed o*, in an unstressed syllable, *unstressed o*.

The letter *o* in stressed syllables

If you determine that the syllable is stressed (see page 42 for how to determine stressed and unstressed syllables), then you will need to make a choice between [o] or [ɔ]: stressed *o* will have no other pronunciations. Unlike the letter *e*, your choice will not often affect the meaning of the word. See the rules below for how to determine whether to pronounce stressed *o* as [o] or [ɔ].

Note: There will be some words not covered in these rules. Rely upon your memory of often repeated words or consult a dictionary.

The letter *o* in unstressed syllables

If you determine that the letter *o* is in an unstressed syllable, then pronounce it as closed, except when it precedes *r* and another consonant. Some vocal pedagogues, however, direct singers to pronounce every unstressed *o* that follows a stressed syllable as open [ɔ]. (See the discussion on page 58 under <u>The letter e</u>, unstressed syllables. The letters *e* and *o* have similar characteristics.) Use this discussion to make your personal choice whether to sing open [ɔ] or closed [o] for unstressed *o*. Then, become aware of your choice and keep it consistent throughout your singing.

The letter o, unstressed

The letter

O

Usually pronounce unstressed *o* as [o]. In the following words, pronounce each unstressed *o* as [o].

Read aloud.

certo	['tʃɛr to]	parlo	['par lo]
sospiro	[so 'spi ro]	momento	[mo 'men to]
p<u>er</u>-do-no	['pɛr do no]	prometto	[pro 'metː to]
pri-mo	['pri mo]	al-me-no	[al 'me no]

Repeat the words a second time and pronounce each unstressed *o* that follows the stressed syllable as open [ɔ]. Listen and feel the difference. (See the discussion above in <u>The letter o</u>).

Read aloud to compare and contrast.

certo	['tʃɛr tɔ]	parlo	['par lɔ]
sospiro	[so ' spi rɔ]	momento	[mo 'men tɔ]
p<u>er</u>-do-no	['pɛr dɔ no]	prometto	[[pro 'metː tɔ]
pri-mo	['pri mɔ]	al-me-no	[al 'me nɔ]

When unstressed *o* is followed by *r* and another consonant, pronounce it as [ɔ].

Read aloud.

tor-men-to	[tɔr 'men to]	tor-na-re	[tɔr 'na re]
cor-pet-to	[kɔr 'petː to]	dor-mi-re	[dɔr 'mi re]

The letter o, stressed

When stressed *o* ends a syllable, usually pronounce it as [o].

Read aloud.

so-no	['so no]	mo-stro	['mo stro]
a-mo-re	[a 'mo re]	o-gni	['o ɲi]
ri-go-re	[ri 'go re]	vo-ce	['vo tʃe]
To-sca	['to ska]	so-la	['so la]

Exceptions: These common words are exceptions to this rule. Pronounce each word with open [ɔ].

cosa   ['kɔ zɑ]   meaning *thing, affair, item*
core   ['kɔ re]   from *cuore*, meaning *heart*
rosa   ['rɔ zɑ]   meaning *pink*
sposa   ['spɔ zɑ]   meaning *bride*
poco   ['pɔ ko]   meaning *little, few*

The letter

o

In the following six circumstances, however, pronounce the stressed *o* when it ends a syllable as open [ɔ], and *not* its usual pronunciation when it ends a syllable of closed [o].

1. When *o* ends a stressed antepenult syllable, pronounce it as [ɔ].

   Read aloud.
   po-ve-ro   ['pɔ rɛ ro]   o-pe-ra   ['ɔ pe rɑ]
   or-fa-na   ['ɔr fɑ nɑ]   po-po-lo   ['pɔ po lo]

   Note: Rely upon the metric stress of the melodic line to help you know when to irregularly give the primary stress to the third-to-last syllable.

2. When *o* is after *i* or *u*, pronounce it as [ɔ].

   Read aloud.
   pio-ve   ['pjɔ ve]   io-sa   ['jɔ zɑ]
   scuo-la ['skwɔ lɑ]   quota   ['kwɔ tɑ]

3. When *o* is final and accented, pronounce it as [ɔ].

   Note: An accent mark over the final vowel indicates that the syllable is stressed.

   Read aloud.
   fa-rò   [fɑ 'rɔ]   sal-pò   [sɑl 'pɔ]
   ciò   [ʧɔ]   fi-ni-rò   [fi ni 'rɔ]
   tornò   [tor 'nɔ]   lascierò   [lɑ ʃɛ 'rɔ]
   potrò   [po 'trɔ]   dileguò   [di le 'gwɔ]

4. When *o* is followed by *gli*, pronounce it as [ɔ].

   Read aloud.
   fo-glio   ['fɔ ʎo]   sco-glio   ['skɔ ʎo]

The letter

5. When *o* is followed by a consonant and a glide, pronounce it as [ɔ].

Read aloud.

glo-ria	['glɔ rja]	To-nio	['tɔ njɔ]
sto-ria	['stɔ rja]	me-mo-ria	[me 'mɔ rja]

6. When *o* is in the noun ending *-oro* and its plural, *ori*, pronounce it as [ɔ].

Read aloud.

tesoro	[te 'zɔ ro]	Lindoro	[lin 'dɔ ro]
Alindoro	[a lin 'dɔ ro]	oro	['ɔ ro]

When stressed *o* is followed by a vowel, pronounce it as [ɔ].

Read aloud.

Diphthongs:	poi [pɔːi]
Triphthongs:	vuoi [vwɔːi]
Two syllables:	balboa [bal 'bɔː a]

When stressed *o* is followed by a consonant in the same syllable, usually pronounce it as [ɔ].

Read aloud.

for-za	['fɔr tsa]	sor-te	['sɔr te]
mor-te	['mɔr te]	por-to	['pɔr to]

Exception: Pronounce these common words with closed [o]:

forma	['for ma]	(meaning *shape, form*)
forse	['for se]	(meaning *doubt*)
giorno	['ʤor no]	(meaning *day*)

In the following three circumstances, however, when *o* is followed by a consonant in the same syllable, pronounce it as closed [o].

1. When *o* is followed by the letter *l* and either *c, f, g, m, p,* or *t*, pronounce *o* as [o].

Read aloud.

dol-ce	['dol ʧe]	vol-to	['vol to]
col-po	['kol po]	a-scol-to	[a 'skol to]

Exception: Pronounce the common word *volta* ['vɔl ta] (meaning *turn*) with open [ɔ].

2. When *o* is followed by the letters *mb, mm,* or *mp,* pronounce *o* as [o].

Read aloud.

om-bra	['om bra]	gom-ma	['gomː ma]
pom-pa	['pom pa]	from-ba	['from ba]

3. When *o* is followed by a single *n* in the same syllable, pronounce it as [o].

Read aloud.

con	['kon]	ron-di-ne	['ron di ne]
mon-do	['mon do]	don-de	['don de]

The letter

O

When stressed *o* is followed by a double consonant, check the dictionary. Sometimes it is pronounced closed [o], sometimes open [ɔ].

Compare and contrast.

Closed		Open	
sot-to	[sotː to]	lot-to	[lɔtː to]
fos-si	[fosː si]	appog-gio	[apː 'pɔdː ʤo]
boc-ca	[bokː ka]	gob-bo	[gɔbː bo]

The letter o in consecutive vowels

oa

Pronounce the strong consecutive vowels *oa* as two syllables.

Read aloud.

bal-bo-a [bɑl 'bɔː a]   so-a-ve [sɔ 'ɑ ve]

oe

Pronounce the strong consecutive vowels *oe* as two syllables.

Read aloud.

e-ro-e [e 'rɔː ɛ]   po-e-ta [pɔ 'ɛ tɑ]

oi

Usually pronounce *oi* as the diphthong [ɔːi].

Read aloud.

poi [pɔːi]   poiche [pɔːi 'ke]

Exceptions: In these common words, pronounce the diphthong with closed [o].

voi [voːi]   noi [noːi]   coi [koːi]

oia, oja (two syllables)

Pronounce *oia* and *oja* as a two syllables [ɔː ja].

Read aloud.

gio-ia ['ʤɔ ːja]   gio-ja ['ʤɔː ja]

See general rules for Consecutive Vowels on page 50.

The letter

u

The letter *u* vowel in a syllable is always pronounced as [u] as in the English word *boot*, never as [ʊ] as in *book*. The sound [ʊ] does not exist in Italian. When [u] is combined with another vowel in a syllable, you will need to decide whether to pronounce it as [u] or the glide [w] See rules below.

The single letter u

When *u* is before a consonant, pronounce it as [u].

Read aloud.

fugare	[fu 'gɑ re]	pupa	['pu pɑ]
cucina	[ku 'ʧi nɑ]	lunga	['lun gɑ]

When *u* is after a vowel, pronounce it as [u].

Read aloud.

più	[pju]	liuto	['lju to]
pausa	['pɑːu zɑ]	Euridice	[eːu ri 'di ʧe]

The letter u in consecutive vowels

See general rules for Consecutive Vowels on page 50.

ua

Usually pronounce *ua* as the glide [wɑ].

Read aloud.

quanto	['kwɑn to]	graduare	[grɑ 'dwɑ re]
squadare	[skwɑ 'dɑ re]	statua	['stɑ twɑ]

ua

Pronounce *ua* as the two syllables [uː ɑ] in small words where there is no accent mark. Notice that the *u* is stressed.

Read aloud.

tua [tuː ɑ]

ue

Usually pronounce *ue* as the glide [wɛ].

> Read aloud.
> guerra   ["gwɛrː rɑ]
> estinguerà [e stin gwɛ 'rɑ]
>
> Exception: The common words *quello* ['kwelː lo] and *questo* ['kwe sto] are pronounced with closed [e].

ue

Pronounce *ue* as two syllables [uː e] in small words where there is no accent mark. Notice that the *u* is stressed.

> Read aloud.
> tue ['tuː e]   due ['duː e]

The letter

u

ui

Usually pronounce *ui* as the glide [wi].

  Note: When *ui* follows *q* or is in the interior of a word, the result is a glide.

> Read aloud.
> qui [kwi]   languir [lɑn 'gwir]

ui

Pronounce *ui* as two syllables [uː i] in small words when it is final in the word and there is no accent mark.

> Read aloud.
> lui ['luː i]   cui ['kuː i]
> fui ['fuː i]

uo

Usually pronounce *uo* as the glide [wɔ].

  When the weak vowel *u*, followed by the strong vowel *o*, is in the initial or interior position of the word, or is final with an accent mark, pronounce the vowel combination as a glide.

> Read aloud.
> uomo   ['wɔ mo]   nuovo ['nwɔ vo]
> può   [pwɔ]   duolo   ['dwɔ lo]
> vuole   ['vwɔ le]   dileguò [di le 'gwɔ]
> fuori   ['fwɔ ri]   cuore   ['kwɔ re]

The letter

u

uo

Pronounce *uo* as the two syllables [uː o] in small words when it is final in the word and there is no accent mark.

t<u>u</u>o [tuː o]   s<u>u</u>o [suː o]

uai

Pronounce *uai* as a triphthong [wɑːi].

buai [bwɑːi]

uie

Pronounce *uie* as a triphthong [wjɛ].

quiete [kwjɛ te]

uio

Pronounce *uio* as a two syllables [uː jɔ].

buio [buː jɔ]

uoi

Pronounce *uoi* as a triphthong [wɔːi].

tuoi [twɔːi]   vuoi [vwɔːi]
suoi [swɔːi]

Italian Consonants in Detail

Pronounce *b* as [b].

b

Note: [b] represents the sound of *b* in the English word *boy*. In Italian [b] is a *dry* consonant pronounced with less aspiration than in English.

Read aloud.

bocca	['bokː ka]	abisso	[ɑ 'bisː so]
bacio	['bɑ ʧo]	batti	['batː ti]
barbara	['bɑr bɑ rɑ]	bambino	[bɑm 'bi no]

bb

Pronounce *bb* as [bː b].

Note: Pronounce [bː b] with a longer duration than the single [b]. Your lips will close for the stop portion of the consonant. The stop is longer than for a single [b], after which the plosive part of the consonant is articulated.

Compare and contrast.

Examples from English which illustrate the rhythm of a double [bː b].

la<u>b b</u>one   gra<u>b b</u>ack

Examples from Italian:

babbo	['babː bo]	labbro	['labː bro]
gabbare	[gabː 'bɑ re]	abbia	['abː bja]
rabbia	['rabː bja]		
abbandonare	[abː ban do 'nɑ re]		

When *c* is followed by *a, o,* or *u,* pronounce it as [k].

C

Note: [k] represents the sound of *k* as in the English word *kit*. In Italian [k] is a *dry* consonant, pronounced with less aspiration than in English. When *c* is pronounced as [k], it is called a hard *c*.

Read aloud.

canta	['kan tɑ]	culto	['kul to]
copia	['ko pja]	cura	['ku rɑ]
stancare	[stɑn 'kɑ re]	pecora	['pe ko rɑ]

When *cc* is followed by *a, o,* or *u,* pronounce it as [kː k].

Note: Pronounce [kː k] with a longer duration than the single [k]. The back of your tongue will lift to touch the soft palate for the stop portion of [k]. There is a short silent pause, after which the plosive part of the consonant is articulated.

Compare and contrast.

Examples from English which illustrate the rhythm of double [kː k]:

pink cat   milk cow

Examples from Italian:

bocca	['bokː ka]	sorccoso	[sɔrkː 'ko zo]
ecco	['ɛkː ko]	accusa	[akː 'ku za]
pecca	['pɛkː ka]	lucca	['lukː ka]

When *c* is followed by *e* or *i,* pronounce it as *ch* [ʧ].

Note: [ʧ] represents the sound of *ch* in the English word *chair.* [ʧ] is an affricative consonant that is made up of the stop of the stop-plosive consonant [t], as in *tip,* combined with the fricative consonant *sh* [ʃ], as in *ship.* A *c* pronounced as [ʧ] is called a *soft c.*

Read aloud.

faci	['fa ʧi]	celare	[ʧe 'la re]
certo	['ʧɛr to]	dolce	['dol ʧe]
dieci	['djɛ ʧi]	ciro	['ʧi ro]
bacio	['ba ʧo]	ciucca	['ʧukː ka]

Note: Even though the *i,* as in *bacio* ['ba ʧo], is silent, it continues to function as an agent which softens the pronounciation of *c* to [ʧ]. (See the rule for silent *i* under The Letter i, page 66.)

When *cc* is followed by *e* or *i,* pronounce it as *soft ch* [tː ʧ].

Note: Pronounce [tː ʧ] with longer duration than [ʧ]. Produce double *cc* as [tː ʧ], with the tip of the tongue lifting to touch the back of the upper front teeth for the stop portion of [t]. There is a short silent pause, then the air escapes in a fricative *sh* [ʃ].

Note: The diacritic [ː] indicates the longer duration of the stop portion of [t]. The symbol [t] is written a second time to emphasize the importance of prolonging the doubled consonant in Italian.

Compare and contrast.

    Examples in English which illustrate the rhythm of a double *cc* [tː tʃ]:

        ha<u>t c</u>heck   sof<u>t c</u>hair

    Examples in Italian:

accenti	[atː 'tʃɛn ti]	traccia	['tratː tʃa]
braccio	['bratː tʃo]	Puccini	[putː 'tʃi ni]

W hen *c* is followed by a *consonant*, pronounce it as [k].

Read aloud.

clav<u>i</u>cola	[kla 'vi ko la]	cl<u>i</u>nica	['kli ni ka]
cr<u>e</u>dere	['krɛ de re]	cruda	['kru da]
cl<u>a</u>ssico	['klasː si ko]	crescendo	[kre 'ʃɛn do]

ch & cch

P ronounce *ch* as [k].

Note: In the digraph *ch*, the *h* is silent. When *ch* is before *e* or *i* the *h* functions as a diacritical mark to harden the pronounciation of *c*. Silent *h* after *c* and before *e* or *i* becomes a diacritical mark and hardens *c* to [k].

Read aloud.

che	[ke]	poichè	[pɔːi 'ke]
chiama	['kja ma]	chi	[ki]
chiesi	['kjɛ zi]	inciuchire	[in tʃu 'ki re]

P ronounce *cch* as [kː k].

Note: Pronounce [kː k] with longer duration than [k].

Read aloud.

pacchetto	[pakː 'ketː to]	m<u>a</u>cchina	['makː ki na]
vecchie	['vɛkː kje]	acchetare	[akː ke 'ta re]
occhi	['ɔkː ki]		

cqu

Pronounce *cqu* as [kː k].

Note: In these words, the *c* is pronounced as [k] and qu is pronounced as [k] , resulting in the prolonged [k].

Read aloud.

acqua ['akː kwa] acquieta [akː 'kwjɛ ta]
acquisire [akː kwi 'zi re]

d

Pronounce *d* as [d].

Note: [d] is the sound of *d* in the English word *day*. In Italian <u>d</u> is a dental consonant, not the alveolar *d* used in English. It is also articulated more dryly, with less aspiration, than in English.

Read aloud.

dare	['da re]	deserto	[de 'zɛr to]
diva	['di va]	ind<u>o</u>cile	[in 'dɔ ʧi le]
padre	['pa dre]	dottore	[dotː 'to re]

Pronounce doubled *dd* as [dː d].

Note: Pronounce [dː d] with your tongue tip touching the back of the upper front teeth for a longer duration than for a single *d*. This is followed by the plosive part of the consonant.

Compare and contrast.

Examples in English which illustrate the rhythm of the double *dd*.
Ne<u>d d</u>id bed <u>down</u>

Examples in Italian:

Nedda	['nɛdː da]	freddo	['fredː do]
add<u>io</u>	[adː 'diː ɔ]	Turiddu	[tu 'ridː du]
bodda	[bɔdː da]	addosso	[adː 'dɔsː so]

Pronounce *f* as [f].

Note: [f] is the sound of *f* in the English word *feet*.

Read aloud.

fato	['fɑ to]	rifare	[ri 'fɑ re]
figura	[fi 'gu rɑ]	figlia	['fi ʎa]
infelice	[in fe 'li ʧe]	confessione	[kon fɛsː 'sjɔ ne]

Pronounce *ff* as [fː f].

Note: Pronounce *ff* [fː f] with longer duration than *f* [f].

Compare and contrast.

Examples of a double *ff* sound in English:
cliff fall   off fool

Examples in Italian:

affani	[afː fɑ ni]	affetto	[afː 'fɛtː to]
maffia	['mafː fjɑ]	gaffa	['gafː fɑ]

---

f

When *g* is followed by *a, o, u,* or a *consonant*, pronounce it as [g].

Note: [g] is the sound of *g* as in the English word *go*. The Italian [g] has a drier, less aspirate sound than in English. When *g* is pronounced as [g] it is called a *hard g*.

Read aloud.

guarda	['gwɑr dɑ]	margari	[mɑr 'gɑ ri]
gala	['gɑ lɑ]	uguale	[u 'gwɑ le]
figura	[fi 'gu rɑ]	agonia	[a go 'niː ɑ]
grato	['grɑ to]	grosso	['grosː so]

When *g* is followed by *e* or *i*, pronounce it as [ʤ].

Note: [ʤ] is the sound of *dg* as in the English word *fudge*. [ʤ] combines the stop portion of the stop-plosive [d] (as in *dog*) with the fricative [ʒ] (as in the English word *vision*). When *g* is pronounced as [ʤ] it is called a *soft g*.

Read aloud.

Gesu	['ʤe zu]	magistero	[mɑ ʤi 'stɛ ro]
geo	[ʤɛː ɔ]	gemma	['ʤɛmː mɑ]
giorni	['ʤor ni]	bugia	['bu 'ʤɑ]

Note: The *i* (as in *giorno*) is silent and acts like a diacritical mark that softens the pronunciation of *g* to [ʤ]. (See rule for the silent *i* in <u>The Letter i,</u> page 66.)

g

gg

g

When *gg* is followed by *a, o, u,* or *consonant* pronounce it as [gː g].

Note: Pronounce *gg* [gː g] with a longer duration than a single *g* [g]. The back of your tongue will lift to touch the soft palate for the stop portion of the consonant. The stop is more prolonged than for a single *g* before the plosive part of the consonant is articulated.

Compare and contrast.

Examples from English which illustrate the rhythm of a double *g*:

dog gone   big gap

Examples from Italian:

fugga	['fugː ga]	agguato	[agː 'gwɑ to]
aggrado	[agː 'grɑ do]	leggo	['lɛgː go]
soggolo	[sɔgː 'go lo]	reggo	['rɛgː go]

When *gg* is followed by *e* or *i,* pronounce it as [dː ʤ]

Note: Pronounce [dː ʤ] with a longer duration of sound than a single [ʤ]. The stop portion of [d] is prolonged before the *zh* [ʒ] is articulated.

Compare and contrast.

Examples from English which illustrate the rhythm of [dː ʤ]:

mad George   bad gem

Examples from Italian:

maggio	['mɑdː ʤo]	guiggiare	[gwidː 'ʤɑ re]
raggio	['rɑdː ʤo]	reggia	['rɛdː ʤa]
figge	['fidː ʤe]	loggia	['lɔdː ʤa]

gh

Pronounce *gh* as [g].

Note: In the digraph *gh* the *h* is silent. In Italian, *h* acts as a diacritical mark to harden the sound of *g* before *e* and *i*.

Read aloud.

ghirlanda	[gir 'lan dɑ]	Respighi	[re 'spi gi]
vaghi	['vɑ gi]	ghermita	[gɛr 'mi ta]
ghetta	['getː ta]	gangherare	[gan ge 'rɑ re]

gli

g

Pronounce the letters *gli* as *elya* [ʎ].

Note: A lateral palatal consonant, this sound does not exist in English, but is similar to the [lj] in *mil<u>li</u>on.* (See page 48 for full explanation of *elya* [ʎ].)
Read aloud.

fo-glia	['fɔ ʎa]	consiglio	[kon 'si ʎo]
Pagliacci	[pa 'ʎaː tʃi]	Guglielmo	[gu 'ʎɛl mo]
figlio	['fi ʎo]	moglie	['mɔ ʎe]

Note: When *gli* stands alone in a syllable, without another vowel, the *i* will be transcribed as [i]:

gli	[ʎi]	e-gli	['e ʎi]

gl, gn, & gu

When *gl* is followed by *a, o,* or *u,* pronounce it as [gl]

Read aloud.

glauca	['glaːu ka]	gloria	['glɔ rja]
glutine	[glu 'ti ne]	glassa	['glasː sa]

When *gn* is in the same syllable, pronounce it as *enya* [ɲ].

Note: A nasal, palatal consonant, this sound does not exist in English, but is similar to the [nj] in *o<u>ni</u>on.* (See page 48 for a full explanation of this sound).
Read aloud.

de-gno	['de ɲo]	compa-gno	[kom 'pa ɲo]
biso-gna	[bi 'zɔ ɲo]	Si-gnori	[si 'ɲo ri]
gnudo	['ɲu do]	gnocco	['ɲɔkː ko]

When *gu* is followed by a *vowel,* pronounce it as [gw].

Read aloud.

sequire	[se 'gwi re]	guarda	['gwar da]
guerra	['gwɛrː ra]	guida	['gwi da]

h

The letter *h* is always silent.

Read aloud.

ho	[ɔ]	ha	[a]
hai	[aːi]	hanno	['anː no]

h
(cont.)

Note: In Italian, the silent *h* often follows *c* and *g* and hardens their pronounciation to [k] and [g]. (See listing for *ch, gh*).

chi	[ki]	ghirlando	[gir 'lɑn do]
che	[ke]	lunghezza	[lun geːʦa]
scherzo	['skɛr ʦo]	ghetto	[geː to]

j

Pronounce the letter *j* as [j].

Note: The letter *j* is only used in older spellings in Italian. The name of the symbol [j] is *jot* [jɔt]. It sounds like *y* in *yes*.

Notice the following:

The old spelling:	gaja	[gɑjɑ]
The current spelling:	gaia	[gɑjɑ]

k

The letter *k* is only used in foreign words and would be pronounced as it is in that language.

l

Pronounce the letter *l* as [l].

Note: [l] is the sound of *l* in *leap*. Pronounce the lateral consonant [l] as a dental sound. Lift the tip of your tongue to touch the back of the upper front teeth instead of the alveolar ridge as usual in English.

Read aloud.

libertà	[li bɛr 'tɑ]	fedele	[fe 'de le]
legale	[le 'gɑ le]	alto	['ɑl to]
luogo	['lwɔ go]	dolore	[do 'lo re]

Pronounce *ll* as [lː l]

Note: [lː l] is pronounced with a more prolonged sound than a single *l* [l].

Compare and contrast.

Examples from English:
tel<u>l L</u>assie   wa<u>ll l</u>ight

Examples from Italian:

folla	['fɔː lɑ]	bello	['bɛː lo]
cartella	[kɑr 'tɛː lɑ]	molle	['mɔː le]

Pronounce the letter *m* as [m], as in the English word *meat*.

marta	['mɑr tɑ]	mano	['mɑ no]
amore	[a 'mo re]	dorma	['dɔr ma]
tema	['te ma]	mondo	['mon do]

m

Pronounce mm as [mː m].

Note: Pronounce with a more prolonged sound than *m* [m].

Compare and contrast.

Examples from English:
dumb man   Mom mummured

Examples from Italian:

mamma	['mɑmː ma]	domma	['dɔmː ma]
gemma	['ʤɛmː ma]	commosso	[komː 'mɔsː so]
sommetta	[somː 'metː ta]	vendemmia	[vɛn 'demː mja]

Pronounce the letter *n* as [n], as in the English word *name*.

Note: [n] in Italian is pronounced dentally. Place the tip of your tongue on the back of the upper front teeth instead of the alveolar ridge as in English.

Read aloud.

nome	['no me]	nozze	[nɔtː tse]
numero	['nu me ro]	funesto	[fu 'nɛ sto]
domani	[do 'mɑ ni]	cantare	[kɑn 'tɑ re]

n

Pronounce double *nn* as [nː n].

Note: Pronounce double *nn* with a more prolonged sound than the single [n].

Compare and contrast.

Examples from English:
Nan knits   can never

Examples from Italian:

donna	['dɔnː na]	Susanna	[su 'zɑnː na]
manna	['mɑnː na]	nonna	[nɔnː na]

When *n* is followed by *the sounds* [k] and [g], pronounce it as [ŋ].

Note: Pronounce *eng* [ŋ] as *ng* in the English word *hung*. The back of your tongue lifts to touch the soft palate.

Read aloud.

bianco	['bjaŋ ko]	ancora	[aŋ 'kɔ ra]
lungo	['luŋ go]	sangue	['saŋ gwe]
inglese	[iŋ 'gle ze]	banca	[baŋ ka]

p

Pronounce the letter *p* as [p], as in the English word *put*.

Note: The Italian [p] is pronounced with less aspiration than in English.

Read aloud.

pianta	['pjɑn to]	porto	['pɔr to]
crepa	['kre pɑ]	compenso	[kom 'pɛn so]
speme	['spɛ me]	placido	['plɑ ʧi do]

Pronounce *pp* [pː p].

Note: Pronounce [pː p] with a longer duration of sound than *p* [p]. Close your lips to articulate the stop portion of the consonant. The stop is longer than for a single [p], after which the plosive part of the consonant is articulated.

Compare and contrast.

Examples from English:
help Paul   clap proudly

Examples from Italian:

drappo	['drɑpː po]	applauso	[ɑpː 'plɑːu zo]
supplice	['supː pli ʧe]	coppo	['kɔpː pɑ]

q

Pronounce *qu* as [kw] as in the English word *queen*.

Note: In Italian the letter *q* is always followed by the vowel *u*.

Read aloud.

qua	[kwɑ]	acqua	['ɑkː kwɑ]
quota	['kwɔ tɑ]	questa	['kwe stɑ]
qui	[kwi]	quando	['kwɑn do]

r

Pronounce the letter *r* in Italian as either a flipped or trilled *r*. Do not pronounce it as the retroflex *r* of English. (See Flipped and Trilled *r*, page 47.)

Note: If desired, the IPA symbol [ɾ] may be used to represent the flipped *r*. See page 47. This text, for simplicity, will use [r] for the flipped and trilled *r*.

Read aloud these words with a single *r* between two vowels as flipped *r*.

fiore	['fjo re]	severo	[se 'vɛ ro]
mistero	[mi 'stɛ ro]	mirare	[mi 'rɑ re]

Read aloud these words with a trilled *r*:

Initial **r**

rosa	['rɔ za]	rabbia	['rab: bja]
raggio	['rad: ʤo]	ruspa	['ru spa]
ricatto	[ri kat: to]	ruzza	['rud: dza]

r after a consonant in the same syllable

cruda	['kru da]	prosa	['pro za]
fronte	['fron te]	struggo	['strug:go]
ingrato	[in 'gra to]	Adrianna	[a 'drjan: na]

r after a stressed vowel and before another consonant

parto	['par to]	guarda	['gwar da]
giorno	['ʤor no]	perdono	['per do no]
morte	['mɔr te]	ricordo	[ri 'kɔr do]

Final *r*

cantar	[kan 'tar]	morir	[mo rir]
danzar	[dan 'tsar]	gioir	[ʤɔ 'ir]
cor	[kɔr]	orror	[ɔr: ror]

rr

Pronounce [r: r] with a more prolonged trill than *r* [r].

Note: A long, trilled *r* is necessary for correct Italian diction, although to many American ears it seems excessive.

Read aloud.

terra	['ter: ra]	errore	[ɛr: 'ro re]
orrido	[ɔr: 'ri do]	Ferrando	[fɛr: 'ran do]
terrore	[ter: 'ro re]	guerra	[gwɛr: ra]

S

When initial in a word before a vowel, pronounce *s* as [s].

Read aloud.

sento	['sɛn to]	sebben	['seb: bɛn]
segreto	[se 'gre to]	sempre	['sɛm pre]
sopore	[so 'po re]	saro	[sa 'rɔ]

S

When the letter s is initial in a syllable, after a consonant, and before a vowel, pronounce it as [s].

Read aloud.

pen-sa-re	[pen 'sɑ re]	ten-sio-ne	[tɛn 'sjɔ ne]
men-so-la	['mɛn so lɑ]	ver-so	['vɛr so]
mo-strar-si	[mo 'strɑr si]	per-so-na	[pɛr 'so nɑ]

When the letter s is initial in a syllable, before an unvoiced consonant, pronounce s as [s].

Read aloud.

sfigurare	[sfi gu 'rɑ re]	sfor-zan-do	[sfɔr 'tsɑn do]
sfiocco	['sfjɔkː ko]	sfac-cia	['sfatː ʧa]
spar-gi	['spɑr ʤi]	spir-to	['spir to]
scrit-to	['skritː to]	scre-zio	['skre tsjɔ]
scrol-lo	['scrɔlː lo]	scru-ma-re	[skru 'mɑ re]
ar-re-sta	[arː 'rɛ stɑ]	ca-sta	['kɑ stɑ]

When the letter s is final, pronounce it as [s].

Read aloud.

Radamès	[rɑ dɑ 'mɛs]	Amneris [ɑm 'ne ris]

When the letter s is between vowels, pronounce it as [z].

Note: Pronounce [z] as in the English word *zero*.
Read aloud.

basilica	[bɑ 'zi li kɑ]	presa	['pre zɑ]
sposo	['spɔ zo]	spinose	[spi 'no ze]
tesoro	[te 'zɔ ro]	rosario	[ro 'zɑ rjɔ]

Note: Although there are some exceptions to this rule for voicing the intervocalic s in spoken Italian (most notably *casa* ['kɑ sɑ], *cosa, cosi,* and *desiderio*), most singers sing [z] in these words.

Note: In a few words with prefixes *pre-* and *ri-,* the intervocalic s must be pronounced [s]. Check the dictionary.

When the letter *s* is initial and is followed by a voiced consonant in the same syllable, pronounce it as [z].

Read aloud.

smanie	['zmɑ nje]	sventura	[zvɛn 'tu rɑ]
sbarra	['zbɑrː rɑ]	sgelo	['zʤɛ lo]
sdegnare	['zde 'ɲɑ re]	slentare	[zlɛn 'tɑ re]

ss

Pronounce double *ss* as [sː s].

Note: Pronounce [sː s] with a more prolonged sound than *s* [s]. Be sure the sound remains unvoiced.

Compare and contrast.

Examples from English:
success sequence   case stands

Examples from Italian:

cassa	['kɑsː sɑ]	lusso	['lusː so]
vissi	['visː si]	esso	['ɛsː so]
possente	[posː 'sɛn te]	oppresso	[opː 'prɛsː so]

sc, sch

When *sc* is followed by *a, o,* or *u,* pronounce it as [sk].

Read aloud.

scusare	[sku 'zɑ re]	cascare	[kɑ 'skɑ re]
scolta	['skol tɑ]	riscontro	[ri 'skon tro]
scuola	['skwɔ lɑ]	discordare	[di skɔr 'dɑ re]

When *sc* is followed *e* or *i,* pronounce it as [ʃ].

Note: Pronounce [ʃ] as *sh* in the English word *she.* The name of the symbol [ʃ] is *esh* [ɛʃ].

Read aloud.

scena	['ʃe nɑ]	scelta	['ʃɛl tɑ]
guscetto	[gu ʃɛtː to]	scintilla	[ʃin 'tilː lɑ]
sciolto	['ʃɔl to]	bascia	['bɑ ʃɑ]

Note: Even though the *i,* as in *sciolto,* is silent, it continues to act as an agent to soften the *sc* to [ʃ]. (See rule for silent *i* in The Letter i, page 66).

S

Pronounce *sch* as [sk].

Note: An *h* after *c* and before *e* or *i*, hardens *c* to [k].
Read aloud.

scherzo	['skɛr tso]	luschero	['lu ske ro]
rischioso	[ri 'skjɔ zo]	schiaffare	[skjaf: 'fa re]
schema	['ske ma]	immischiarsi	[im: mi 'skjar si]

t

Pronounce the letter *t* as [t] as in the English word *team*.

Note: In Italian, [t] is a dental, dry consonant. Lift the tip of your tongue to touch the back of the front teeth instead of the alveolar ridge as you would in English and give less aspiration on the plosive part of the consonant.

Read aloud.

timore	[ti 'mo re]	punto	['pun to]
guinta	['gwin ta]	testa	['tɛs ta]
bistro	['bis tro]	terzo	['tɛr tso]
tanto	['tan to]	mite	['mi te]

Pronounce double *tt* [t: t] with a longer duration than a single [t].

Note: Lift the tip of the tongue to touch the back of the front teeth. Your tongue tip remains in that position for a brief pause, then releases plosively, but with a dryer, less aspirate sound than in English.

Compare and contrast.
Examples in English:
Pat tells   met Tim

Examples in Italian:

ditta	['dit: ta]	moffetta	[mof: 'fet: ta]
ricetta	[ri ʧɛt: ta]	batti	['bat: ti]
Masetto	[ma 'zet: tɔ]	Violetta	[vjɔ 'let: ta]

V

Pronounce the letter *v* as [v] as in the English word *victor*.
Read aloud.

avanti	[a 'van ti]	virtù	[vir 'tu]
voce	['vo ʧe]	viola	['vjɔ la]
favore	[fa 'vo re]	malvivo	[mal 'vi vo]

Pronounce double *vv* as [vː v]

Note: [vː v] with a more prolonged sound than [v].

Compare and contrast.
Examples in English:
ha*ve* *ve*rses   sa*ve* *V*ictor

Examples in Italian:
avverso [ɑvː 'vɛr so]   avvolto [ɑvː 'vɔl tɑ]

The letter *w* is used only in foreign words. Pronounce it as you would in that language.	**W**
The letter *x* is used only in foreign words. Pronounce it as you would in that language.	**x**
The letter *y* is used only in foreign words. Pronounce it as you would in that language.	**y**
The consonant *z* in Italian has two pronunciations: [ts] (as in *eats*) or [dz] (as in *beads*.) There are no consistent rules that tell us which pronunciation to use, although [ts] is more frequent. You will need to refer to a reliable dictionary for correct pronunciation.	**z**

Note: These words use the unvoiced combination sound [ts], which is composed of the stop portion of [t] followed by the fricative [s].

Read aloud.

zio	['tsiː o]	terzo	['tɛr tso]
zitto	['tsitː to]	grazia	['grɑ tsjɑ]
danza	['dɑn tsɑ]	delizia	[de 'li tsjɑ]

Z

Note: These words use the voiced combination sound [dz], which is composed of the stop portion of [d] followed by the fricative [z].

zelo	['dze lo]	Zerlina	[dzɛr 'li na]
bronzo	['brɔn dzo]	donzella	[don 'dzɛlː la]
Azucena	[a dzu 'tʃe na]	Zuniga	[dzu 'ni ga]

The double zz is pronounced either as [tː ts] or [dː dz]. Check a dictionary to know whether the word should be pronounced with [tː ts] or [dː dz]. Pronounce the zz with a more prolonged sound than a single z.

Pay attention to the difference between the sounds of [dz] and [dʒ]. Do not confuse these two sounds.

Examples in English comparing [dz] with [dʒ].

feeds	[fidz]	fudge	[fʌdʒ]
beads	[bidz]	budge	[bʌdʒ]

Examples in Italian comparing [dː dz] with [dː dʒ].

vizza	[vidː dza]	figge	[fidː dʒe]
mezzo	[mɛdː dzo]	reggia	[rɛdː dʒa]

Pronounce these words with [tː ts].

mezzo	['mɛtː tso]	(of fruit, over-ripe)
nozze	['nɔtː tse]	
guizzare	[gwitː 'tsa re]	
mazza	['matː tsa]	
pizza	['pitː tsa]	

Pronounce these words with [dː dz].

mezzo	['mɛdː dzo]	(half, medium)
mezzana	[mɛdː 'dza na]	
bizzaro	[bidː 'dza ro]	
gazza	['gadː dza]	

Latin
Diction

La

Chart of Latin Sounds

The following chart lists the sounds of the Latin language in alphabetic order. Refer to this chart to quickly check the sound of a spelling. There are some special circumstances and exceptions to the sounds which cannot be presented easily in a simple chart. Detail is included in the discussion of the individual sounds.

Latin Letter & Position in Word		IPA	Example &	IPA	Page
a	a	[ɑ]	mala	[ˈmɑ lɑ]	104
	æ	[ɛ]	æternæ	[ɛ ˈtɛr nɛ]	104
	au, a diphthong	[ɑːu]	causa	[ˈkɑːu zɑ]	104
	ay, a diphthong	[ɑːi]	Raymundi	[rɑːi ˈmun di]	105
b	b	[b]	bonæ	[ˈbɔ nɛ]	108
c	c, cc before a, o, u, or a *consonant*	[k]	corda	[ˈkɔr dɑ]	108
	c, cc before e, æ, œ, i or y	[ʧ]	lucis	[ˈlu ʧis]	109
	c between ex and e, æ, œ, i or y	[ʃ]	excelsis	[ɛk ˈʃɛl sis]	109
	c final	[k]	fac	[fɑk]	109
	ch	[k]	Christum	[ˈkri stum]	109
d	d	[d]	domine	[ˈdɔ mi nɛ]	109
e	e	[ɛ]	testi	[ˈtɛ sti]	105
	eu, a diphthong	[ɛːu]	euge	[ˈɛːu ʤɛ]	105
	eu, two syllables	[ɛ u]	Deum	[ˈdɛ um]	105
f	f	[f]	finis	[ˈfi nis]	109
g	g before a, o, u or a *consonant*	[g]	plagas	[ˈplɑ gɑs]	110
	g before e, æ, œ, i or y	[ʤ]	regina	[rɛ ˈʤi nɑ]	110
	gn	[ɲ]*	Agnus	[ˈɑ ɲus]	110
h	h	silent	Hosanna	[ɔ ˈzɑnː nɑ]	110
i	i	[i]	liber	[ˈli bɛr]	106
	i between two *vowels*	[j]	alleluia	[ɑlː lɛ ˈlu jɑ]	106

* The IPA symbol enya [ɲ] represents a sound similar to the *ni* of the English word *onion* [ˈʌn jən]. See page 110.

Latin Letter & Position in Word			IPA	Example	& IPA	Page
j	j		[j]	Jesu	['jɛ zu]	111
k	k		[k]	kalendæ	[kɑ 'lɛn dɛ]	111
l	l		[l]	laudamus	[lɑːu 'dɑ mus]	111
m	m		[m]	morte	['mɔr tɛ]	111
n	n		[n]	non	[nɔn]	111
	n before [g] or [k]		[ŋ]	sancto	['sɑŋ ktɔ]	112
				sanguis	['sɑŋ gwis]	
o	o		[ɔ]	nobis	['nɔ bis]	106
	œ		[ɛ]	cœlestis	[ʧɛ 'lɛs tis]	106
p	p		[p]	pater	['pɑ tɛr]	112
	ph		[p]	Prophetas	[prɔ 'fɛ tɑs]	112
q	qu		[kw]	quoniam	['kwɔ ni ɑm]	112
r	r	flipped	[ɾ]	Maria	[mɑ 'ri ɑ]	112
		trilled	[r]	regina	[rɛ 'ʤi nɑ]	113
s	s	usually	[s]	tristis	['tri stis]	113
	s between two *vowels*		[z]	miserere	[mi zɛ 'rɛ ɾɛ]	113
	s final		[s]	vivos	['vi vɔs]	113
	s final after *final voiced consonant*		[z]	omnipotens	[ɔ 'mni pɔ tɛnz]	114
	sc before *a, o, u* or a *consonant*		[sk]	scuto	['sku tɔ]	114
	sc before *e, æ, œ, i,* or *y*		[ʃ]	scio	['ʃi ɔ]	114
	sch before *a, o,* or *u*		[sk]	Pascha	['pɑ skɑ]	114
t	t		[t]	tantum	['tɑn tum]	114
	ti between a *vowel* and a letter other than *s, t,* or *x*		[tsi]	gratia	['grɑ tsi ɑ]	114
	th		[t]	Sabaoth	['sɑ bɑ ɔt]	115
u	u		[u]	crucem	['kru ʧɛm]	107
	u following *ng* or *q* and preceding a *vowel*		[w]	qui	[kwi]	107
				sanguis	['sɑŋ gwis]	

Latin • Chart of Sounds

Latin Letter & Position in Word	IPA	Example	& IPA	Page
V v	[v]	vivos	['vi vɔs]	115
W w (This letter not used in Latin)				115
X x in initial *ex:*				
before a *vowel*	[gs]*	exalto	[ɛg 'salt ɔ]*	115
before *c* followed by *a, o, u*	[ksk]	excuso	[ɛk 'sku zɔ]	116
before *c* followed by *e, æ, œ, i* or *y*	[kʃ]	excelsis	[ɛk 'ʃɛl sis]	116
before *h*	[gs]*	exhibeo	[ɛg 'si bɛ ɔ]*	116
before *s* followed by *vowel*	[gs]*	exsules	[ɛg 'su lɛs]*	116
before *s* followed by *consonant*	[ks]	exspiro	[ɛk 'spi rɔ]	116
before other *consonants*	[ks]	extendo	[ɛk 'stɛn dɔ]	117
x in interior of word	[ks]	dextro	['dɛk strɔ]	117
x final	[ks]	pax	[paks]	117
Y y	[i]	hymnus	['im nus]	107
Z z	[dz]	Lazaro	['la dza rɔ]	117

* In words pronounced with [gs], some people choose to use an acceptable variation of [gz] *exalto* [ɛg 'zal tɔ].

Special Features of Latin

Liturgical Latin

There are two systems of pronunciation in Latin. One is liturgical and the other is classical.

Classical Latin is the original language attributed to Caesar and Cicero. Although classical Latin has had a long history, it is not currently spoken by any culture as a native tongue and exists only as a scholarly language.

Liturgical, Roman, or ecclesiatical Latin is the language used in the vocal literature of the church. The system of pronounciation presented in this book is liturgical Latin and is appropriate for choral masses, cantatas and oratorios. The material follows the guidelines set forth by Rev. Michael de Angelis in a publication entitled the Correct Pronunciation of Latin According to Roman Usage, St. Gregory Guild, 1937.

Latin rules of pronunciation are regular and straightforward. Vowels usually have only one possible pronunciation; there are only three diphthongs. Other consecutive vowels are pronounced as two syllables. Many consonants have similarities to other languages, although there is one consonant, the letter *x* as in *excelsis*, which often poses pronunciation questions. See The letter x on page 115, for answers about how to pronounce this letter.

Perhaps the greatest challenge in Latin diction is to determine the stress patterns of the words. There are no easy, regular rules. Therefore, we have indicated primary stress in the IPA transcriptions and have included a complete IPA transcription and translation for the five parts of the "Ordinary of the Mass". For words not included in this book, refer to a dictionary, a Liber Usualis, or other sources listed in the bibliography. Within these sources you can find translations and pronunciation transcriptions for many other sacred Latin texts.

Syllabification

Single consonant

*The small diacritical mark
placed above and before a
syllable in IPA transcription
indicates that syllable receives
primary stress:*
miserere [mi zɛ 'rɛ rɛ]

Place a single consonant between vowels with the second
syllable.

mi-se-re-re	[mi zɛ 'rɛ rɛ]
a-men	['ɑ mɛn]
no-bis	['nɔ bis]
na-tu-ra	[nɑ 'tu rɑ]
glo-ri-a	['glɔ ri ɑ]
sa-lu-ta-re	[sɑ lu 'tɑ rɛ]

The consonant *x* is usually placed with the preceding vowel.
(The letter *x* has several pronunciations. See The letter x,
page 115.)

dix-it	['dik sit]
ex-au-di	[ɛg 'sɑu di]
dex-te-ram	['dɛk stɛ rɑm]

Two consonants

Usually divide two consonants between two syllables.

tor-men-tum	[tɔr 'mɛn tum]
mun-di	['mun di]
tan-go	['tɑn gɔ]
mit-to	['mitː tɔ]

However, there are many instances when you will place
consonant combinations with the second syllable:

1) Place the consonant digraphs *ch, gn, ph, th* (combined
letters pronounced as single consonants) with the
second syllable.

ma-chi-na	['mɑ ki nɑ]	a-gnus	['ɑ ɲus]
Pro-phe-tas	[prɔ 'fɛ tɑs]		
Ca-tho-li-cam	[kɑ 'tɔ li kɑm]		

2) When *l, r,* or *t* follow *b, c, d, g,* or *p* place both
consonants with the second syllable.

bl, br:	te-ne-bræ	['tɛ nɛ brɛ]
cl, cr, ct:	fa-ctum	['fɑ ktum]
	sæ-clum	['sɛ klum]
	se-pul-cra	[sɛ 'pul krɑ]
pl, pr, pt:	pro-pter	['prɔ ptɛr]

3) Place *qu, mn, sc, sp,* and *st* with the second syllable.

qu:	re-qui-em	['rɛ kwi ɛm]
mn:	o-mnes	['ɔ mnɛs]
sc:	a-scen-dit	[ɑ 'ʃɛn dit]
sp:	in-spe-ra-tus	[in spɛ 'rɑ tus]
st:	Chri-stum	['kri stum]

Exception: In compound words, put the consonant with the preceding syllable.

ad-i-re	[ɑd 'i rɛ]
in-i-qui-ta-tis	[in i kwi 'tɑ tis]

Three consonants

Usually divide three consonants as one followed by two.

san-cto	['sɑɲ ktɔ]
cun-cta	['kuɲ ktɑ]
Ec-cle-si-a	[ɛkː 'klɛ zi ɑ]

Put the combination *str* with the second syllable.

no-stri	['nɔ stri]

Exception: Prefixes will be put into separate syllables and may not follow the previous rules for syllabification.

abs-ti-ne-o	[ɑbs ti 'nɛ ɔ]

Consecutive vowels

Most consecutive vowels form two syllables, although some form diphthongs. (See the detailed discussion of consecutive vowels page 101.)

Divide these vowels into two syllables.

De-o	['dɛ ɔ]
glo-ri-a	['glɔ ri ɑ]
fi-li-um	['fi li um]
per-pe-tu-a	[pɛr 'pɛ tu ɑ]
Re-qui-em	['rɛ kwi ɛm]
Di-es I-ræ	['di ɛs 'i rɛ]

The penultimate syllable is the second to last syllable. The antepenultimate is the third to last syllable.

Stressing

The topic of primary stress in Latin is complex and requires familiarity with the language. The rules presented here are meant to be simple guidelines. A singer can rely on the metric setting of the words in the musical score, can refer to the IPA transcriptions located later in this section, or can refer to a dictionary for additional help with stressing.

Two syllables:

In words of two syllables, give the primary stress to the penultimate syllable.

tan-go ['tɑn gɔ]   De-us ['de us]
un-de ['un dɛ]

More than two syllables:

Sometimes in words of more than two syllables, the primary stress will be given to the penultimate.

Ray-mun-dus [rɑːi 'mun dus]
be-a-ta [be 'ɑ tɑ]

Otherwise, the primary stress will be given to the antepenultimate.

Do-mi-nus ['dɔ mi nus]
glo-ri-a ['glɔ ɾi ɑ]

Elision

In certain words with a dropped *final e*, retain the primary stress of the original spelling.

tan-ton [tɑn 'tɔn] for tan-to-ne [tɑn 'tɔ nɛ]
il-lic [ilː 'liʧ] for il-li-ce [ilː 'li ʧɛ]

Latin Vowels

Latin is a language of pure vowels. There are only five pure vowel sounds, [ɑ, ɛ, i, ɔ, u], although there are six orthographic letters, *a, e, i, o, u* and *y*. In Latin, the two letters, *i* and *y*, have the same pronunciation of [i], as *ee* in *beet*.

The pronunciation of Latin vowels is not influenced by stressing and unstressing as it is in English and Italian. The vowels *e* and *o* are always pronounced [ɛ] and [ɔ]. The unstressed schwa [ə] sound does not exist in Latin. The only time a vowel has a pronunciation that is different than the five vowel sounds listed above is when *i* and *u* are pronounced as glides.

The letters *i* and *u* are pronounced as the glides *j* [j] and *w* [w] when they adjoin certain letters. When *i* stands between two vowels, as in *alleluia* [ɑlː lɛ 'lu jɑ], it will be pronounced as the glide *j* [j]. When the letter *u* follows *q* or *ng* and precedes another vowel, as in *qui* [kwi] or *sanguis* ['sɑn gwis], it will be pronounced as the glide *w* [w].

There are only three diphthongs in Latin: *ay, au,* and *eu*. Latin diphthongs are transcribed in the International Phonetic Alphabet as two pure vowels (as [ɑu] in *laudamus*) and both vowels must be pronounced clearly and distinctly. Latin diphthongs are pronounced with one longer vowel sound and a second shorter sound. English speakers must be careful not to reduce the second vowel sound to a brief glide, but to give it the full vowel value.

Consecutive Vowels

Most consecutive vowels in Latin will be two syllables, as in *be-a-ta* or *De-o*. However, in Latin, two consecutive vowels may be pronounced as either a single vowel, a diphthong, a glide, or as two separate syllables.

The digraphs *æ* and *œ* are a single vowel sound.

Pronounce the digraphs printed as *æ* and *œ* as the single sound *eh* [ɛ] as in bed.

cæ-li	['ʧɛ li]	hœ-dis	['ɛ dis]
cœ-lum	['ʧɛ lum]	sæ-cu-lum	['sɛ ku lum]
bo-næ	['bɔ nɛ]	mœ-re-bat	[mɛ 'rɛ bɑt]

However, when there is a dieresis over one of the vowels, treat the vowels as two distinct sounds.

Mi-cha-ël	['mi kɑ ɛl]	Ra-pha-ël	['rɑ fɑ ɛl]
Is-rä-el	['is rɑ ɛl]	po-ë-ma	[pɔ 'ɛ mɑ]

The vowels *au, ay* and *eu* combine to form diphthongs.

The vowel combinations *au* and *ay* are always pronounced as diphthongs and *eu* is sometimes a diphthong. Both vowel sounds of a diphthong are distinctly articulated, with the first vowel longer and the second one shorter in duration.

When a single diphthong is written under a series of notes, vocalize on the first vowel and move to the second vowel at the last moment before the next syllable, with an assigned metrical time appropriate to the musical context. But be careful that the second vowel is given full vowel value and is not reduced to a glide.

Two dots over a vowel is called a dieresis.

Pronounce *au* and *ay* as diphthongs.

lau-da-mus [lɑːu 'dɑ mus]
ex-au-di [ɛg 'sɑːu di]
Ray-mun-di [rɑːi 'mun di]

Pronounce *eu* sometimes as a diphthong,
sometimes as two syllables.

When *eu* begins a word, it tends to be a
diphthong.

eu-ge ['ɛːu ʤɛ]
Eu-se-bi-i [ɛːu 'zɛ bi i]

When *eu* is in a position other than initial in
the word, it is pronounced as two syllables.

me-us ['mɛ us]

The vowels *u* and *i* are sometimes pronounced as glides [w]
and [j].

When there is a combination of two vowels and the first
vowel is either the glide [w] or [j], pronounce the second
vowel with greater stress and longer duration.

The glide *w* [w] occurs when *u* follows *ng* or *q*
and precedes another vowel.

qu: qui [kwi]
quo-ni-am ['kwɔ ni ɑm]
ngu: san-guis ['sɑŋ gwis]

The glide [j] occurs when *j* precedes another
vowel.

Ju-dex ['ju dɛks]
Je-sus ['jɛ zus]

The glide [j] occurs when *i* is between two
vowels.

al-le-lu-ia [ɑlː lɛ 'lu jɑ]

In Latin [ai] and [ou] are
always pronounced as two
separate syllables, not as
diphthongs as in English.

Consecutive vowels are usually pronounced as two separate
syllables, except for the spellings previously listed. The
following spellings are examples:

ai: la-i-cus ['lɑ i kus]
a-it ['ɑ it]
ou: pro-ut ['prɔ ut]
co-u-tun-tur [kɔ u 'tun tuɾ]
ei: me-i ['mɛ i]
de-i-tas ['dɛ i tɑs]
e-le-i-son [ɛ lɛ i zɔn]
One exception: The interjection *Hei* [ɛi] is a
single syllable.

ea:	be-a-ta	[bɛ ˈɑ tɑ]
eo:	De-o	[ˈdɛ ɔ]
ie:	Ky-ri-e	[ˈki ɾi ɛ]
ia:	me-mo-ri-a	[mɛ ˈmɔ ɾi ɑ]
	glo-ri-a	[ˈglɔ ɾi ɑ]
ua:	per-pe-tu-a	[pɛr ˈpɛ tu ɑ]
uo:	Tu-o	[ˈtu ɔ]
eu:	me-us	[ˈmɛ us]
ii:	fi-li-i	[ˈfi li i]
	a-tri-is	[ˈɑ tɾi is]
aa:	A-A-ron	[ˈɑ ɑ ɾɔn]

*Each vowel, including a
repeated vowel in such words
as filii or AAron, must be
clearly articulated—in a
smooth, not staccato, manner.*

Latin Vowels in Detail

Vowels in Latin are extremely easy to pronounce because of the few variations. Single vowels are, for the most part, pronounced with a single sound.

The letter

a

The letter *a* will always be pronounced [ɑ], the sound of *ah* as in *father*, with the one exception of the digraph æ, which is pronounced [ɛ], as the sound of *e* in *bet*. As an American singer, you must be cautioned never to use the neutral sounds of *uh* [ʌ] as in *up* or *schwa* [ə] as in *a-bove* in Latin. In addition, the [ɑ] sound must be clear and open, never rounded as the sound of *aw* [ɔ] in *caw* or *caught*.

Read aloud.

tu-ba	['tu bɑ]	sal-va	['sɑl vɑ]
spar-gens	['spɑr ʤɛnz]	gra-tis	['grɑ tis]
ma-la	['mɑ lɑ]	a-ni-mas	['ɑ ni mɑs]

æ

The letters æ form a digraph and are pronounced as the single vowel sound [ɛ] as in *bet*.

Read aloud.

æ-ter-næ	[ɛ 'tɛr nɛ]	mæ-re-bat	[mɛ 'rɛ bɑt]
vi-æ	['vi ɛ]	me-æ	['mɛ ɛ]
cæ-lis	['ʧɛ lis]	bo-næ	['bɔ nɛ]

au

Pronounce *au* as the diphthong [ɑu]. Give the first vowel longer duration than the second, but give the full vowel quality to both vowel sounds.

Read aloud.

cau-sa ['kɑːu zɑ]   au-di-ti-o-ne [ɑːu di tsi 'ɔ nɛ]

ay

Pronounce *ay* as the diphthong [ɑːi]. Give the first vowel longer duration than the second but give the full vowel quality to both vowels. Be careful not to use the more open vowel [ɪ] as in the English word *bid*. Keep the vowel *i* pure [i].

Read aloud.

Ray-mun-di   [rɑːi 'mun di]

The letter e

There are differing opinions among authorities about whether to pronounce the vowels *e*, *æ*, and *œ* as closed [e] or open [ɛ]. Some suggest that all of these vowels should be pronounced as closed [e] as in *chaotic*, while others suggest that all vowels be pronounced as open [ɛ]. A third group of Latin scholars prefers a combination of [e] and [ɛ]. In this book, we suggest that you always pronounce the letters *e*, *æ*, and *œ* with the sound of open [ɛ] as in *bet* in keeping with current choral tradition.

Be sure that the sound of [ɛ] is well articulated. Do not open it so far that it resembles the sound of [æ] as in *bat*. The vowels in the words *bet*, *bed*, *head*, *said*, and *pet* can be a guide.

Read aloud.

per-fru-i	['pɛr fru i]	est	[ɛst]
te-sti	['tɛ sti]	e-va-de-re	[ɛ 'vɑ dɛ ɾɛ]
tre-mor	['trɛ mɔɾ]	mi-se-re-re	[mi zɛ 'rɛ ɾɛ]
eleison	[ɛ 'lɛ i zɔn]	deo	['dɛ ɔ]

eu

Pronounce *eu* as a diphthong only when it is initial in a word.

Read aloud.

eu-ge ['ɛːu ʤɛ]   Eu-se-bi-i [ɛːu 'zɛ bi i]

Note: The word *eun-tes* ['ɛuːn tɛs] has an irregular stress. Longer duration is given to the second vowel.

Otherwise, pronounce *eu* as two syllables.

me-us ['mɛ us]   De-um ['dɛ um]   De-us ['dɛ us]

The letter

The letter *i* is always pronounced as [i], the sound of *ee* in *beet,* with one exception: when *i* stands between two vowel sounds, it will be pronounced as the glide [j], the sound of *y* in *you.* This vowel is never pronounced [ɪ] as in *bit.*

Read aloud.

i-ræ	['i ɾɛ]	Ju-di-can-ti	[ju di 'kɑn ti]
di-es	['di ɛs]	ul-ti-o-nis	[ul ti 'ɔ nis]
stri-cte	['stri ktɛ]	il-lis	[ilː lis]
scri-ptus	['skri ptus]	mi-rum	['mi ɾum]
li-ber	['li bɛɾ]	sit	[sit]

Read aloud.

al-le-lu-ia [alː lɛ 'lu ja]   e-ia ['ɛ ja]

Be aware of the difference between the sound of [j] and [i] in words with consecutive vowels. Read aloud this common word pronouncing *ia* as two syllables. Do not use a glide:

glo-ri-a ['glɔ ɾi ɑ]

The letter

The letter *o* is always pronounced as open [ɔ] as in *bought, awe,* or *autumn.* Be sure to articulate [ɔ] with rounded lips. Many American singers fail to adequately round their lips and [ɔ] begins to sound like [ɑ]

Read aloud using a well formed [ɔ].

non	[nɔn]	la-bor	['lɑ bɔɾ]
cor	[kɔɾ]	le-o-nis	[lɛ 'ɔ nis]
vo-ca	['vɔ kɑ]	do-lo-ro-sa	[dɔ lɔ 'rɔ zɑ]
o-ra	['ɔ ɾɑ]	no-bis	['nɔ bis]

œ

The letters *œ* are a digraph pronounced as the single sound of [ɛ] as in *bet.*

Read aloud.

cœ-le-stis [ʧɛ 'lɛ stis]

The letter

u

The letter *u* is pronounced as [u], the sound of *oo* in the word *boot*, with only one exception (See Exception below), when it is pronounced as the glide [w] as in *were*. In Latin, this vowel is never pronounced as open [ʊ] as in *book* nor as the diphthong [ju] as in the English word *abuse* or *fuse*.

Read aloud these words with *u* before a consonant.

u-nam	['u nɑm]	fa-ci-mus	['fɑ ʧi mus]
tu	['tu]	san-tus	['sɑn tus]
Je-su	['jɛ zu]	mun-di	['mun di]
la-cu	['lɑ ku]	cru-cem	['kru ʧɛm]

Read aloud these words with *u* before or after another vowel.

per-pe-tu-a	[pɛr 'pɛ tu ɑ]
me-us	['mɛ us]
al-le-lu-ia	[ɑlː lɛ 'lu jɑ]
lau-da-mus	[lɑːu 'dɑ mus]
fi-li-um	['fi li um]
mor-tu-os	['mɔr tu ɔs]

Exception:

Read aloud these words with the letter *u*, when it follows *ng* or *q* and precedes another vowel, pronouncing *u* as the glide [w].

qu:	qua-rum	['kwɑ ɾum]
	tam-quam	['tɑm kwɑm]
	qui	[kwi]
	quod	[kwɔd]
	quæ-rems	['kwɛ ɾɛmz]
ngu:	san-guis	['sɑŋ gwis]

The letter

The letter *y* has only one sound. It is always pronounced as [i], the sound of *ee* as in *beet*.

Read aloud.

hy-mnus ['i mnus]   mar-ty-res ['mɑr ti ɾɛs]

The letter *y* is also pronounced [i] in the diphthong *ay*:

Ray-mun-dus   [rɑːi 'mun dus]

Latin Consonants in Detail

Many of the Latin consonants have the same sounds as English or Italian and their pronounciation is very regular. The relative simplicity of the pronunciation choices for the vowel and consonants of Latin, make it an easy language to learn to pronounce.

b

Pronounce the consonant *b* [b] as in the English word *bone*.

Read aloud.

li-be-ra ['li bɛ ɾa]   bo-næ ['bɔ nɛ]

c

The following rules relate to the pronunciation of the letter *c* when it occurs as a single consonant before a vowel or a consonant or as the final letter of the word. For the pronunciation of the letter combination of *sc*, see <u>The letter s,</u> page 113; and for *xc*, see <u>The letter x,</u> page 115.

Pronounce *c* or *cc*, when before *a, o, u* or a *consonant*, as [k], as in the English word *kit*. When *c* is pronounced as [k], it is called *hard c*.

Read aloud these words using *c* before *a, o,* or *u.*

cum	[kum]	cor-da	['kɔr da]
sæ-cu-la	['sɛ ku la]	lu-cam	['lu kɑm]
cau-sa	['kaːu za]	pec-ca-ta	[pɛkː 'ka ta]
cre-do	['krɛ dɔ]	lo-cu-tus	[lɔ 'ku tus]

Read aloud these words using *c* before a consonant.

cre-a-tu-ra	[krɛ a 'tu ɾa]
fa-ctum	['fa ktum]
la-cri-mo-sa	[la kri 'mɔ za]
sæ-clum	['sɛ klum]

Note: In Latin, pronounce double consonants, as in the word *peccata*, with a more prolonged sound as in Italian. Double consonants will be transcribed using the diacritical mark [ː] and a repeated consonant symbol to indicate prolongation.

Pronounce *c* or *cc* before *e, æ, œ, i,* or *y* as [ʧ], as *ch* in the English word *chair*. When *c* is pronounced [ʧ], it is called *soft c*.

Read aloud.

lu-ce-at ['lu ʧɛ ɑt]
lu-cis ['lu ʧis]
ci-nis ['ʧi nis]
ac-ci-pe ['ɑtː ʧi pɛ]
ec-ce ['ɛtː ʧɛ]
be-ne-di-ci-mus [bɛ nɛ 'di ʧi mus]

Pronounce *c* as [ʃ], the sound of *sh* in the English word *she*, when *c* stands between *ex* and the vowel *e, æ, œ, i,* or *y*. The symbol [ʃ] is called *esh* [ɛʃ]. (See <u>The letter x,</u> page 115 for a fuller description.)

Read aloud.

ex-cel-sis [ɛk 'ʃɛl sis]

Pronounce *c* final as [k].

Read aloud.

fac [fɑk]   nunc [nunk]

Pronounce *ch* as [k].

Read aloud.

Chri-stum ['kri stum]   ma-chi-na ['mɑ ki nɑ]

Pronounce the letter *d* as the sound of *d* in *dog*. However, the Latin *d* is more dental and less aspirate than the English *d*.

Read aloud.

do-mi-ne ['dɔ mi nɛ]   De-um ['dɛ um]
a-do-ra-tur [ɑ dɔ 'rɑ tuɾ]   De-i ['dɛ i]

d

Pronounce the letter *f* as in the English word *feet*.

Read aloud.

of-fe-ri-mus [ɔfː 'fɛ ɾi mus]   fi-nis ['fi nis]
fa-vil-la [fɑ 'vilː lɑ]   fons [fɔnz]

f

g

Pronounce the letter *g* before *a, o, u,* or a *consonant* other than *n* as [g], as in the English word *gone.* When *g* is pronounced as [g], it is called *hard g.*

Read aloud.

a-gas	['ɑ gɑs]	gla-di-us	['glɑ di us]
pla-ga	['plɑ gɑ]	er-go	['ɛr gɔ]
glo-ri-a	['glɔ ri ɑ]		

Pronounce *g* before *e, æ, œ, i* or *y,* as [ʤ] in the English word *fudge.* When *g* is pronounced as [ʤ], it is called *soft g.*

vir-gi-ne	['vir ʤi nɛ]	ge-re	['ʤɛ rɛ]
re-sur-get	[rɛ 'sur ʤɛt]	re-gi-na	[rɛ 'ʤi nɑ]
co-get	['kɔ ʤɛt]	ge-ni-tum	['ʤɛ ni tum]
in-ge-mi-sco	[in ʤɛ 'mi skɔ]		

gn

Pronounce *gn* as [ɲ]. The symbol *enya* [ɲ] represents a sound similar to the *ni* in *onion* ['ʌn jən]. However, [ɲ] is a pre-palatal consonant, made with a single articulatory action. The blade of the tongue lifts to touch the boundary between the alveolar ridge and the hard palate.

Read aloud.

A-gnus	['ɑ ɲus]	di-gnæ	['di ɲɛ]
re-gni	['rɛ ɲi]	i-gnem	['i ɲɛm]

h

The letter *h* is always silent in Latin, except for two irregular words listed under Exceptions.

Ho-san-na	[ɔ 'zɑnː nɑ]	ho-di-e	['ɔ di ɛ]
ho-mi-ni-bus	[ɔ 'mi ni bus]		

Exceptions: In these two words, *h* is pronounced [k]. In ancient manuscripts these words were spelled *nichel* and *michi.*

ni-hil	['ni kil]	mi-hi	['mi ki]

The letter *j* is pronounced as the glide *jot* [j]. The symbol [j] represents the sound of *y* in *you* and is often called a semi-consonant or semi-vowel.

Read aloud.

Je-su	['jɛ zu]
ma-je-sta-tis	[mɑ jɛ 'stɑ tis]
cu-jus	['ku jus]
ju-di-ca-re	[ju di 'kɑ ɾɛ]

j

Pronounce the letter *k* as in the English word *kit*.

ka-len-dæ	[kɑ 'lɛn dɛ]
kæ-sa	['kɛ zɑ]

k

The letter *l* is pronounced as *clear l* [l], the sound of *l* as in *leap*. The Latin *l* is articulated more dentally than in English.

Read aloud.

la-tro-nem	[lɑ 'trɔ nɛm]	lu-ce-at	['lu ʧɛ ɑt]
tol-lis	['tɔlː lis]	il-lud	['ilː lud]
lu-mi-ne	['lu mi nɛ]		

l

Pronounce the letter *m* as in the English word *me*.

Read aloud.

me	[mɛ]	mor-te	['mɔr tɛ]
sum	[sum]	mun-di	['mun di]
do-mi-ne	['dɔ mi nɛ]	sæ-clum	['sɛ klum]

m

Pronounce the letter *n* as in the English word *note*.

Read aloud.

ne	[nɛ]	an-te	['ɑn tɛ]
sunt	[sunt]	ven-tu-ra	[vɛn 'tu ɾɑ]
in-ter	['in tɛɾ]	tre-men-da	[trɛ 'mɛn dɑ]

n

n

cont.

Pronounce the letters *gn* in the same syllable as *enya* [ɲ]. (See The letter g)

Read aloud.

Ma-gni-fi-cat	[mɑ ˈɲi fi kɑt]
ma-gna	[ˈmɑ ɲɑ]

Pronounce the letter *n* before *g* or *k* as [ŋ]. The symbol *eng* [ŋ] represents the *ng* in *song*. English words also use [ŋ] before *g* and *k* as in *languid* or *bank*.

nunc	[nuŋk]	san-guis	[ˈsaŋ gwis]
san-cto	[ˈsaŋ ktɔ]	san-ctus	[ˈsaŋ ktus]

p

The letter *p* is pronounced as in the English word *put*. The Latin *p* is less aspirate than in English.

pi-e	[ˈpi ɛ]	pro-pter	[ˈprɔ ptɛɾ]
pi-us	[ˈpi us]	pa-ter	[ˈpɑ tɛɾ]
Spi-ri-tu	[ˈspi ɾi tu]	Pi-la-to	[pi ˈlɑ tɔ]

Pronounce the letters *ph* as [f].

Pro-phe-tas	[prɔ ˈfɛ tɑs]
phre-ne-ti-ci	[frɛ ˈnɛ ti tʃi]

q

In Latin, the letter *q* always combines with *u* and is pronounced as kw [kw].

Read aloud.

quæ-rens	[ˈkwɛ ɾɛnz]	re-qui-em	[ˈɾɛ kwi ɛm]
qua-si	[ˈkwɑ zi]	quo-ni-am	[ˈkwɔ ni ɑm]
Fi-li-o-que	[fi li ˈɔ kwɛ]		

r

The Latin *r* is pronounced as flipped [ɾ] or trilled [r], as in Italian. It is never the retroflex *r* of English, as in the word *run*. When *r* is between two vowels or is final, pronounce it as flipped *r*.

Read aloud these words with *r* between two vowels.

Ky-ri-e	[ˈki ɾi ɛ]	e-rat	[ˈɛ ɾɑt]
glo-ri-a	[ˈglɔ ɾi ɑ]	me-mo-ra-ri	[mɛ mɔ ˈɾɑ ɾi]
o-re-mus	[ɔ ˈɾɛ mus]	sa-lu-ta-re	[sɑ lu ˈtɑ ɾɛ]

Read aloud these words with final r.

sem-per	['sɛm pɛɾ]	con-fun-dar	[kɔn 'fun dɑɾ]
mi-ser	['mi zɛɾ]	cla-mor	['klɑ moɾ]

When r is not between two vowels or final, pronounce it with either flipped or trilled r. Soloists will usually use the trilled r in these words, while choral singers use flipped r.

Read aloud these words with an r before a vowel.

re-gi-na	[rɛ 'ʤi nɑ]	no-stri	['nɔ stri]
re-spi-ce	[rɛ 'spi ʧɛ]	Chri-stum	['kri stum]

Read aloud these words with a double rr.

ter-ra	['tɛrː rɑ]	ter-ræ	['tɛrː ræ]

Read aloud these words with r preceding a consonant.

per-so-næ	[pɛr 'sɔ næ]	mor-ti-us	['mɔr ti us]
æ-ter-na	[ɛ 'tɛr nɑ]	a-sper-ges	[ɑ 'spɛr ʤɛs]
no-stram	['nɔ strɑm]		

S

The letters s and ss are pronounced as in the English word sit.

Read aloud.

re-mis-si-o-nem	[rɛ misː si 'ɔ nɛm]
bap-tis-ma	[bɑp 'tis mɑ]
tri-stis	['tri stis]
di-scus-si-o	[di 'skusː si ɔ]
sunt	['sunt]
spi-ri-tum	['spi ɾi tum]
al-tis-si-mus	[ɑlː 'lisː si mus]
sa-lu-tem	[sɑ 'lu tɛm]
est	[ɛst]

When s is between two vowels, pronounce it as the voiced z [z] sound as in the English word zero.

Read aloud.

mi-se-re-re	[mi zɛ 'rɛ ɾɛ]
Je-su	['jɛ zu]
Ec-cle-si-am	[ɛkː 'klɛ zi ɑm]

When s is final, pronounce it as [s].

Read aloud.

vi-vos	['vi vɔs]	e-is	['ɛ is]
mor-tu-os	['mɔr tu ɔs]	tu-is	['tu is]
re-ges	['rɛ ʤɛs]	se-des	['sɛ dɛs]

When final *s* follows a final voiced consonant, it is pronounced [z] as in the English word *tens* [tɛnz].

Read aloud.

 o-mni-po-tens [ɔ 'mni pɔ tɛnz]

When *sc* is before *a, o, u* or a *consonant*, pronounce it as [sk].

Read aloud.

sca-bel-lum	[skɑ 'bɛlː lum]
scu-to	['sku tɔ]
re-qui-e-scat	[rɛ kwi 'ɛ skɑt]
Scri-ptu-ras	[skri 'ptu rɑs]

When *sc* is before *e, æ, œ, i* or *y*, pronounce it as [ʃ].

Read aloud.

su-sci-pi-at	['su ʃi pi at]	sci-o	['ʃi ɔ]
de-scen-dit	[dɛ 'ʃɛn dit]	vi-sce-ra	['vi ʃɛ rɑ]
a-scen-dit	[ɑ 'ʃɛn dit]	su-sci-pe	['su ʃi pɛ]

When *sch* is before *a, o,* or *u*, pronounce it as [sk].

Read aloud.

scho-la	['skɔ lɑ]
scho-las-ti-ca	[skɔ 'lɑs ti kɑ]
Pa-scha	[pɑ skɑ]

Pronounce the letter *t* [t] as in the English word *tote*. However, the Latin *t* is more dental and less aspirate than in English.

Read aloud.

et	[ɛt]	tan-tum	['tɑn tum]
tem-po-ra	['tɛm pɔ rɑ]	i-te-rum	['i tɛ rum]
te-sta-men-tum	[tɛ stɑ 'mɛn tum]		

Pronounce the letters *ti* as [ts] when between any vowel and any letter except *s, t,* or *x*. Otherwise, *ti* is pronounced [ti], as in *majestatis* [mɑ jɛ 'stɑ tis], where it is before the consonant *s*.

Read aloud.

gra-ti-a	['grɑ tsi ɑ]
ter-ti-a	['tɛr tsi ɑ]
Pon-ti-o	['pɔn tsi ɔ]
o-ra-ti-o-nem	[ɔ rɑ tsi 'ɔ nɛm]
deprecationem	[dɛ prɛ kɑ tsi 'ɔ nɛm]
con-sub-stan-ti-a-lem	[kɔn sub stɑn tsi 'ɑ lɛm]

The letters *th* form a digraph that is pronounced with the single sound [t]. The letter *h* in Latin is silent.

Read aloud.

Sa-ba-oth	['sɑ bɑ ɔt]
Ca-tho-li-cam	[kɑ 'tɔ li kɑm]
thro-num	['trɔ num]

Pronounce the letter *v* as in the English word *vet*.

Read aloud.

vox	[vɔks]	vi-sce-ra	['vi ʃɛ ɾɑ]
vi-vos	['vi vɔs]	no-vum	['nɔ vum]
voluntatis	[vɔ lun 'tɑ tis]		
vi-si-bi-li-um	[vi zi 'bi li um]		

The letter w is not used in Latin spellings.

The letter *x* in Latin has several different pronunciations, [gs], [gz], [ks], [kʃ] and [ksk], depending upon its position in the word and the adjoining letters. The spellings for these pronunciations are listed below.

Note: In words pronounced with [gs], some people choose to use an acceptable variation of [gz].

When *x* is in initial *ex* before a vowel, pronounce it as [gs].

Initial *ex* before any vowel is [ɛgs]. The sound of [ɛgs] can be heard in the English words *egg sandwich*.

Read aloud.

ex-al-to	[ɛg 'sɑl tɔ]
ex-er-ce-o	[ɛg 'sɛr ʧɛ ɔ]
ex-o-pto	[ɛg 'sɔ ptɔ]

X

When *x* is in initial *ex* before *c*, pronounce it as described below:

1. Initial *ex* before *c* followed by *e, æ, œ i,* or *y* is [ɛkʃ].

   The symbol [ʃ], called esh, is the sound of *sh* in *she*. The sound of [kʃ] can be heard in the English words *pink shells* or *peck shells*.

   Read aloud.

ex-cel-sis	[ɛk 'ʃɛl sis]
ex-ces-sus	[ɛk 'ʃɛsː sus]

2. Initial *ex* before *c* followed by *a, o,* or *u* is [ɛksk].

   The sound of [ksk] can be heard in the English words *Nick's car.*

   Read aloud.

ex-can-to	[ɛk 'skɑn tɔ]
ex-car-ni-fi-ca-re	[ɛk skɑr ni fi 'kɑ ɾɛ]
ex-cu-so	[ɛk 'sku zo]

When *x* is in initial *ex* before *h*, pronounce it as [gs].

Read aloud.

ex-hi-be-o [ɛg 'si bɛ ɔ]

When *x* is in initial *ex* before *s*, pronounce it as described below:

1. Initial *ex* before an *s* followed by a vowel is [ɛgs].

   Read aloud.

ex-sur-ge	[ɛg 'sur dʒɛ]
ex-su-les	[ɛg 'su lɛs]

2. Initial *ex* before an *s* followed by a consonant is [ɛks].

   Read aloud.

ex-spi-ro	[ɛk 'spi ɾɔ]
ex-ster-no	[ɛk 'stɛr nɔ]
ex-spe-cto	[ɛk 'spɛ ktɔ]

When *x* is in initial *ex* before *other consonants*, pronounce it as [ks].

1. Initial *ex* before consonants other than *c, h,* or *s* is [ks].

Read aloud.

ex-po-sci-te	[ɛk 'spɔ ʃi tɛ]
ex-pu-ngo	[ɛk 'pu ŋgɔ]
ex-ten-do	[ɛk 'stɛn dɔ]

When *x* is in the interior of a word, pronounce it as [ks] whether it precedes a vowel or a consonant.

Read aloud.

re-sur-rex-it	[rɛ zurː 'rɛk sit]
dex-te-ram	['dɛk stɛ ɾam]
e-rex-it	[ɛ 'rɛk sit]
cru-ci-fi-xus	[kru ʧi 'fik sus]

When *x* is final, pronounce it as [ks].

Read aloud.

pax	[pɑks]	vox	[vɔks]
lux	[luks]	ex	[ɛks]
Rex	[rɛks]	sup-plex	['supː plɛks]

The letter *z* is pronounced as [dz], as in the English word *beads* [bidz]. It is never [ts] as it is sometimes in Italian.

Read aloud.

La-za-ro	['lɑ dzɑ ɾɔ]

The Ordinary of the Mass

Kyrie

Kyrie eleison.
['ki ɾi ɛ   ɛ lɛ i zɔn]
Lord, have mercy.

Christe eleison.
['kri stɛ   ɛ lɛ i zɔn]
Christ, have mercy.

Kyrie eleison.
['ki ɾi ɛ   ɛ 'lɛ i zɔn]
Lord, have mercy.

Gloria

Gloria in excelsis Deo.
['glɔ ɾi ɑ in ɛk 'ʃɛl sis 'dɛ ɔ]
Glory to God in the highest.

Et in terra pax hominibus bonæ voluntatis.
[ɛt in 'tɛrː ɾɑ pɑks ɔ 'mi ni bus 'bɔ nɛ vɔ lun 'tɑ tis]
And on earth peace to men of good will.

Laudamus te. Benedicimus te.
[lɑu 'dɑ mus   tɛ   bɛ nɛ 'di ʧi mus   tɛ]
We praise You. We bless You.

Adoramus te. Glorificamus te.
[ɑ dɔ 'rɑ mus   tɛ   glɔ ɾi fi 'kɑ mus   tɛ]
We worship You. We glorify You.

Gratia agimus tibi propter magnam gloriam tuam.
['grɑ tsi ɑ   'ɑ ʤi mus   'ti bi   'prɔ ptɛr   'mɑ ɲɑm   'glɔ ɾi ɑm   'tu ɑm]
We give You thanks for Your great glory.

Domine Deus, Rex cœlestis, Deus Pater omnipotens,
['dɔ mi nɛ   'dɛ us   rɛks   tʃɛ 'lɛs tis   'dɛ us   'pɑ tɛr   ɔ 'mni pɔ tɛnz]
Lord God, heavenly king, God the Father almighty.

Domine Fili unigenite, Jesu Christe.
['dɔ mi nɛ   'fi li   u ni 'ʤɛ ni tɛ   'jɛ zu   'kri stɛ]
Lord Jesus Christ, the only-begotten Son.

Domine Deus, Agnus, Dei, Filius Patris.
['dɔ mi nɛ   'dɛ us   'ɑ ɲus   'dɛ i   'fi li us   'pɑ tris]
Lord God, Lamb of God, Son of the Father.

Qui tollis peccata mundi,
[kwi   'tɔlː lis   pɛkː 'kɑ tɑ   'mun di]
You, Who take away the sins of the word,

miserere nobis.
[mi zɛ 'rɛ rɛ   'nɔ bis]
have mercy on us.

Qui tollis peccata mundi,
[kwi   'tɔlː lis   pɛkː 'ka ta   'mun di]
You, Who take away the sins of the world,

suscipe deprecationem nostram.
['su ʃi pɛ   dɛ prɛ ka ʧi 'ɔ nɛm   'nɔ stram]
receive our prayer.

Qui sedes ad dexteram Patris,
[kwi   'sɛ dɛs   ad   'dɛks tɛ ram   'pa tris]
You, Who sit at the right hand of the Father,

miserere nobis.
[mi zɛ 'rɛ rɛ   'nɔ bis]
have mercy on us.

Quoniam tu solus sanctus. Tu solus Dominus.
['kwɔ ni am   tu   'sɔ lus   'saŋ ktus.   tu   'sɔ lus   'dɔ mi nus]
For You alone are holy. You alone are Lord.

Tu solus Altissimus, Jesu Christe.
[tu   'sɔ lus   al 'tis si mus   'jɛ zu   'kri stɛ]
You alone, O Jesus Christ, are most high,

Cum Sancto Spiritu,
[kum   'saŋ ktɔ   'spi ri tu]
With the Holy Spirit,

in gloria Dei Patris. Amen.
[in   'glɔ ri a   'dɛ i   'pa tris.   'a mɛn]
in the glory of God the Father. Amen.

Credo

Credo in unum Deum,
['krɛ dɔ   in   'u num   'dɛ um]
I believe in one God.

Patrem omnipotentem, factorem cœli et terræ,
['pa trɛm   ɔ mni pɔ 'tɛn tɛm   fa 'ktɔ rɛm   'ʧɛ li   ɛt   'terː rɛ]
The Father almighty, maker of heaven and earth, and

visibilium omnium, et invisibilium.
[vi zi 'bi li um   'ɔ mni um   ɛt   in vi zi 'bi li um]
of all things visible and invisible.

Et in unum Dominum Jesum Christum,
[ɛt   in   'u num   'dɔ mi num   'jɛ zum   'kri stum]
And I believe in one Lord, Jesus Christ,

Ordinary
of the
Mass

Filium Dei unigenitum.
['fi li um 'dɛ i u ni 'ʤe ni tum]
the only-begotten Son of God.

Et ex Patre natum ante omnia sæcula.
[ɛt ɛks 'pɑ trɛ 'nɑ tum 'ɑn tɛ 'ɔ mni ɑ 'sɛ ku lɑ]
Born of the Father before all ages.

Deum de Deo, lumen de lumine,
['dɛ um dɛ 'dɛ ɔ 'lu mɛn dɛ 'lu mi nɛ]
God of God, Light of Light,

Deum verum de Deo vero.
['dɛ um 'vɛ ɾum dɛ 'dɛ ɔ 'vɛ ɾɔ]
true God of true God.

Genitum, non factum,
['ʤe ni tum nɔn 'fɑ ktum]
Begotten, not made,

consubstantialem Patri:
[kɔn sub stɑn ʧi 'ɑ lɛm 'pɑ tri]
of one substance with the Father.

per quem omnia facta sunt.
[pɛɾ kwɛm 'ɔ mni ɑ 'fɑ ktɑ sunt]
By Whom all things were made.

Qui propter nos homines,
[kwi 'prɔ ptɛɾ nɔs 'ɔ mi nɛs]
Who for us men

et propter nostram salutem
[ɛt 'prɔ ptɛɾ 'nɔ strɑm sɑ 'lu tɛm]
and for our salvation

descendit de cælis.
[dɛ 'ʃɛn dit dɛ 'ʧɛ lis]
came down from heaven.

Et incarnatus est de Spiritu Sancto
[ɛt in kɑɾ 'nɑ tus ɛst dɛ 'spi ɾi tu 'sɑŋ ktɔ]
And He became flesh by the Holy Spirit

ex Maria Vergine: Et homo factus est.
[ɛks mɑ 'ri ɑ 'vir ʤi nɛ ɛt 'ɔ mɔ 'fɑ ktus ɛst]
of the Virgin Mary: And was made man.

Crucifixus etiam pronobis:
[kru ʧi 'fik sus 'ɛ tsi am prɔ 'nɔ bis]
He was also crucified for us,

sub Pontio Pilato passus, et sepultus est.
[sub 'pɔn tsi ɔ pi 'lɑ tɔ 'pɑs sus ɛt sɛ 'pul tus ɛst]
suffered under Pontius Pilate, and was buried.

Et resurrexit tertia die,
[ɛt rɛ surː rɛk sit 'tɛr tsi ɑ 'di ɛ]
And on the third day He rose again,

secundum Scripturas.
[sɛ 'kun dum skri 'ptu rɑs]
according to the Scriptures.

Et ascendit in cælum:
[ɛt ɑ 'ʃɛn dit in 'ʧɛ lum]
He ascended into heaven

sedet ad dexteram Patris.
['sɛ dɛt ɑd 'dɛks tɛ rɑm 'pɑ tris]
and sits at the right hand of the Father.

Et iterum venturus est cum gloria,
[ɛt 'i tɛ rum vɛn 'tu rus ɛst kum 'glɔ ri ɑ]
He will come again in glory

judicatre vivos et mortuos:
[ju di 'kɑ rɛ 'vi vɔs ɛt 'mɔr tu ɔs]
to judge the living and the dead:

cujus regni non erit finis.
['ku jus 'rɛ ɲi nɔn 'ɛ rit 'fi nis]
And of His kingdom there will be no end.

Et in Spiritum Sanctum Dominum et vivificantem:
[ɛt in 'spi ri tum 'saŋ ktum 'do mi num ɛt vi vi fi 'kɑn tɛm]
And I believe in the Holy Spirit, the Lord and Giver of life,

qui ex Patre Filioque procedit.
[kwi ɛks 'pɑ trɛ fi li 'ɔ kwɛ prɔ 'ʧɛ dit]
Who proceeds from the Father and the Son.

Qui cum Patre et Filio simul adoratur
[kwi kum 'pɑ trɛ ɛt 'fi li ɔ 'si mul ɑ dɔ 'rɑ tur]
Who together with the Father and the Son is adored

et conglorificatur:
[ɛt kɔn glɔ ri fi 'kɑ tur]
and glorified,

qui locutus est per Prophetas.
[kwi lɔ 'ku tus ɛst pɛr prɔ 'fɛ tɑs]
and Who spoke through the prophets.

Et unam sanctam catholicam
[ɛt 'u nɑm 'saŋ ktɑm kɑ 'tɔ li kɑm]
and one holy, Catholic,

et apostolicam Ecclesiam.
[ɛt ɑ pɔ 'stɔ li kɑm ɛk 'klɛ zi ɑm]
and Apostolic Church.

Ordinary
of the
Mass

Confiteor unum baptisma
[kɔn 'fi tɛ ɔr 'u num bɑp 'tis mɑ]
I confess one baptism

in remissionem peccatorum.
[in rɛ misː si 'ɔ nɛm pɛkː kɑ 'tɔ rum]
for the remission of sins.

Et exspecto resurrectionem mortuorum.
[ɛt ɛk 'spɛ ktɔ rɛ zurː rɛk tsi 'ɔ nɛm mɔr tu 'ɔ rum]
And I await the resurrection of the dead.

Et vitam venturi sæculi. Amen.
[ɛt 'vi tɑm vɛn 'tu ri 'sɛ ku li 'ɑ mɛn]
And the life of the world to come. Amen.

Sanctus

Sanctus, Sanctus,
['sɑŋ ktus 'sɑŋ ktus]
Holy, holy

Sanctus Dominus Deus Sabbaoth.
['sɑŋ ktus 'dɔ mi nus 'dɛ us 'sɑ bɑ ɔt]
holy Lord God of hosts.

Pleni sunt cæli et terra gloria tua.
['plɛ ni sunt 'ʧɛ li ɛt 'tɛrː rɑ 'glɔ ri ɑ 'tu ɑ]
Heavens and earth are filled with Your glory.

Hosanna in excelsis.
[ɔ 'zɑnː nɑ in ɛk 'ʃɛl sis]
Hosanna in the highest.

Benedictus

Benedictus qui venit in nomine Domini
[bɛ nɛ 'di ktus kwi 've nit in 'nɔ mi nɛ 'dɔ mi ni]
Blessed is He Who comes in the name of the Lord.

Hosanna in excelsis.
[ɔ 'zɑnː nɑ in ɛk 'ʃɛl sis]
Hosanna in the highest.

Agnus Dei

Agnus Dei qui tollis peccata mundi:
['ɑ ɲus 'dɛ i kwi 'tɔlː lis pɛkː 'kɑ tɑ 'mun di]
Lamb of God, you take away the sins of the world.

miserere nobis.
[mi zɛ 'rɛ rɛ 'nɔ bis]
have mercy on us.

Agnus Dei qui tollis peccata mundi:
['ɑ ɲus 'dɛ i kwi 'tɔl lis pɛkː 'kɑ tɑ 'mun di]
Lamb of God, you take away the sins of the world.:

dona nobis pacem.
['dɔ nɑ 'nɔ bis 'pɑ ʧɛm]
grant us peace.

German Diction

The accepted standard of German for public performance is called Bühnenaussprache, *or "stage German." Used by professional German singers, actors, and broadcasters, this pronunciation is the basis for the principles of diction which follow.*

Many people unfamiliar with the German language consider it a dark, gutteral language because of the presence of several sounds and speech patterns foreign to American English. In reality, the majority of German vowels and consonants are clear and forward, promoting good vocalism.

As you begin to study German diction, you will find several traits of the language that will ease your work. The rules of spelling and pronunciation are regular, with fewer exceptions than in Italian or English. You will notice that there are usually no more than one or two pronunciations of an orthographic letter, and that there are few orthographic spellings for a particular sound. The clear principles of syllabification will help you recognize sound groups to guide your pronunciation.

You will find also that many sounds are common to German and English. Other sounds are closely related to their English allophones. You will need to make only minor adjustments in the shape or use of the articulators to produce the German sound. These "fine tunings" are discussed in detail in the "Special Features" section, with reminders and drills in the "Vowels and Consonants in Detail" section to help you master the changes.

You will discover several unfamiliar mixed vowel sounds (called *umlauts*) represented by the orthographic symbols *ä*, *ö*, and *ü*, and two other new sounds: the lingua-velar and lingua-palatal fricative pronunciations of *ch*. As you read the descriptions and go through the exercises, you will learn to feel the shapes of these German sounds as well as the vocal focus and breath connection which they can bring to your singing.

To begin your adventure with German, I suggest you first read the "Special Features" section dealing with specific sounds. Complete the drills, paying special attention to the sounds of the *umlauts* and *ch*. Next, become familiar with the overview of sounds presented in the initial chart. Finally, with this overview as a base, begin the Syllabification section and work your way straight through the text. Once this is done, apply your knowledge to the careful study of your song texts. Welcome to the rich world of the German Lied!

Chart of German Sounds

The following chart lists the sounds of the German language in alphabetic order. Refer to this chart to quickly check the sound of a spelling. Although German is quite regular in its forms, there are some special circumstances and exceptions which cannot be presented easily in a simple chart. Detail is included in the discussion of the individual sounds.

German Letter & Position in Word			IPA	Example & IPA		Page
a	a	before *one* consonant	[ɑ]	Vater	['fɑ tər]	146
	aa	"	[ɑ]	Saal	[zɑl]	146
	ah	"	[ɑ]	Mahl	[mɑl]	146
	a	before *two* consonants	[a]	Wasser	['va sər]	147
	ai		[aɪ]	Mai	[maɪ]	137, 148
	ay		[aɪ]	Bayern	['baɪ ərn]	137, 148
	au		[aʊ]	Baum	[baʊm]	137, 148
ä	ä *	before *one* consonant	[ɛː]	spät	[ʃpɛːt]	149
	äh *	"	[ɛː]	Krähe	['krɛː ə]	149
	ä *	before *two* consonants	[ɛ]	Männer	['mɛ nər]	149
	äu		[ɔY]	Träume	['trɔY mə]	138, 150
b	b	initial in word or syllable	[b]	Buch, geben	[bux] ['ge bən]	159
	b	final in word or syllable	[p]	Dieb	[dip]	159
	b	before *t* and *st*	[p]	lebst	[lepst]	159
c	c	before a *front* vowel (*i, e, y*)	[ts]	Citrone	[tsi 'tro nə]	160
	c	before a *back* vowel (*a, o, u*)	[k]	Café	[ka 'fé]	159
	ch	after a *front* vowel, consonant	[ç]	ich, welche	[ɪç] ['vɛl çə]	140, 161
	ch	after a *back* vowel	[x]	Bach, doch	[bax] [dɔx]	140, 162
	chs	when *s* is part of the root word	[ks]	sechs	[zɛks]	163
	ck		[k]	backen	['ba kən]	160
d	d	initial in word or syllable	[d]	anders	['an dərs]	163
	d	final in word or syllable	[t]	Tod, Widmung	[tot] ['vɪt muŋ]	163
	dt		[t]	Stadt	[ʃtat]	163
e	e	stressed syllable and before *one* consonant	[e]	ewig, beten	['e vɪç] ['be tən]	150
	ee		[e]	Seele	['ze lə]	150
	eh		[e]	sehr	[zer]	150
	e	before *two* consonants	[ɛ]	Bett, helfen	[bɛt] ['hɛl fən]	151
	e	final or in an unstressed syllable	[ə]	Liebe, gesund	['li bə] [gə 'zʊnt]	151
	ei		[aɪ]	ein	[aɪn]	137, 152
	ey		[aɪ]	Meyer	['maɪ ər]	137, 152
	eu		[ɔY]	heulen	['hɔY lən]	138, 152

* *The umlauts ä, ö, and ü are sometimes written ae, oe, and ue. These spellings do not alter the pronunciation.*

German Letter & Position in Word			IPA	Example & IPA		Page
f	f		[f]	fein, Tafel	[faɪn] ['tɑ fəl]	164
g	g	initial in word or syllable	[g]	Gott, fragen	[gɔt] ['frɑ gən]	164
	g	final in word or syllable,	[k]	Tag, Flugzeug	[tɑk] ['fluk tsɔʏk]	164
	g	before *t* or *st*	[k]	fragst	[frɑkst]	164
	g	in suffix - *ig*	[ç]	König, Ewigkeit	['kø nɪç] ['e vɪç kaɪt]	164
	g	in some words of French origin	[ʒ]	Genie	[ʒe 'ni]	165
h	h	initial in a word or element**	[h]	Held, Gottheit	[hɛlt] ['gɔt haɪt]	165
	h	*after* a vowel	*silent*	Wahn, gehen	[vɑn] ['ge ən]	165
i	i	before *one* consonant	[i]	Bibel	['bi bəl]	152
	ie	"	[i]	Liebe	['li bə]	152
	ih	"	[i]	ihr	[ir]	152
	ieh	"	[i]	Vieh	[fi]	152
	i	in the *stressed* ending -*ik*	[i]	Musik	[mu 'zik]	153
	i	before *two* consonants	[ɪ]	Kinder, ist	['kɪn dər] [ɪst]	153
	i	in the suffixes -*in*, -*nis*,	[ɪ]	Müllerin, Bildnis	['mʏ lə rɪn] ['bɪlt nɪs]	153
	i	in the suffix -*ig*	[ɪ]	willig	['vɪ lɪç]	153
	i	in the *unstressed* ending -*ik*	[ɪ]	Lyrik	['ly rɪk]	153
j	j		[j]	Jahr, ja	[jɑr] [ja]	165
	j	in some words of French origin	[ʒ]	Journalist	[ʒur na 'lɪst]	166
k	k		[k]	Klause	['klɑu zə]	166
				zurück	[tsu 'ryk]	
l	l		[l]	hell, loben	[hɛl] ['lo bən]	166
m	m		[m]	Mond	[mont]	167
				träumen	['trɔʏ mən]	
n	n		[n]	Nonne, Wein	['nɔ nə] [vaɪn]	167
	ng	in same element**	[ŋ]	lang, singen	[laŋ] ['zɪ ŋən]	167
		in separate elements**	[n | g]	hingehen	['hɪn ge ən]	168
	nk	in one element**	[ŋk]	danken	['daŋ kən]	168
		in separate elements**	[n | k]	Anklang	['an klaŋ]	168
o	o	before *one* consonant	[o]	Rose, Ton	['ro zə] [ton]	154
	oh	"	[o]	Sohn, wohl	[zon] [vol]	135
	oo	"	[o]	Moos, Boot	[mos] [bot]	135
	o	before *two* consonants	[ɔ]	Ort, kommen	[ɔrt] ['kɔ mən]	154
o	ö *	before *one* consonant	[ø]	Öde, hören	['ø də] ['hø rən]	155
	öh *	"	[ø]	Höhe, fröhlich	['hø ə] ['frø lɪç]	155
	ö *	before *two* consonants	[œ]	Göttlich	['gœt lɪç]	155

** For a definition of element, see page 130.

German Letter & Position in Word			IPA	Example & IPA		Page
p	p	as in English "cupful"	[p]	prosit, Puppe	['pro zɪt] ['pʊ pə]	168
	pf		[pf]	Pferd, stumpf	[pfɛrt] [ʃtʊmpf]	169
	ph		[f]	Phrase, phantastisch	['fra zə] [fan 'tas tɪʃ]	169
q	qu		[kv]	Quelle	['kvɛ lə]	169
				erquicken	[ɛr 'kvɪ kən]	
r	r	flipped or trilled; *never* the American [ɹ]	[r]	Regen	['re gən]	169
				Herr	[hɛr]	
s	s	initial in word or element,	[z]	Silber, Absicht	['zɪl bər] ['ap zɪçt]	170
	s	between vowels	[z]	Rose	['ro zə]	170
	s	final in word or syllable	[s]	Glas, lösbar	[glɑs] ['løs bɑr]	170
	ss, ß		[s]	müssen, Kuß	['mʏ sən] [kʊs]	170
	sch	in *same* element **	[ʃ]	schnell, Tisch	[ʃnɛl] [tɪʃ]	171
	sch	in *two* elements **	[s|ç]	Häuschen	['hɔʏs çən]	171
	sp	initial in word or element **	[ʃp]	spielen, Aussprache	['ʃpi lən] ['aʊs ʃpra xə]	171
	sp	in all other environments	[sp]	Knospe	['knɔs pə]	171
	st	initial in word or element **	[ʃt]	Stein, Frühstück	[ʃtaɪn] ['fry ʃtʏk]	171
	st	in all other environments	[st]	ist, trösten	[ɪst] ['trø stən]	171
t	t		[t]	Ton, Sonntag	[ton] ['zɔn tɑk]	172
	th	in *same* element **	[t]	Thema, Theater	['te ma] [te 'ɑ tər]	172
	th	in *two* elements **	[t|h]	Rathaus, mithören	['rɑt haʊs] ['mɪt hø rən]	172
	ti	in the endings -tion, -tient	[tsj]	Nation, Patient	[na 'tsjon] [pa 'tsjɛnt]	172
	tsch	in *same* element **	[tʃ]	deutsch	[dɔʏtʃ]	172
	tz		[ts]	Platz, sitzen	[plats] ['zɪ tsən]	172
u	u	before *one* consonant	[u]	Musik, Blume	[mu 'zik] ['blu mə]	156
	uh	"	[u]	Stuhl, Uhr	[ʃtul] [ur]	156
	u	before *two* consonants	[ʊ]	Mutter, Bruch	['mʊ tər] [brʊx]	156
ü	ü *	before *one* consonant	[y]	für, grün	[fyr] [gryn]	157
	üh *	"	[y]	fühlen	['fy lən]	157
	ü *	before *two* consonants	[ʏ]	Müller, Glück	['mʏ lər] [glʏk]	157
v	v	all German words, final in foreign words	[f]	Vater, brav	['fɑ tər] [brɑf]	172
	v	other positions in foreign words	[v]	Vase, November	['va zə] [no 'vɛm bər]	172
w	w		[v]	Welt, Schwester	[vɛlt] ['ʃvɛ stər]	173

* *The umlauts ä, ö, and ü are sometimes written ae, oe, and ue. These spellings do not alter the pronunciation.*

** *For a definition of element, see page 130.*

German Letter & Position in Word			IPA	Example & IPA		Page
x	x		[ks]	Hexe	['hɛ ksə]	173
y	y	as *ü* in derivations from Greek:				
		before *one* consonant	[y]	Lyrik, Physik	['ly rɪk] ['fy zɪk]	158
		before *two* consonants	[ʏ]	Rhythmus, idyllisch	['rʏt mʊs] [i 'dʏ lɪʃ]	158
	y	elsewhere, as in the foreign language:				
			[i]	Tyrol, Pyjama	[ti 'rɔl] [pi 'dʒɑ ma]	158
			[j]	York	[jɔrk]	158
z	z		[ts]	Zimmer, Hertz	['tsɪ mər] [hɛrts]	173
	zw		[tsv]	zwei, zwischen	[tsvaɪ] ['tsvɪ ʃən]	174

Syllabification

Dividing words into elements and syllables helps determine the placement of stress as well as the open or closed sound of the vowels and the pronunciation of certain consonants. Separate German words into syllables according to the following rules.

Single Consonant

When a single consonant stands between two vowels, divide the word after the first vowel.

An element is a word, prefix, or suffix, which forms a self-contained unit within a larger word. An element may be multi-syllabic.

Va-ter	['fɑ tər]	Flü-gel	['fly gəl]
he-ran	[hɛ 'ran]	ge-ge-ben	[gə 'ge bən]

An *h* after a vowel indicates that the sound of the vowel is long and closed. The *h* is silent and remains with the preceding vowel. Divide the word after the *h*.

steh-len	['ʃte lən]	müh-se-lig	['my ze lɪç]
eh-e	['e ə]	Hoh-e-lied	[ho ə 'lit]

Exception: When the *h* is part of the suffixes *-heit* or *-haft*, or when it begins the second element of a compound word, separate it from the preceding vowel and give it aspiration.

ß, called Eszett [ɛs 'tsɛt], occurs instead of ss in final position and before t. Pronounce it [s].

Ho-heit	['ho haɪt]
Hun-de I haus	['hʊn də ˌhaʊs]
dog I house	

A digraph is the combination of two written consonants that produce a single consonant sound.

Treat *ß*, the digraphs *ch, ph, th*, and the consonant combinations *sch* and *st* as single consonants which begin the next syllable.

Bü-cher	['by çər]	lau-schen	['laʊ ʃən]
Stra-ße	['ʃtrɑ sə]	Pro-phet	[pro 'fet]
la-sten	['la stən]	zi-ther	['tsɪ tər]

Multiple Consonants

When a cluster of two or more consonants follows a vowel, begin the next syllable with the last of the consonants.

Bet-te	['bɛ tə]	Was-ser	['va sər]
Städ-ten	['ʃtɛ tən]	wer-den	['ver dən]
Knos-pen	['knɔs pən]	be-merk-ten	[bə 'mɛrk tən]

Prefixes and Suffixes

Divide prefixes and suffixes from the root word as separate elements.

Prefixes		Suffixes	
zu ‖ gleich	[tsu 'glaɪç]	Mäd ‖ chen	['mɛːt çən]
be ‖ glü-cken	[bə 'glʏ kən]	Rös ‖ lein	['røz laɪn]
Zu ‖ eig-nung	['tsu aɪg nʊŋ]	Land ‖ schaft	['lant ʃaft]
ab ‖ bren-nen	['ap brɛ nən]	Fröh ‖ lich ‖ keit	['frø lɪç kaɪt]
durch ‖ spie-len	['dʊrç ʃpi lən]	scherz ‖ haft	['ʃɛrts haft]

Become familiar with the common prefixes and suffixes listed below to clarify seeming exceptions to the first two rules of syllabification.

Common Prefixes

ab-	[ap]	*her-	[her]				
an-	[an]	hin-	[hɪn]				
auf-	[aʊf]	miß-	[mɪs]				
aus-	[aʊs]	mit-	[mɪt]				
be-	[bə]	nach-	[nax]				
bei-	[baɪ]	über-	['y bər]				
*da-	[da]	um-	[ʊm]				
*dar-	[dar]	un-	[ʊn]				
durch-	[dʊrç]	unter-	['ʊn tər]				
ein-	[aɪn]	ur-	[ur]				
ent-	[ɛnt]	ver-	[fɛr]				
er-	[ɛr]	vor-	[for]				
fort-	[fɔrt]	weg-	[vɛk]				
ge-	[gə]	zer-	[tsɛr]				
		zu-	[tsu]				

Common Suffixes

-bar	[bɑr]
-chen	[çən]
-haft	[haft]
-heit	[haɪt]
-keit	[kaɪt]
-lein	[laɪn]
-lich	[lɪç]
-los	[los]
-nis	[nɪs]
-sal	[zɑl]
-sam	[zɑm]
-schaft	[ʃaft]
-tum	[tum]
-wärts	[vɛrts]

*Vowel color varies in these prefixes. See page 136.

Compound Words

Divide a compound word between the word elements and then by syllables.

Zug ‖ luft	['tsuk lʊft]
Mond ‖ schein	['mont ʃaɪn]
Don-ners ‖ tag	['dɔ nərs tɑk]
Ar-beits ‖ tisch	['ar baɪts tɪʃ]
A-bend ‖ es-sen	['a bənt ɛ sən]

Learn to recognize common connective syllables which often indicate a compound word:

e as in Scheidegruß
en as in Lindenbaum
er as in Rädergebraus
es as in Liebesgaben.

Stressing

Meis-ter | si-nger   ['maɪ stər ˌzɪ ŋər]

German, like English, is a strongly metric language with similar patterns of stress. The primary stress in most German words falls on the root syllable, which in simple words is usually the first syllable. In IPA, it is indicated by the diacritical mark ['] placed above and before the stressed syllable. Secondary stress may occur in multi-syllabic and compound words, and is indicated by the diacritical mark [ˌ] placed below and before the syllable receiving the secondary stress. Syntax may cause the stress to vary from these general rules. When in doubt, check a reliable dictionary.

Simple words: In simple words, stress the first syllable.

Mut-ter	['mʊ tər]	Schu-le	['ʃu lə]
le-ben	['le bən]	ha-ben	['ha bən]

Nouns and words used as nouns are always capitalized in German.

Compound words: The placement of stress varies in compound words.

Nouns: In compound nouns, stress the first element. Secondary stress may fall on the second element.

Haus	tür	['haʊs tyr]	Schnee	ball	['ʃne bal]
Früh	jahr	['fry jar]	Dank	sa-gung	['daŋk za gʊŋ]
Wald	ein-sam-keit	['valt	ˌaɪn zam kaɪt]		

Adverbs: In compound adverbs, stress the second syllable. Most of the elements which make up compound adverbs are found in the list of common prefixes, page 131.

hi-nauf	[hɪ 'naʊf]	hi-naus	[hɪ 'naʊs]
he-rein	[hɛ 'raɪn]	da-her	[da 'her]
um-sonst	[ʊm 'zɔnst]	da-für	[da 'fyr]

Prefixes: Placement of stress varies in words with prefixes.

In words with the inseparable prefixes *be-, emp-, ent-, er-, ge-, ver-,* and *zer-,* stress the word root.

Ver-ständ-nis	[fɛr 'ʃtɛnt nɪs]
zer-reiß-en	[tsɛr 'raɪ sən]
be-glü-cken	[bə 'glʏ kən]
ge-ge-ben	[gə 'ge bən]
ent-flieh-en	[ɛnt 'fli ən]
er-reicht	[ɛr 'raɪçt]

Prefixes *cont.*

Stress the prefixes *ab-, an-, aus-, auf-, bei-, ein-, mit-,* and *ur-.*

ab I wärts	['ap vɛrts]
aus I ge-hen	['aʊs ge ən]
Bei I fall	['baɪ fal]
ein I si-ngen	['aɪn zɪ ŋən]
mit I leid	['mɪt laɪt]
ur I al-te	['ur al tə]

The prefixes *da-, dar-, durch-, her-, hin-, in-, miß-, ob-, über-, um-, un-, unter-, voll-, vor-,* and *zu-* are usually stressed.

durch I zieh-en	['dʊrç tsi ən]
miß I brauch	['mɪs braʊx]
Vor I sicht	['for zɪçt]
zu I kom-men	['tsu kɔ mən]
Um I weg	['ʊm vek]
un I klar	['ʊn klɑr]
her I kom-men	['her kɔ mən]

However:

zu-frie-den	[tsu 'fri dən]
miß -gönnt	[mɪs 'gœnt]

When a prefix separates from the verb and stands alone at the end of a phrase or sentence, it bears the primary stress of the sentence: "Ich komme vom Gebirge her."[ɪç 'kɔmə fɔm gə'bɪrgə 'her] Der Wanderer

Words and word endings of foreign origin:

Stress is frequently on the last syllable of borrowed words and German words of foreign origin such as those that end with *-ei*. In the borrowed ending *-ieren,* stress the *-ie.*

Stu-dent	[ʃtu 'dɛnt]	Pa-pier	[pɑ 'pir]
Phy-sik	[fy 'zik]	Bi-bli-o-tek	[bɪ bli o 'tek]
Ma-le-rei	[mɑ lə 'raɪ]	hal-bie-ren	[hal 'bi rən]

Stress sometimes shifts from the prefix to the root word for emphasis or to change the connotation of the word: 'unmenschlich = inhuman (cruel); un'menschlich = inhuman (excessive)-as in "an inhuman pace."

Special Features of German Pronunciation

The following sections introduce you to the characteristic sounds, speech patterns, and rules of pronunciation used in German. Practice whispering, speaking, and singing the examples. The poetic "tongue twisters" included with the discussion of each letter may be spoken and sung on various vocalise patterns. These exercises will help you overcome the unfamiliar muscular sensations of pronouncing German and lead you to fluent German pronunciation habits.

Except where indicated by an *, the poetic exercises are excerpted from Der kleine Hey: Die Kunst des Sprechens with the permission of the publisher, B. Schott's Söhne.

The Distinctive Sounds of German Vowels

Pronounce each of the German vowel letters with a pure, distinct sound. The vowels *a*, *e*, *o*, and the unstressed *e* require special practice to avoid American speech patterns.

a The letter *a* may be pronounced as [ɑ] or [a]. In German it never rounds to [ɔ] or slips to the neutral [ə] in an unaccented syllable as it does in English.

Compare and contrast.

	English		German	
America	[ə 'mɛ ɾɪ kə]	Amerika	[ɑ 'me ri kɑ]
alter	['ɔl tər]	Altar	[al 'tɑr]
majestic	[mə 'dʒɛs tɪk]	Majestät	[mɑ jɛs 'tɛːt]

e Pronounce *stressed e* as [e], [ɛ], or [ə], but never use the off-glide of English. When you pronounce [e], place the arch of your tongue more forward and closer to the aveolar ridge than its English counterpart, creating a sound close to that of [i].

Compare and contrast.

	English		German	
sail	[seɪl]	Seele	['ze lə]
way	[weɪ]	Weh	[ve]

Pronounce *unstressed e* with a more forward sensation than its English counterpart. Never open it to [ɛ] or round it to [ʊ]. Slightly round your lips toward [œ] and place your tongue in a higher position for the German [ə] than for the English [ə] or [ʌ].

Compare and contrast.

	English		German	
comma	['kɑ mə]	Komme	['kɔ mə]
about	[ə 'baʊt]	gebaut	[gə 'baʊt]

o Pronounce *o* as [o] or [ɔ]. Never pronounce the off-glide as in its English counterpart. Pronounce [o] with firmly rounded lips and long duration.

Compare and contrast.

	English		German	
note	[noʊt]	Not	[not]
sew	[soʊ]	Sohn	[zon]

General Rules for Open and Closed Vowels

In German each vowel has an open and closed sound, the closed sound being of longer duration as well. (See the chart on the right.) A few simple rules, which apply to all of the vowels, determine when to pronounce a vowel with its open or closed sound. Common words that are exceptions to these rules are included in the German Vowels Section.

Closed Vowels

Pronounce a vowel with its closed sound and with long duration when it occurs in the following situations:

When a vowel letter is doubled.

Saal [zɑl]   Moos [mos]   Meer [mer]

When the vowel letter is before *h* in the same syllable.

mehr [mer]   ihrer   ['i rər]
hohe ['ho ə]   bemühen [bə 'my ən]

When the vowel letter is before a single consonant.

Grab [grɑp]   Ton [ton]   Bru-der ['bru dər]
re-den ['re dən]   ö-de ['ø də]   Flü-gel ['fly gəl]

Open Vowels

Pronounce a vowel letter with its open sound and a short duration when it is before a double consonant and, usually, when it is before two or more different consonants. This rule includes the letter *x*, which functions as the phonetic consonant [ks].

schlaffen ['ʃla fən]   Sonne   ['zɔ nə]   Hexe ['hɛ ksə]
nicht   [nɪçt]   helfen   ['hɛl fən]   unter [ʊn tər]

Exceptions:

A vowel letter before ß, *st*, *ch*, or the combination of *r* plus a dental consonant (*d*, *t*, *l* and *n*) can be open or closed. When in doubt, consult a reliable dictionary. Look at the list below and become familiar with the pronunciation of frequently encountered words that have these consonants.

Closed (exceptions)
Schoß   [ʃos]   groß   [gros]   Trost   [trost]
hoch   [hox]   Gruß   [grus]   Buch   [bux]
suchen   ['zu xən]   Erde   ['er də]   erst   [erst]
werden   ['ver dən]   zart   [tsɑrt]

Open (regular)
Roß   [rɔs]   doch   [dɔx]   kosten   ['kɔ stən]
Kuß   [kʊs]   Spruch   [ʃprux]   Hertz   [hɛrts]
Sehnsucht   ['zen zʊxt]

Letter	Rule	Sound
a*	closed	[ɑ]
	open	[a]
e	closed	[e]
	open	[ɛ]
i	closed	[i]
	open	[ɪ]
o	closed	[o]
	open	[ɔ]
u	closed	[u]
	open	[ʊ]
ä*	closed	[ɛː]
	open	[ɛ]
ö	closed	[ø]
	open	[œ]
ü, y	closed	[y]
	open	[ʏ]

*See page 146 for further explanation.

A closed vowel in a verb stem will remain closed despite inflective endings. Learn to recognize verb endings illustrated by the conjugation of leben, *to live*.
leben, leb<u>ten</u>, ge<u>lebt</u>

ich lebe   wir leb<u>en</u>
du leb<u>st</u>   ihr leb<u>t</u>
er leb<u>t</u>   sie leb<u>en</u>

The closed or open character of these vowels remains constant when the plural of a noun or the degree of an adjective is formed by the process of umlaut. Buch [bux], Bücher [by çər]; hoch [hox]höher [hø ər], höchst [høçst]

See the chart of prefixes and suffixes on page 131 for many of the common exceptions to the rules for open and closed vowels.

Exceptions: *cont.*

The vowels in monosyllabic words, prefixes, and suffixes are pronounced irregularly in German, just as they are in most languages. Learn the most common exceptions to the rules included in the discussion of the individual vowel sounds.

Pronounce the vowel in the prefixes, *her-*, *da-*, and *dar-* with its closed sound when stressed and its open sound when unstressed.

'dadurch	['da durç]	da'heim	[da 'haɪm]
'darbieten	['dar ˌbi tən]	da'rum	[da 'rʊm]
'herstellen	['her ʃtɛ lən]	her'nieder	[hɛr 'ni dər]

Notice that the word *her* is always pronounced with a closed vowel.

"Barfuß auf dem Eise schwankt er hin und her;"
['barfus | aʊf dem | aɪzə ʃvaŋt | er hɪn | ʊnt her]

"Der Leiermann"

Unstressed e

Pronounce the letter *e* as *schwa* [ə] when it occurs in final, unstressed syllables and in the prefixes *ge-* and *be-*. You may find the *schwa e* in consecutive unstressed syllables when an adjectival ending is added to a verb form: *helfen* ['hɛl fən] - *helfenden* ['hɛl fən dən].

Liebe	['li bə]	wogen	['vo gən]
Müller	['mʏ lər]	Gebot	[gə 'bot]
Bremer I hafen	[bre mər 'ha fən]		

The German Diphthongs

The three German diphthong sounds, [aɪ], [aʊ], and [ɔʏ] are pronounced in a similar manner to their English counterparts, with the first vowel sound receiving the primary stress and longer duration. However, in singing German the definition and duration of the second vowel is usually less emphasized than in English. To achieve the sound of the German diphthong, shift from the first to the second vowel using the appropriate tongue and lip motion, but keeping the jaw in the position of the first vowel. You may find it helpful to think of the German diphthong as the first vowel sound *colored* by the second vowel sound. This is especially true when you pronounce the two darker sounds, [aʊ] and [ɔʏ].

Authorities vary as to the most accurate way of transcribing the sounds of the German diphthongs. Siebs, who wrote for a German-speaking audience, used [ae], [ao], and [ɔø]. Other authorities employ [aɪ], [aʊ], and [ɔɪ] or [ɔy] or [ɔY]. In an attempt to capture the coloration of the German sounds for American-speaking singers — and to avoid confusing the diphthong transcription [ae] with the the single vowel transcription [æ] as in *cat* — this text will use the symbols [aɪ], [aʊ], and [ɔY].

[aɪ] The diphthong [aɪ] may be spelled *ai, ay, ei,* or *ey.* The sound is similar to the diphthong in the English word *bite.* Although the IPA transcription is the same in English and German, the transition from [a] to [ɪ] is smoother and the [ɪ] less clearly defined in the German diphthong. Prolong the [a] and glide smoothly to an unstressed [ɪ] by allowing the jaw to remain still as the tongue changes position.

Note the differences in the pronounciation of [aɪ] from the smooth blend in German through the "middle-ground" of English to the almost bi-syllabic character of Italian.

Compare and contrast.

German		English		Italian	
Mai	[maɪ]	my	[maɪ]	mai	[mai]
dein	[daɪn]	dine	[daɪn]	daino	['daino]

[aʊ] The diphthong [aʊ] is spelled *au.* The sound is like the diphthong found in the English word *house,* but with a smoother transition from vowel to vowel. Although Siebs states that any darkening of the first vowel sound [a] should be avoided, the most respected German singers do darken (color) the initial vowel [a] with the sound of [ʊ]. Awareness of this darker, rounder [a] is especially important for American singers in areas of the country where [aʊ] is normally pronounced with a broad, flat sound.

Compare and contrast.

German		English		Italian	
Haus	[haʊs]	house	[haʊs]	cauto	['kaːu to]
baut	[baʊt]	about	[ə 'baʊt]	baule	['baːu le]

Shift from the first vowel to the second vowel of a German diphthong by changing the tongue and/or lip position, but not the jaw.

Compare the sounds of bright *ah* [a] and dark *ah* [ɑ] in the following diphthongs.

feil	[faɪl]	faul	[fɑʊl]
Reich	[raɪç]	Rauch	[rɑʊx]
Bein	[baɪn]	Baum	[bɑʊm]
Wein‖laub	['vaɪn lɑʊp]		

[ɔY] The diphthong [ɔY] may be spelled *eu* or *äu.* The sound is pronounced like the diphthong in the English word *toy,* but with a smoother transition from vowel to vowel and a more rounded second vowel sound. Feel the German [ɔY] more forward in the mouth than its English equivalent.

Compare and contrast.

German	English	Italian
treu [trɔY]	Troy [trɔɪ]	tuoi [twɔi]

Exercise for the diphthongs [ai], [ɑʊ], and [ɔY].

Read aloud.

Ein leuchtender Tau   [aɪn 'lɔYçtəndər tɑʊ]
Weilt heut auf der Au. [vaɪlt hɔYt | ɑʊf der | ɑʊ]
Ein säuselnder Hauch [aɪn 'zɔYzəlndər hɑʊx]
Streift leise euch auch. [ʃtraɪft 'laɪzə | ɔYç | ɑʊx]

The Mixed Vowels

In the German language there are four mixed vowels that are indicated by the placement of an umlaut, (¨), over the letters *o* and *u,* as in *schön* and *früh.* Each mixed vowel is composed of two vowel sounds —a front vowel and a back vowel — that are *mixed* together, i.e. pronounced at the same time.

To articulate each mixed vowel, place the tongue in the arched position of the forward vowel and then, *without moving the tongue,* round the lips to the position of the back vowel. Once the vowel is formed, maintain the lip and tongue position until the beginning of the next phoneme to avoid a diphthongal off-glide. As you pronounce the sounds and words in the exercises, notice how it feels to pronounce the two sounds *simultaneously.* Do not glide from one sound to another.

The symbol, (¨), found over the vowels a, o, and u in German, is called an umlaut ['ʊmlaʊt]. *The umlauts ä, ö, and ü are sometimes spelled ae, oe, and ue. The sound remains the same.*

Chart of Tongue and Lip Positions for the Mixed Vowels

	Tongue position		Lip position		Mixed vowel
closed ü	[i]	+	[u]	=	[y]
open ü	[ɪ]	+	[ʊ]	=	[ʏ]
closed ö	[e]	+	[o]	=	[ø]
open ö	[ɛ]	+	[ɔ]	=	[œ]

Compare and contrast the following sounds.

Tongue Vowel		Mixed Vowel		Lip Vowel	
Miete	['mi tə]	müde	['my də]	Mut	[mut]
misten	['mɪs tən]	müssen	['mʏ sən]	Muster	['mʊs tər]
Sehne	['ze nə]	Söhne	['zø nə]	Sohn	[zon]
helle	['hɛ lə]	Hölle	['hœ lə]	Holde	['hɔl də]

The sound of [ʏ] is familiar to fans of the "Pink Panther" films in Inspector Cloussau's fractured pronunciation of the English word bump *[bʏmp]. The sound {ø} occurs when he answers the* phone *{føn}.*

The Interpretive Use of Consonants

To a greater degree than in Italian or English, the consonants in German are used as carriers of expression. Pronounce all German consonants clearly. Do not be afraid to emphasize them: you can, like the great German singers, enhance the meaning of the text by coloring a word with expressive, emphasized consonants. The type and amount of emphasis will change with the character of the text. Use a word-by-word translation of the text and become sensitive to the flow of the musical line to help determine which consonants might be emphasized. As in English, you may shift the emphasis when words are repeated. However, emphasize consonants only to enliven the expression: Be careful not to destroy the vocal line!

When emphasizing a consonant, three guidelines must be followed:

Pronounce consonants before the musical beat. The vowel must be placed on the beat to avoid slowing the tempo.

In consonant clusters, emphasize only one consonant. The consonant emphasized will generally be the sharpest of the group. For example:

s<u>t</u>ille not <u>st</u>ille   <u>fr</u>isch not f<u>r</u>isch

Within a word, emphasize only those consonants following a short, open vowel. For example:

"Hinab zum Tale rauschen, so fri<u>sch</u> und wunderhell"
[hɪ 'nap tsum 'tɑlə 'rɑʊʃən zo frɪʃ | ʊnt 'vʊndər hɛl]
"Wohin?"

Notice that a consonant will not be emphasized after a long, closed vowel.

"Durch der Menschen stille, sti<u>ll</u>e Brust."
[dʊrç der mɛnʃən 'ʃtɪlə 'ʃtɪlːlə brʊst]
"Nacht und Träume"

"O Tod, wie bitter, wie bi<u>tt</u>er bist du."
[o tot vi bɪtər vi bɪtːtər bɪst du]
"O Tod..." from *Vier ernste Gesänge*

ch - The Ach-Laut and Ich-Laut

The consonant combination *ch* has two sounds in German, both foreign to English speakers (except, perhaps, those who hiss at their cats). These are the lingua-velar and lingua-palatal consonants mentioned in the introduction.

[ç]   To produce [ç], the forward *ich-laut*, — literally, "ich-sound" — speak the name *Hugh* and emphasize the initial aspirate sound. Isolate the initial sound [ç ç ç ç], then precede it with a bright [i], [iç iç iç iç], allowing the energized stream of air to flow over your arched tongue. You will feel the air flow between the center of your tongue arch and your alveolar ridge.

In German words, the consonant combination ch is pronounced with an aspirated sound, either [ç] or [x]. It is [k] or [ʃ] only in words borrowed from Greek or French.

To pronounce the German word *ich*, repeat the process using the open sound of the letter *i*, [ɪç ɪç ɪç]. Once you find the sound, you will notice that the sound naturally adjusts it's position slightly, depending on the sounds surrounding it. The ich-laut remains an aspirated sound, however, and never becomes the fricative [ʃ] or plosive [k].

Compare and contrast.

English		German	
dish	[dɪʃ]	dich	[dɪç]
wrecked	[ɹɛkt]	Recht	[rɛçt]

[x] Produce [x], the back *ach-laut*, — literally, "ach- sound" — by directing an energetic air stream between the velum and the arched back of the tongue. You may think of the sound as a *fricative* [k]. Try pronouncing the velar-plosive [k] several times [k k k k], then prolong the sound of the attack, [kxxx]. Finally, remove the initial [k], attacking and sustaining the sound of [x]. The Ach-Laut is always an aspirated sound. It is never pronounced as the plosive [k].

Compare and contrast.

English	German
boxs [bɑks]	Bachs [baxs]
fluke [fluk]	Fluch [flux]

Exercise:

Speak the following progression of "ich-" and "ach-lauts" from the most forward to the most back position, then reverse the pattern.

ichi eche ächä acha ocho uchu
[içi eçe ɛçɛ ɑxɑ oxo uxu]

The ich-laut and ach-laut are produced in the position closest to that of the preceding vowel: [ç] after forward vowels and diphthongs, [x] after back vowels and the back diphthong [ɑʊ].

Dental Consonants

To articulate the consonants *d*, *t*, and *n*, place the tip of the tongue forward, touching the gum line behind the upper teeth. The tip of the tongue is more forward than the linguo-alveolar English counterparts. Notice also that less air escapes with the explosion of *d* and *t* in German than in English, producing what is sometimes called a *dry* sound.

[d]

[t]

[n]

Compare and contrast.

English	German
dandy [dæn dɪ]	dadurch [da 'dʊrç]
total [toʊ təl]	total [to 'tal]
none [nʌn]	Nonne ['nɔ nə]

The consonants d, t, n, and l are dental consonants in German. Dental consonants are sometimes referred to as linguo-dental consonants.

[l] Pronounce [l] as a clear sound formed by touching the tip of the tongue to the gum line behind the upper teeth with the base of the tongue in a low position. This sound is like *l*

[l]
cont..

in the English word *let*. Avoid the alveolarized dark *l* as in *all*, which is the most common sound of *l* in English.

Compare and contrast.

English		German	
feel	[fiɫ]	viel	[fil]
fail	[feɪɫ]	fehl	[fel]
built	[bɪɫt]	Bild	[bɪlt]

Voicing and Unvoicing of Consonants - b, d, g

Voiced

Pronounce the consonants *b*, *d*, and *g* with their normal, voiced sound when they are initial in a word or syllable.

Bett	[bɛt]	Lie-der	['li dər]
We-ge	['ve gə]	ja-gen	['jɑ gən]
hin-geh-en	['hɪn ge ən]	To-des-qual	['to dəs ˌkvɑl]

Unvoiced

Pronounce *b*, *d*, and *g* like their unvoiced counterparts *p*, *t*, and *k* when they occur before *t* and *st*, or final in a word or syllable. Unvoice both sounds of the combinations *-bt* and *-gd* when they are final.

Dieb	[dip]	Tod	[tot]	Weg	[vek]
end-lich	['ɛnt lɪç]	Jagd	[jakt]	gibt	[gipt]
ab-fahren	['ap fɑ rən]	er-folg-reich	[ɛr 'fɔlk raɪç]		

Voicing or unvoicing of the single consonants b, d, and g depends entirely upon the position of the consonant in the word. Articulation will change in different forms of the same word. For example, notice the g and d in the following words as the form of the word changes:

Weg [vek]

becomes We-ge ['ve gə];

Leid [laɪt]

becomes leider ['laɪ dər]

Exceptions:

ig Pronounce the combination *-ig* usually as [ɪç] when final in a word or syllable. See page 153 for a more detailed explanation.

billig	['bɪ lɪç]	emsig	['ɛm zɪç]
wichtig	['vɪç tɪç]	Ewigkeit	['e vɪç kaɪt]

ng Pronounce the digraph *ng* as the sound [ŋ]. Do not pronounce the g.

singen	['zɪ ŋən]	Hoffnung	['hɔf nʊŋ]

Contractions

The plosive consonants *b*, *d*, and *g* are sometimes placed before *l*, *n*, or *r* through the omission of an *e* in a contracted word. When this happens, the plosive consonant begins the second syllable and remains voiced. Although this may sound confusing, in many instances your ear will guide you.

Wa-ge-ner ['vɑ gə nər] becomes Wa-gner ['vɑ gnər]
re-ge-net ['re gə nət] becomes re-gnet ['re gnət]
gol-de-ne ['gɔl də nə] becomes go-ldne ['gɔ ldnə]
Wan-de-rer ['van də rər] becomes Wan-drer['van drər]

Double Consonants

In spoken German, a double consonant is generally pronounced the same way as a single consonant in simple words. The effect is to open the preceding vowel rather than to elongate the consonant sound. Pronounce double consonants with longer duration in two instances:

Compound Words

In compound words, when the final consonant of the first word is the same as the first consonant of the second word, pronounce both. Since there must be no intervening vocalic sound, the effect is that of imploding the first consonant and exploding the second. A similar sound occurs in English when the same consonant ends one word and begins the next.

Compare and contrast.

English	German	
quit talking	Fest l tag	['fɛstːtɑk]
ban noise	hin l nehmen	['hɪnːne mən]
if free	Schif l fahrt	['ʃɪfːfɑrt]

Emphasis

In German speech, double consonants are often used for emphasis. Where we might say, "Everything's going my way," our German counterpart would exclaim, "Es geht mir alles gut!" and emphasize the double *ll*. Outstanding singers of German Lieder make judicious use of this technique to enliven both diction and meaning.

German

The long duration of a double consonant is indicated in IPA transcriptions by a colon [ː]. This text reflects the standard undoubled patterns of speech in the transcription of individual words. Prolonged double consonants are indicated only where context warrants their use.

When emphazing double consonants, choose only the ones that will strengthen the emotional or onomatopoetic impact of the text. A word-by-word translation of the Lied text will help you select the words with double consonants that you may choose to emphasize.

Speak the following lines, emphasizing the onomatopeotic impact of "zappelt" and the emotional effect of "nimmer" by lengthening the double consonants:

> "...das Fischlein zappelt dran."
> [das ˈfɪʃlaɪn tsapːpəlt dran]
> (the little fish wriggled on the line)
> "Die Forelle"

> "ich finde sie ni<u>mm</u>er, und nimmer<u>m</u>ehr."
> [ɪç ˈfɪndə zi ˈnimːmər | ʊnt nɪmər mer]
> (I find it {peace} never, and nevermore.)
> "Gretchen am Spinnrade"

A glottal stop is a slight interruption in the flow of sound, as heard in the English phrase the/apple. In singing terms, glottal stop is sometimes referred to as a glottal stroke indicating the easy gentle handling of this sound.

Use of the Glottal Stop

Initial position

In German, unlike French and Italian, most words beginning with a vowel will be preceded by a glottal stop. Except for instances when strong emotion needs to be shown, as in "und <u>a</u>ch, sein Kuß !" from *Gretchen am Spinnrade* use a gentle glottal stroke to maintain good vocalism and a legato singing line.

> Practice the following phrases using a gentle glottal stroke before the initial vowels.

> an alle
> [an | ˈalə]

> Am offenen Abend
> [am | ˈɔfənən | ˈɑbənt]

> Dein Abschied
> [daɪn | ˈapʃit]

> Etwas in ihm ist anders
> [ˈɛtvas | ɪn | im | ɪst | ˈandərs]

> Uralte Eichen am Ufer der Elbe
> [ˈur | altə | ˈaɪçən | am | ˈufər der | ˈɛlbə]

> Ankunft ist um acht Uhr Abends
> [ˈankʊnft | ɪst | ʊm | axt | ur | ˈɑbənts]

Within a word

Use a glottal stop within a word in two instances:

In a compound word, when the second element begins with a vowel, separate it from the first element with a glottal stroke.

Land ǀ urlaub	['lant ǀ ˌurlɑʊp]
Mannes ǀ art	['manəs ǀ art]
Ein ǀ akter	['aɪn ǀ aktər]
Erd ǀ apfel	['ert ǀ ˌapfəl]

Prefixes also constitute separate elements. Use a glottal stroke to separate them from a root word which begins with a vowel.

Er ǀ innerung	[ɛr ǀ 'ɪnərʊŋ]
aus ǀ atmen	['ɑʊs ǀ ˌatmən]
über ǀ all	['y bər ǀ ˌal]
un ǀ endlich	[ʊn ǀ 'ɛnt ǀ lɪç]
hin ǀ arbeiten	['hɪn ǀ arbaɪtən]
Vor ǀ ahnung	['for ǀ ˌɑ nʊŋ]

Exception:

When the prefixes *her-*, *hin-*, *dar-*, and *vor-* are combined with another prefix which begins with a vowel, do not use a glottal stroke. The medial consonant begins the second syllable. Refer to the chart on page 131 to help you recognize prefixes which may be combined.

her + ab = he-rab	[hɛ 'rap]
dar + an = da-ran	[da 'ran]
hin + ein = hi-nein	[hɪ 'naɪn]
vor + aus = vo-raus	[fo 'rɑʊs]

German Vowels in Detail

The German language contains six vowels plus three mixed-vowels indicated by an umlaut. Each vowel letter has an open and closed sound; *e* and *y* each have an additional sound possibility. The orthographic letters and their sixteen respective sounds are indicated in the chart below.

The Letter	The Sound				
a	[ɑ]	or	[a]		
e	[e]	or	[ɛ]	or	[ə]
i	[i]	or	[ɪ]		
o	[o]	or	[ɔ]		
u	[u]	or	[ʊ]		
y	[y]	or	[ʏ]	or	[i]
ä	[ɛː]	or	[ɛ]		
ö	[ø]	or	[œ]		
ü	[y]	or	[ʏ]		

The letter

The German letter *a* has both closed and open sounds in singing as well as speech.

Caution: Be careful not to pronounce the vowel letter *a* as [ɔ] or [ə] in German, as you would in English when it occurs in a word like *caught* [kɔt] or *about* [ə 'baʊt]. The letter *a* is only pronounced [a] or [ɑ].

a, aa, ah

Pronounce *a*, *aa*, or *ah* as [ɑ], f<u>a</u>ther, when followed by a single consonant.

Note: Even though dark [ɑ] is more open (the jaw is dropped more) than bright [a], you will find it called *closed a* because it follows the rules for a closed vowel.

Read aloud.

Vater	['fɑ tər]	Grab	[grɑp]
Staat	[ʃtɑt]	Saal	[zɑl]
Bahn	[bɑn]	fahren	['fɑ rən]

Exceptions: Several prefixes and one syllable words are pronounced with the bright [a] when followed by a single consonant.

Read aloud these exceptions.

Word		Prefix	
am	[am]	ab- [ap] as in abordnen ['ap | ɔrdnən]
man	[man]	an- [an] as in anerkannt ['an | ɛrkant]

Pronounce *a* as bright [a] when it occurs before a double consonant or multiple consonants in the same element.

Note: Even though bright [a] is more closed than dark [ɑ], you will find it called *open a* because it follows the rules for a open vowel.

Pronounce the German bright [a], as in the French word *voilà!* or the initial sound found in the diphthong [aɪ] in the English word *high*. Some manuals of singer's diction eliminate this sound because the contrast of [a] and [ɑ] is subtle when sustained in singing. Although tonal duration is predetermined in singing, you can nevertheless sing [a], and by closing more quickly, you can define a short [a].

Read aloud.

Tasse	['ta sə]	Rast	[rast]
Dach	[dax]	Sack	[zak]
fangen	['fa ŋən]		

Compare and contrast.

[ɑ]			[a]
Kahn	[kɑn]	—	kann	[kan]
Abend	['ɑ bənt]	—	Apfel	['a pfəl]
Wahl	[vɑl]	—	Wald	[valt]
Sahne	['zɑ nə]	—	sandte	['zan tə]
Vater	['fɑ tər]	—	Wasser	['va sər]

The letter

a

a *cont.*

Read aloud.

> Vom Wasser haben wir's gelernt... "Das Wandern"
> [fɔm 'vasər 'habən virs gə'lɛrnt]

Practice the following exercise for both open and closed *a*.

> Nah dem Hage Tannen schwanken,
> [nɑ dem 'hagə 'tanən'ʃvaŋkən]

> Alles strahlet Abendprangen
> ['aləs 'ʃtralət | 'abənt 'praŋən]

ai, ay

Pronounce *ai* and *ay* as the diphthong [aɪ]. Also see *ei,* page 152 and diphthongs, page 136.

Note: Remember to glide smoothly through the unstressed [ɪ] without closing the jaw.

Read aloud.

Mai	[maɪ]	Laich [laɪç]	Kaiser ['kaɪ zər]
Saite	['zaɪ tə]	Bayern['baɪ ərn]	Tokayer [to 'kaɪ ər]

au

Pronounce *au* as the diphthong [ɑʊ]. Produce the initial vowel with rounded lips and then move to the second vowel sound by further rounding the lips rather than by closing the jaw. Also see page 137.

Read aloud.

Haus	[hɑʊs]	Laub [lɑʊp]	Auge ['ɑʊ gə]
auf	[ɑʊf]	Faust [fɑʊst]	lauschen ['lɑʊ ʃən]

Practice the following exercise for the diphthong [ɑʊ].

> Es schaut aus blauem Auge
> [ɛs ʃɑʊt | ɑʊs 'blɑʊəm | 'ɑʊgə]

> So traurig auf die Frau;
> [zo 'trɑʊrɪç | ɑʊf die frɑʊ]

Gr

Pronounce ä or äh as long [ɛː] when followed by a single consonant.

The letter

ä

Pronounce long [ɛː] by opening the [ɛ], as when pronouncing the English word *candid* in an affected "upper-crust" manner. Although the [ɛː] is similar to [ɛ], you must allow the chin to drop slightly lower than for [ɛ].

Compare and contrast.

[ɛ]	[ɛː]	[e]
Betten ['bɛ tən]	bäten ['bɛː tən]	beten ['be tən]
esse ['ɛ sə]	äße ['ɛː sə]	Esel ['e zəl]
Vetter ['fɛ tər]	Väter ['fɛː tər]	Fetisch ['fe tɪʃ]

Read aloud.

ähnlich ['ɛːn lɪç]	Schwäne ['ʃvɛː nə]
spät [ʃpɛːt]	Mädchen ['mɛːt çən]
erklären [ɛr 'klɛː rən]	nähen ['nɛː ən]

Pronounce ä as short [ɛ] when it occurs before a double consonant or multiple consonants in the same element.

Read aloud.

Äpfel ['ɛ pfəl]	Kälte ['kɛl tə]
lächelnd ['lɛ çəlnt]	stärke ['ʃtɛr kə]
nächtlich ['nɛçt lɪç]	ärgern ['ɛr gərn]

Practice speaking the following exercise for the open and closed sounds of the letter ä.

Die lässigen Wächter erwähnen und zählen
[di 'lɛsɪgən 'vɛçtər ɛr'vɛːnən | ʊnt 'tsɛːlən]

Die schwärmenden Schwäne nah den prächtigen Kähnen.
[di 'ʃvɛrməndən 'ʃvɛːnə nɑ den 'prɛçtɪgən 'kɛːnən]

äu

Pronounce *äu* as the diphthong [ɔʏ]. See the spelling *eu*, page 152, and diphthongs, page 136.

Caution: Remember that when you pronounce the German [ɔʏ], you must round your lips more than for the English [ɔɪ]. Allow the jaw to remain still and the lips slightly protruded. The arch of the tongue must not rise too far as you move to the second vowel: an obtrusive off-glide (Bäu-ime for Bäu-me) must be avoided.

Read aloud.

Fräulein	['frɔʏ laɪn]	Bäume	['bɔʏ mə]
Häuser	['hɔʏ zər]	läuten	['lɔʏ tən]
Bläue	['blɔʏ ə]	Täubchen	['tɔʏp çən]

The letter

Pronounce *e*, *ee*, or *eh* as [e] when followed by a single consonant.

Pronounce the German [e] with the high point of the tongue closer to the roof of the mouth than in English and without a trace of the diphthongal [ɪ] off-glide found in English speech. To our ears "O, Weh!" [| o 've] sounds almost like [| o 'vi] when well pronounced.

Read aloud.

ewig	['e vɪç]	Regen	['re gən]
mehr	[mer]	Elend	['e lənt]

Exceptions: Several prefixes and one syllable words are pronounced with [ɛ] when followed by a single consonant.

Words:

der [dɛr]　des [dɛs]　wes [vɛs]

Prefixes:

er- [ɛr]	as in erachten	[ɛr | 'ax tən]
her- [hɛr]	as in herauf	[hɛ 'raʊf]
zer- [tsɛr]	as in zerfliesse	[tsɛr 'fli sə]
But: her- [her]	as in 'herkommen	['her kɔ mən]

Note: The noun, *Weg*, (written with capital *W*) is always pronounced [vek]. The adverb, prefix, and suffix *weg* is pronounced [vɛk].

The letter

e

Pronounce *e* as [ɛ] when it occurs before a double consonant or multiple consonants in the same element.

Pronounce [ɛ] with the tongue slightly more forward and and the jaw more open than [ɛ] in the English word *met.*

Compare and contrast.

[e]		[ɛ]	
den	[den]	denn	[dɛn]
beten	['be tən]	betten	['bɛ tən]
stehlen	['ʃte lən]	stellen	['ʃtɛ lən]

Read aloud.

Welt	[vɛlt]	emsig	['ɛm zɪç]
Herz	[hɛrts]	wenn	[wɛnn]

Pronounce *e* as *schwa* [ə] when it occurs in final, unstressed syllables and in the prefixes *ge-* and *be-*. (See page 136).

Pronounce the German *schwa* with the lips very slightly rounded toward [œ]. The sound quality varies slightly in openness according to its environment, but it is consistently more forward and has a higher tongue position than either the English [ʌ] or [ə].

Caution: Be careful not to open the schwa all the way to [ɛ] or to over-round it to the French *schwa.*

Read aloud.

Hilfe	['hɪl fə]	liebevoll	['li bə fɔl]
lispeln	['lɪs pəln]	spiegelnden	['ʃpi gəln dən]
Tränen	['trɛː nən]	suchen	['zu xən]
beglücken	[bə 'glʏ kən]	gegeben	[gə 'ge bən]
schöner	[ʃø nər]	Himmel	['hɪ məl]

Practice speaking the following exercise for the sounds of the letter *e.*

Es streben der Seele Gebete
[ɛs 'ʃtrebən der 'zelə gə'betə]

Den helfenden Engeln entgegen;
[den 'hɛlfəndən | 'ɛŋəln | ɛnt'gegən]

ei, ey

The letter

e

Pronounce *ei* and *ey* as the diphthong [aɪ] Also see *ai*, page 148, and diphthongs, page 136.

Read aloud.

dein	[daɪn]	Leib	[laɪp]
bleiben	['blaɪ bən]	Veilchen	['faɪl çən]
Heine	['haɪ nə]	Meyer	['maɪ ər]

Practice speaking the following exercise for the diphthong [aɪ].

Es schreit ein Meislein im Gezweig,
[ɛs ʃraɪt | aɪn 'maɪslaɪn | ɪm gə'tsvaɪç]

Daß weit wie breit sei Maienzeit!
[das vaɪt vi braɪt zaɪ 'maɪən tsaɪt]

eu

Pronounce *eu* as the diphthong *äu* [ɔʏ]. Also see *äu*, page 148, and diphthongs, page 136.

Read aloud.

neu	[nɔʏ]	heute	['hɔʏ tə]	Reue	['rɔʏ ə]
Freude	['frɔʏ də]	treulich	['trɔʏ lɪç]	atreus	['ɑ trɔʏs]

Practice speaking the following exercise for the diphthong [ɔʏ].

Heulsturm drauend beuget Bäume,
['hɔʏlʃtʊrm 'drɔʏənt 'bɔʏgət 'bɔʏmə]

Streut das Heu, verscheucht die Leute!
[ʃtrɔʏt das hɔʏ fɛr'ʃɔʏçt di 'lɔʏtə]

i, ie, ih, ieh

The letter

Pronounce *i*, *ie*, *ieh*, or *ih* as [i] when followed by a single consonant.

Pronounce *i* similar to the letters *ea* in the English word *pea*, with the lips neither spread nor rounded.

Read aloud.

Liebe	['li bə]	ihr	[ir]
hier	[hir]	Melodie	[me lo 'di]
Poesie	[po e 'zi]	Phantasie	[fan tɑ 'zi]

Exceptions: In a small group of borrowed words
ending in *-ie*, *-ien*, *-ier*, and *-ient*, pronounce the
letter *i* as the glide [j].

Read aloud.

Lilie	['lɪ ljə]	Familie	[fɑ 'mi ljə]
Italien	[i 'tɑ ljən]	Patient	[pɑ 'tsjɛnt]
Portier	[pɔr 'tje]		

Exceptions: In the following words and suffixes, *i* is pronounced as open [ɪ] when followed by a single consonant.

Words:

in, im	[ɪn] [ɪm]	bin	[bɪn]
bis	[bɪs]	mit	[mɪt]
hin	[hɪn]	April	[a 'prɪl]

Suffixes:

-ig	[-ɪç]	as in *fertig*	[fɛr tɪç]
-nis	[-nɪs]	as in *Bildnis*	['bɪlt nɪs]
-in	[-ɪn]	as in *Studentin*	[ʃtu 'dɛn tɪn]

Pronounce *i* as [ɪ] when followed by a double consonant or multiple
consonants in the same element.

Compare and contrast.

[i]		[ɪ]	
Lied	[lit]	litt	[lɪt]
bieten	['bitən]	bitten	['bɪtən]
ziemlich	['tsimlɪç]	Zimmer	['tsɪmər]

Read aloud.

Bitte	['bɪ tə]	Winter	['vɪn tər]
spricht	[ʃprɪçt]	frisch	[frɪʃ]
Gericht	[gə 'rɪçt]	blitzen	['blɪ tsən]

In the combination *-ik*, pronounce *i* as closed [i] if
the syllable is stressed and open [ɪ] if the syllable
is unstressed.

Musik	[mu 'zik]	Tragik	['trɑ gɪk]
Fabrik	[fab 'rik]	Lyrik	['ly rɪk]

Practice speaking the following exercise for the
sounds of *i*.

Ist dies Idyll hier nicht des Friedens Bild?
[ɪst dis | 'idʏl hir nɪçt dɛs 'fridəns bɪlt]

Wie innig wirkt's, wie tief, wie himmelsmild!
[vi | 'ɪnɪç vɪrkts vi tif vi 'hɪmːməls,mɪlt]

The letter

i

The letter

Pronounce *o* as [o] when followed by a single consonant.

Pronounce [o] as a long, pure sound with no trace of the diphthongal [ʊ] release used in the English diphthong [oʊ].

Read aloud.

Hof	[hof]	Brot	[brot]	schon	[ʃon]
wohl	[vol]	vor	[for]	Strom	[ʃtrom]
Rose	['ro zə]	Boden	['bo dən]		

Exceptions: Several words are pronounced with [ɔ] when followed by a single consonant.

op	[ɔp]	Doktor	['dɔk tɔr]
von	[fɔn]	Marmor	['mar mɔr]
vom	[fɔm]	Bischof	['bɪ ʃɔf]

Pronounce *o* as [ɔ] when followed by a double consonant or multiple consonants in the same element.

Pronounce [ɔ] similar to the sound of the letters *au* in the English word *caught*. Protrude and round the lips slightly more for the German [ɔ] than for its English equivalent.

Exception: In one important word, the letter o is pronounced as [o] when followed by two consonants: Mond [mont].

Compare and contrast.

[o]		[ɔ]	
wohne	['vo nə]	Wonne	['vɔ nə]
Ofen	['o fən]	offen	['ɔ fən]

Read aloud.

Sommer	['zɔ mər]	voll	[fɔl]	Dorf	[dɔrf]
sonst	[zɔnst]	kommt	[kɔmt]	Wort	[vɔrt]

Practice the following exercise for the sounds of *o*.

Oben thront der Nonnen Kloster
['obən tront der 'nɔnən 'klostər]

Voll von Trost, voll hoher Wonne
[fɔl fɔn trost fɔl 'hoər 'vɔnə]

Wohnen dorten fromme Nonnen
['vonən 'dɔrtən 'frɔmə 'nɔnən]

Loben Gott vor Morgenrot
['lobən gɔt for 'mɔrgən‚rot]

ö, öh, oe

Pronounce *ö, öh,* and *oe* as [ø] when followed by a single consonant.

Produce the mixed vowel, *closed umlaut* ö by *simultaneously* forming the tongue vowel [e] and the lip vowel [o].

Note: In pronouncing all the rounded umlaut sounds, maintain the lip position until the beginning of the next sound to avoid a diphthongal off-glide.

Compare and contrast.

[e]	[ø]	[o]
Sehne ['ze nə]	Söhne ['zø nə]	Sohn [zon]

Read aloud.

schön	[ʃøn]	öde	['ø də]
löhnen	['lø nən]	hörbar	['hør bar]
Herzöge	['hɛr tsøgə]	König	['kø nɪç]

Pronounce *ö* and *oe* as [œ] when followed by a double consonant or multiple consonants in the same element.

Pronounce the open sound of *umlaut ö* by *simultaneously* forming the tongue vowel [ɛ] and the lip-rounded vowel [ɔ]. The mouth is more open than it is for [o], but the lips must maintain enough rounding to prevent *können* from becoming confused with *kennen*.

Note: It is interesting that, lacking the English sound [ʌ], Siebs Deutsche Hochsprache uses [oe] as the vowel sound in the borrowed word *lunch*.

Compare and contrast.

[ɛ]	[oe]	[ɔ]
helle ['hɛ lə]	Hölle ['hœ lə]	Holde ['hɔl də]

Read aloud.

Götter	['gœ tər]	können	['kœ nən]
Wörter	['vœr tər]	plötzlich	['plœts lɪç]
köstlich	['kœst lɪç]		

Practice speaking the following exercise for the sound of ö.

Göttlich schön erlöst Versöhnen,
['gœtlɪç ʃøn ɛr'løst fɛr'zønən]

Böse mögen's schnöd verhöhnen.
['bøzə 'møgəns ʃnøt fɛr'hønən]

u, uh

The letter

u

Pronounce *u* or *uh* as [u] when followed by a single consonant.

Pronounce German long, closed *u* like *oo* in the English word *boot*, but with more firmly rounded lips. Avoid any hint of a *schwa* release by maintaining the lip position until the next sound begins. *Genug* [gə'nuk] must not become *genuag* [gə'nuək].

Note: In German *u* is always a pure sound. It never has the glide sound [ju], found in the English word *muse*.

Read aloud.

du [du] Muse ['mu zə] nur [nur] Fuß [fus]

zu [tsu] fuhren ['fu rən] Gesuch [gə 'zux]

Exceptions: In the following words and prefixes, pronounce the letter *u* as [ʊ] when followed by a single consonant.

Word:	Prefix:
um [ʊm]	un- [ʊn] as in unendlich [ʊn | 'ɛnt lɪç]
zum [tsʊm]	um- [ʊm] as in umarmen [ʊm | 'ar mən]

Pronounce *u* as [ʊ] when followed by a double consonant or multiple consonants in the same element.

Pronounce [ʊ] like the *oo* sound in the English word *book*, but with the lips more rounded and slightly protruded. The German sound is more forward and brighter in color than its English counterpart.

Compare and contrast.

[u]		[ʊ]	
Fuß	[fus]	Fluß	[flʊs]
Buhle	['bu lə]	Bulle	['bʊ lə]

Read aloud.

Mutter	['mʊ tər]	drucken	['drʊ kən]
Sturm	[ʃtʊrm]	Busch	[bʊʃ]
muß	[mʊs]	Brust	[brʊst]

Practice speaking the following exercise for the sound of *u*.

Dulden mußt du nun zur Stund',
['dʊldən mʊst du nun tsur ʃtʊnt]

Und der Fluch schuf Blut und Wunde!
[ʊnt der flux ʃuf blut | ʊnt 'vʊndə]

ü, üh, ue

Pronounce *ü*, *üh* or *ue* as [y] when followed by a single consonant.

Pronounce the mixed vowel, *closed umlaut u*, by *simultaneously* forming a closed [i] and a firmly rounded closed [u]. You will feel a downward pull on the upper lip, creating a beak-like sensation. The proper shape may also be found by whistling a pitch at medium range and then, without changing the mouth formation, shifting from a whistle to a vocal sound.

Compare and contrast.

[i]	[y]	[u]
Miete ['mi tə]	müde ['my də]	Mut [mut]

Read aloud.

üben ['y bən] Flügel ['fly gəl] grün [gryn] süß [zys]
für [fyr] glühen ['gly ən] düster ['dy stər]

Pronounce *ü*, *üh* or *ue* as [ʏ] when followed by a double consonant or multiple consonants in the same element.

Pronounce *open umlaut u* by *simultaneously* forming the tongue vowel [ɪ] and the lip-rounded vowel [ʊ]. Although the shape is more relaxed than [y], the lips must maintain enough rounding to prevent *stücken* ['ʃtʏ kən] from becoming confused with *sticken* ['ʃtɪ kən].

Compare and contrast.

[ɪ]	[ʏ]	[ʊ]
misten ['mɪ stən]	müssen ['mʏ sən]	Muster ['mʊ stər]

Read aloud.

Hütte ['hʏ tə] Glück [glʏk] wünschen ['vʏn ʃən]
flüstern ['flʏ stərn] Küsse ['kʏ sə] Müllerin ['mʏlə rɪn]

Practice speaking the following exercise for the sounds of *u*.

Müssen kühn wir überbrücken -
['mʏsən kyn vir 'ybər,brʏkən]

Blüt' wie Früchte rühmlich pflücken.
[blyt vi 'frʏçtə 'rymlɪç 'pflʏkən]

The letter

y

The letter *y* appears only in words of foreign origin. In the majority of cases, the derivation is Greek, and *y* will follow the rules for the letter *ü*. Words of other derivation are given the sound found in the original language, usually *i*.

In these words, pronounce the letter *y* as [y].

    Lyrik　['ly rɪk]　　typisch　['ty pɪʃ]　　Mythe　['my tə]

In these words, pronounce the letter *y* as [ʏ].

    Nymphe　['nʏm fə]　Myrte　['mʏr tə]　　Zephyr　['tse fʏr]

In these words, pronounce the letter *y* as [i].

    Tyrol　[ti 'rol]　　Zylinder　[tsi 'lɪn dər]

In these words, pronounce the letter *y* as [j].

    York　　[jɔrk]　　Yeoman　['jo mən]

German Consonants in Detail

b

When initial in a word or syllable, pronounce *b* as in English, though crisply plosive.

Read aloud.

Bett	[bɛt]	Bibel	['bi bəl]	über	['y bər]
lieben	['li bən]	Ebbe	['ɛ bə]	Bube	['bu bə]

Note: The stop-plosive consonants, *b - p, d - t,* and *k - g,* are pronounced more crisply and with less escape of air in German than in English.

Pronounce *b* as *p* before *t* or *st* and at the end of a word or word element.

Read aloud.

Knab	[knɑp]	abnehmen	['ap ne mən]
Grabstein	['grɑp ʃtaɪn]	gibt	[gipt]
Herbst	[hɛrpst]	erbebt	[ɛr 'bept]

Practice speaking the sounds of *b*.

Bleich und betrübt blickt die blonde Braut.
[blaɪç ʊnt bə'trypt blɪkt di 'blɔndə braʊt]

Lobpreiset, liebpredigt, ihr Boten.
['lopːpraɪzət 'lipːpredɪçt | ir 'botən]

c

In German, the single letter *c* occurs only in words of foreign origin, where it usually retains the pronunciation used in the original language. The following rules generally apply.

Pronounce *c* as a strongly articulated, linguo-velar plosive [k] before *a, o, u,* or any consonant except *h*.

Read aloud.

Café	[ka 'fe]	Crème	[krɛ mə]
Coca-Cola	['ko ka ˌko la]		

C

In words of Latin orgin, prounce *c* before *e* or *i*, or the umlauts, *ä*, *ö*, or *ü* as[ts]. Note that this sound is found in classical rather than ecclesiastical Latin.

Read aloud.

Cis (C#)	[tsɪs]	Cäcilie	[tsɛ 'tsi ljə]
Citrone	[tsi 'tro nə]	cito	['tsi to]
Cicero	['tsi tse ro]	Casar (Caesar)	['tsɛː zar]

Note: In modern spelling, *k* is often substituted for *c* when the sound is hard, and *z* is used when the sound is soft:
Kapelle for *Capelle; Zigarette* for *Cigarette.*

In many words of Italian origin, pronounce *c* before *e* or *i* as the Italianate soft sound [ʧ].

Read aloud.

Cembalo	['tʃɛm ba lo]	Cello	['tʃɛ lo]
Celesta	[tʃe 'lɛ sta]		

A few words of French origin retain the French sound of [s] for *c*.
Read aloud.

Farce	['far sə]	Force	['fɔr sə]
Cinemascope	[sɪ ne ma 'skop]		

ck

Pronounce *ck* like *k* in the English word *bake,* but with a sharper, more energized articulation than *k* alone.

Read aloud.

Ecke	['ɛ kə]	Stück	[stʏk]
beglücken	[bə 'glʏ kən]		

Practice speaking, using an energetic [k].

Denk' was drückt und zwickt, Schicksals Tücke schickt!
[dɛŋk vas drʏkt | ʊnt tsvɪkt 'ʃɪkzɑls 'tʏkə ʃɪkt]

The two fricative sounds of *ch* are a special characteristic of the German language.

When *ch* follows the letters *i, e,* the umlauts *ä, ö, ü,* the diphthongs *au, eu, ai, ei,* or a consonant, pronounce it as the "Ich-Laut" [ç]. In the diminutive suffix *-chen* and in a few borrowed words pronounce initial *ch* as [ç].

Produce the "Ich-Laut" *ch* by forming the mouth for [j] as in *yes* and directing an energetic flow of air over the arch of the tongue. For a full discussion of the production of [ç] see page 140.

Practice, gradually increasing speed. Notice how the position adjusts slightly to match the position of each vowel.

ichi, eche, ächä, öchö, üchü

[içi eçe ɛːçɛː øçø yçy]

Read aloud.

mich	[mɪç]	Milch	[mɪlç]
Bächlein	['bɛç laɪn]	rechts	[rɛçts]
Bücher	['by çər]	leuchten	['lɔ yç tən]
Cherub	['çe rʊp]	Chemie	[çe 'mi]
Chirurg	[çi 'rʊrk]	Mädchen	['mɛːt çən]
Liedchen	['lit çən]	Kätzchen	['kɛts çən]

Practice speaking [ç] in text.

Nicht schlechte Wächter scheuchen
[nɪçt 'ʃlɛçtə 'vɛçtər ʃɔ yçən]

Wichte, welche frech lächelnd,
[vɪçtə vɛlçə frɛç 'lɛçəlnt]

Ziemlich bezecht - möchten flüchtig entweichen.
['tsimlɪç bə'tsɛçt 'mœçtən 'flyçtɪç | ɛnt'vaɪçən]

Note: [ç] and [x] are aspirated sounds. Do not substitute the fricative [ʃ] or plosive [k]. Give special practice to the diminutive suffix *-chen* [çən], which must not slip to [ʃən] or [kən].

ch

When *ch* follows the letters *a*, *o*, *u*, or the diphthong *au*, pronounce it as the "Ach-Laut" [x].

Produce the back aspirate "Ach-Laut" *ch* by directing an energized air stream between the velum and the arched back of the tongue. Like its forward counterpart, it adjusts position slightly with each vowel, but it never migrates as far back as the uvular aspirate found in Hebrew. For a full discussion of the production of [x], see page 141.

Practice.

[axa ɔxɔ oxo ʊxʊ uxu]

Read aloud.

hoch	[hox]	Buch	[bux]
lachen	['la xən]	auch	[aʊx]
Bruch	[brʊx]	Sprache	['ʃprɑ çə]
Nacht	[naxt]	Loch	[lɔx]
jauchzet	['jɑʊx tsət]	taucht	[tɑʊxt]

Note: Back vowels are those on the *a - u* side of the vowel chart.

Practice speaking text with the sounds of [ç] and [x].

Auch ich weich' nicht solch frechem Wicht,
[aʊx | ɪç vaɪç nɪçt zɔlç 'freçəm vɪçt]

Doch leicht bricht nicht solch Joch.
[dɔx laɪçt brɪçt nɪçt zɔlç jɔx]

Deucht's euch auch Nacht - Reichsacht doch wacht!
[dɔʏçts | ɔʏç | aʊx naxt 'raɪçs | axt dɔx vaxt]

In words of Greek origin, *ch* is usually pronounced [k].

Read aloud.

Chor [kor]   Christ [krɪst]   Charakter [ka 'rak tər]

In words borrowed from French, *ch* retains the French sound of [ʃ].

Read aloud.

Chef [ʃɛf]   Chaise ['ʃɛː zə]
Chose ['ʃo zə]   Chanson [ʃɑ̃ sɔ̃]

chs

Pronounce the combination *chs* as [ks] when it is an integral unit of a word stem.

Read aloud.

sechs	[zɛks]	Ochse	[ˈɔ ksə]
Fuchs	[fʊks]	wachsen	[ˈva ksən]

When an *s* is added to *ch* as a part of a suffix, a part of a verb ending, or the beginning of a compound word, pronounce *chs* as [çs] or [xs]. The sound is that of *ch* plus *s*. See *ch* pages 161-162.

Read aloud.

höchstens [ˈhøç stəns]
hoch + -stens (adjective + suffix)

lachst [laxst]
lach|st (verb + ending) see page 171.

Sprechstimme [ˈʃprɛç ʃtɪ mə]
Sprech + stimme (compound word)

d

Like the letter *b*, *d* is voiced when initial in a word or syllable. It is strictly a voiced linguo-dental plosive, without the glottal stroke often included in the American English sound.

Read aloud.

Dank	[daŋk]	du	[du]	dadurch	[da ˈdʊrç]
drei	[draɪ]	Räder	[ˈrɛː dər]	anders	[ˈan dərs]

Practice speaking the dental *d*.

Den Dido durch den Dolch dort duldet!
[den ˈdido dʊrç den dɔlç dɔrt ˈdʊldət]

Pronounce *d* as an energetically plosive *t* before *t* or *st* and at the end of a word or word element.

Note: Pronounce *d* and *t* as dental consonants, with the tongue stroke against the gum line of the front teeth rather than against the alveolar ridge, as in English.

Read aloud.

Bild	[bɪlt]	Tod	[tot]
Hand	[hant]	Stadt	[ʃtat]

Kindheit [ˈkɪnt haɪt]
freundlich [ˈfrɔʏnt lɪç]
sandte [ˈzan tə]

f

Pronounce the letter *f* as in English.

Read aloud.

fein	[faɪn]	Ofen	['o fən]
offen	['ɔ fən]	Erfolg	[ɛr 'fɔlk]
funf	[fʏnf]	scharf	[ʃarf]

Exercises for the sound of *f* are included with those for *v* on pages 172-173.

g

The letter *g* has three primary sounds.

When initial in a word or syllable, pronounce *g* as a voiced stop-plosive, the "hard" sound of [g].

Read aloud.

geben	['ge bən]	Geist	[gaɪst]
Gegend	['ge gənt]	obgleich	[ɔp 'glaɪç]
gnädige	['gnɛː dɪ gə]	vergnügen	[fɛr 'gny gən]

When *g* or the combinations *-gd*, *-gst*, and *-gt* are final in a word or word element after any letter but *i* or *n*, pronounce *g* as an unvoiced [k]. The sound of this [k] lies mid-way between [g] and [k], unvoiced, but less crisply plosive than in a word spelled with *k* or *ck*. See the entry under *n* on pages 167-168 for the combination *ng*.

Read aloud.

Tag	[tɑk]	genug	[gə 'nʊk]
lag' (lage)	[lɑk]	Magd	[mɑkt]
tragst	[trɛː kst]	birgt	[bɪrkt]
taglich	['tɛːk lɪç]	Siegfried	['zik frit]

The letter group ig

Pronounce the combination *ig* as [ɪç] when final in a word or word element.

Read aloud.

ewig	['e vɪç]	König	['kø nɪç]
eckig	['ɛk ɪç]	wichtig	['vɪç tɪç]
Ewigkeit	['e vɪç kaɪt]	freudigste	['frɔʏ dɪç stə]

Exception: When the suffixes *-lich* or *-reich* are added to a word ending in *-ig,* pronounce *-ig* as [ɪk].

ewiglich	['e vɪk lɪç]	wonniglich	['vɔ nɪk lɪç]
königlich	['kø nɪk lɪç]	Königreich	[kø nɪk raɪç]

g

In a word borrowed from French *g* usually retains its French sound.

Read aloud.

Genie	[ʒe 'ni]	Loge	['lo ʒə]
Gigue	['ʒi gə]	Regisseur	[re ʒi 'sør]

Practice speaking the sounds of the letter *g.*

Gar gnädig gibt Gott tägliche Gaben genug.*
[gar 'gnɛːdɪç gipt gɔt 'tɛːklɪçə 'gabən gə'nuk]

h

When initial in a word or word element, pronounce *h* with the aspirant [h] found in the English word *house.*

Read aloud.

Hut	[hut]	Himmel	['hɪ məl]
Hauch	[haʊx]	herzhaft	['hɛrts haft]
erhaben	[ɛr 'ha bən]	hierher	[hir 'her]
Haushalt	['haʊs halt]		

Practice speaking the following text with initial *h.*

Hinterm Haus heult der Hofhund heiß hungrig hervor.*
['hɪntərm haʊs hɔʏlt der 'hɔf͵hunt haɪs 'huŋrɪç hɛr'for]

Except when initial in a word or element, *h* is silent, merely serving as a sign that the preceding vowel is closed in character.

Read aloud.

ruhig	['ru ɪç]	sehen	['ze ən]
Ehe	['e ə]	frühe	['fry ə]
mühselig	['my ze lɪç]		

j

Pronounce *j* like *y* in the English word *yes!* The sound is related to the articulation of the vowel [i]. Pronounce it energetically and move quickly to the following vowel.

Read aloud.

ja	[ja]	Jahr	[jɑr]
jeder	['je dər]	Jüngling	['jʏŋ lɪŋ]
jauchzen	['jaʊx tsən]	Majestät	[ma jɛs 'tɛːt]

A few words borrowed from the French retain the soft French sound of [ʒ].

Read aloud.

Journal   [ʒʊr 'nɑl]   Jury   [ʒy 'ri]

Practice speaking the energized sound of the letter *j*.

Jubelnd, johlend und jauchzend,
['jubəlnt 'jolənt | ʊnt 'jɑʊxtsənt]

Jetzt im Janner des Jahrs.
[jɛtst | ɪm 'janər dɛs jɑrs]

---

k

Pronounce *k* as in the English word *kick*. It is a crisp, energized plosive.

Read aloud.

Kind	[kɪnt]	Kette	['kɛ tə]
keine	['kaɪ nə]	Knospen	['knɔs pən]
krumm	[krʊm]	Rock	[rɔk]
Kerker	['kɛr kər]		

Practice speaking with a crisp initial *k*.

Komm kecker Kerl mit Kunde vom kummerkranken Kind.*
[kɔm 'kɛkər kɛrl mɪt 'kʊndə fɔm 'kʊmːmər,kraŋkən kɪnt]

---

l

Pronounce the clear *l* used in German as a linguo-dental consonant, similar to *l* in *billion* or *Lee*.

Read aloud.

hell	[hɛl]	Felder	['fɛl dər]
leben	['le bən]	moll	[mɔl]
allen	['a lən]	lieblich	['lip lɪç]
lispeln	['lɪs pəln]	huld	[hʊlt]

Note: *l* is a clear, liquid sound in German, produced with the tongue tip at the gum line. If *hell* (bright) sounds like its English allophone *hell* (Hades), so does your German.

Practice speaking the sound of clear *l*.

Lisple, lieblich, Liebeslallen.
['lɪsplə 'liplɪç 'libəs,lalən]

Pronounce *m* as in English.

Read aloud.

Mann	[man]	Kummer	['kʊ mər]
manchmal	['mançˌmɑl]	Samt	[zamt]
Schmerz	[ʃmɛrts]	Kampf	[kampf]

Practice speaking with a resonant *m*.

Nimmt mit Himmels Milde Marias Muttermacht-
[nɪmt mɪt 'hɪmːməls 'mɪldə maˈrias 'mʊtərˌmaxt]

Stumm Schmerz und Schmach von mir.
[ʃtʊmː ʃmɛrts | ʊnt ʃmax fɔn mir]

Pronounce *n* like the *n* in the English word *night*.

Note: Remember that *n* is a linguo-dental consonant in German. The tongue is placed more forward than in English, the tip just touching the gum line rather than the alveolar ridge.

Read aloud.

nun	[nʊn]	neben	['ne bən]
Sinn	[zɪn]	Wonnen	['vɔ nən]
unklar	['ʊn klɑr]	angenehm	['an gə nem]
Tannenbaum	['ta nən bɑʊm]		

Caution: Make sure that no *schwa* sound intervenes between a forward vowel or an *r* and a following *n*.

nein	[naɪn]	*not*	[naɪ ən]
fern	[fɛrn]	*not*	[fɛ ərn]

Practice speaking with a resonant *n*.

Nun nahen neue Wonnen, nun glänzt und grünt manch Land;
[nun 'nɑən 'nɔʏə 'vɔnən nun glɛntst | ʊnt grynt manç lant]

Pronounce the combination *ng* as the single sound [ŋ] when the letters are part of the same word element. Note that *ng* is pronounced [ŋk] only in dialect, and that the combination [ŋg] as in the English word *hunger* does not exist in German.

Read aloud.

Hoffnung	['hɔf nʊŋ]	singen	['zɪ ŋən]
Finger	['fɪ ŋər]	Wange	['va ŋə]
England	['ɛŋ lant]	Angst	[aŋst]

Exception: When *ng* occurs through the combination of a prefix and word or at the juncture in a compound word, the letters retain their individual sounds.

Read aloud.

angehen ['an ge ən] hingeben ['hɪn ge bən]
Eingeweide ['aɪn gə ˌvaɪ də]

Pronounce the combination *nk* as [ŋk] when the letters are part of the same word unit.

Read aloud.

Dank [daŋk] links [lɪŋks]
dunkel ['dʊ ŋkəl] wanken ['va ŋkən]

Exception: When *nk* occurs through the combination of a prefix and word or at the juncture in a compound word, *n* retains its normal sound.

Read aloud.

Einklang ['aɪn klaŋ] anklagen ['an klɑ gən]
unklar ['ʊn klɑr]

Practice speaking text employing the sounds of [ŋ] and [ŋk].

Bangen, verlangen nach prangenden Wangen!
['baŋən fɛr'laŋən nax 'praŋəndən 'vaŋən]

Wanken und schwanken, dem Undank zanken...
['vaŋkən | ʊnt 'ʃvaŋkən dem | 'ʊndaŋk 'tsaŋkən]

p

Pronounce the German *p* as a more sharply articulated version of the English *p* found in *pepper*.

Read aloud.

Papier [pɑ 'pir] plötzlich ['plœts lɪç]
Knospe ['knɔs pə]

Connect the two consonants of the combination *pf* in a quick and energetic manner without an intervening *schwa*. It is most easily accomplished when the position for the *p* is as close to that of *f* as possible. Practice the cartoon noise *fffffp:pf*, stopping the *f* with the closure for *p* then releasing the plosive back into the fricative *f*. Another aid in pronunciation is to practice saying *cupful* with an exaggerated *pf*, gradually shortening and finally eliminating the first syllable.

p

Read aloud.

Pfui! [pfʊ i]   Pferd [pfɛrt]
Pfad [pfɑt]   Apfel ['a pfəl]

Exercises for the sounds of *p* and *pf* are included with those for *v*, pages 172-173.

In words of Greek origin, pronounce the combination *ph* as *f*.

Read aloud.

Philosophie [fi lo zo 'fi]   Physik [fy 'zik]

The letter *q* is found only in the combination *qu*. Pronounce the combination as [kv], the *v* clearly voiced and without a trace of *schwa* between the two consonants.

q

Read aloud.

Quelle   ['kvɛ lə]   quälen   ['kvɛː lən]
erquicken [ɛr 'kvɪ kən]   bequem   [bə 'kvem]

Practice speaking the combination of [kv].

Erquickende Quelle quillt quirlend empor.
[ɛr 'kvɪkəndə 'kvɛlə kvɪlt 'kvɪrlənt ɛm 'por]

In singing use the flipped *r* almost exclusively. In most environments it will receive 2-3 flaps; at the end of an unaccented syllable, only one tap. The number of flaps and their intensity will vary with the emotional value of the word. Note that at rapid tempi, final *-er* or *r* followed by another consonant may sometimes be pronounced as [ɐ]. The sound of [ɐ] is similar to [ʌ], except that it is more open.

r

"Lieber durch Leiden" ['libɐ dʊɐç 'laɪdən]
"Rastlose Liebe"

Note: Avoid the American *burred r* [ɹ] at all times when singing German!

Read aloud.

Räder	['rɛː dər]	Rhein	[raɪn]
Tür	[tyr]	Garten	['gar tən]
irrt	[ɪrt]	Werke	['vɛr kə]
erreichen	[ɛrːˈraɪ çən]		

Practice speaking text with the sound of *r*.

Schwer heran braust Sturmeswetter,
[ʃver hɛˈran braʊst ˈʃtʊrməsˌvɛtːər]

Dräuend rasselt Donners Grollen!..
[ˈdrɔʏənt ˈrasːəlt ˈdɔnːnərsˈgrɔlːən]

Rings umher durch scharf Gerölle
[rɪŋs | ʊmˈher dʊrç ʃarf gəˈrœlːə]

Rinnen klare Wasser nieder -
[ˈrɪnːnən klɑrə ˈvasːər ˈnidər]

S

Pronounce *s*, *ss*, or *ß* as the unvoiced sibilant [s] when final in a word or syllable.

Read aloud.

Haus	[haʊs]	Fluß	[flʊs]
meistens	[ˈmaɪs təns]	deshalb	[ˈdɛs halp]
wissen	[ˈvɪ sən]	Knospe	[ˈknɔs pə]

When a single *s* stands between two vowels or is initial in a word or syllable, pronounce [z], like the voiced *s* in *rose*.

Read aloud.

Rose	[ˈro zə]	Silber	[ˈzɪl bər]
lesen	[ˈle zən]	Musik	[mu ˈzik]
sorgsam	[ˈzɔrk zam]	Sehnsucht	[ˈzen zʊxt]

Practice speaking text with the sounds of *s*.

Es senkt sich sacht die Sonne,
[ɛs zɛŋkt zɪç zɑxt di ˈzɔnə]

Sanft säuselt's längs dem Flusse.
[zanft ˈzɔʏzəlts lɛŋs dem ˈflʊsə]

sch

S

Pronounce the combination *sch* as [ʃ]. In the initial position followed by a vowel, it is pronounced sharply and with more energy than its English equivalent. For exercises using the sound of *sch*, see *sp* and *st* at the bottom of this page.

Read aloud.

Schall	[ʃal]	Schauer	['ʃɑʊ ər]
Schande	['ʃan də]	schnell	[ʃnɛl]
Asche	['a ʃə]	Mensch	[mɛnʃ]
erlauscht	[ɛr 'lɑʊʃt]	Abschluß	['ap ʃlʊs]
Bursch	[bʊrʃ]		

sp & st

When the combinations *sp* and *st* are initial in a word or word element, pronounce the *s* [ʃ], as in sheep.

spielen	['ʃpi lən]	spät	[ʃpeːt]
Aussprache	['ɑʊs ʃprɑ xə]	Stunde	['ʃtʊn də]
still	[ʃtɪl]	frühstück	['fry ʃtʏk]

In all other positions, pronounce *sp* and *st* as [sp] and [st].

Wespe	['vɛs pə]	lispeln	['lɪs pəln]
Liebespaar	['li bəs ˌpɑr]	finster	['fɪn stər]
rastlos	['rast los]	zuerst	[tsu ǀ 'erst]

Practice speaking text with the sounds of *sp*, *st*, and *sch*.

Feststämmig stolz strebt sein Geäst
['fɛstʃtɛmɪç ʃtɔlts ʃtrept zaɪn gəǀɛst]

Stromwärts, und weist nach Ost und West.
['ʃtromvɛrts ǀ ʊnt vaɪst nax ǀ ɔst ǀ ʊnt vɛst]

Spät aus spitz'gen Speichers Spalte
[ʃpeːt ǀ ɑʊs 'ʃpɪtsgən 'ʃpaɪçərs 'ʃpaltə]

Schrillen Schreis den Schloßschenk schreckend!
['ʃrɪlːən ʃraɪs den 'ʃlɔsʃɛŋk 'ʃrɛkənt]

t

Pronounce single or double *t* as well as the combination *th* in a single word element as [t], more dental and plosive than the English *t*.

Note: The archaic spelling of *th* for *t* is found in some song texts and a few words in modern German.
Example: Muth = Mut, Theil = Teil

Read aloud.

Tod	[tot]	Mut	[mut]
Gott	[gɔt]	Thron	[tron]
Theater	[te 'ɑ tər]	Rath	[rɑt]
Theil	[taɪl]		

However in two elements, each letter is sounded.
Example: Rat I haus [rɑt haʊs]

Practice speaking text with the sound of *t*.

Nicht enttauscht, verderbt durch Welttand,
[nɪçt | entː'tɔyʃt fɛr'dɛrpt dʊrç 'vɛltːtant]

Trifft dir Tod, der Trennungs traur'ge Trübsal.
[trɪft dir tot der 'trɛnʊŋs 'traʊrgə 'trypzɑl]

In borrowed words ending in the suffixes *-tion* and *-tient*, pronounce the combination of *ti* as [tsj].

Read aloud.

Nation	[na 'tsjon]	Aktion	[ak 'tsjon]
Funktion	[fʊŋk 'tsjon]	Patient	[pa 'tsjɛnt]

V

Pronounce *v* as [f] in all words of German origin and in the final position of any word.

Read aloud.

Vater	['fɑ tər]	vergessen	[fɛr 'gɛ sən]
davon	[da 'fɔn]	Volkslied	['fɔlks lit]
Archiv	[ar 'kif]	bravster	['brɑf stər]

In words of foreign origin, voice *v* as in the English word *vine*.

Read aloud.

Vase	['vɑ zə]	Vokal	[vo 'kɑl]
November	[no 'vɛm bər]	Universität	[u ni vɛr si 'tɛːt]
nervös	[nɛr 'vøs]		

Practice speaking the sounds of *f*, *pf*, and *v*.

Vielfach verfolgt von pfiffigen Pfaffen
['filfaç fɛr'fɔlkt fɔn 'pfɪfɪgən 'pfafən]

Verpflegt vom Freund - ein Pfui! vom Feind...
[fɛr'pflekt fɔm frɔʏnt aɪn pfʊɪ fɔm faɪnt]

Pronounce the letter *w* as a clearly voiced *v*. The movement from unvoiced [f] to voiced [v] needs special practice.

W

Compare and contrast.

auffinden ['aʊfːfɪn dən]	aufwinden ['aʊf vɪn dən]
auffallen ['aʊfːfa lən]	aufwallen ['aʊf va lən]

Read aloud.

Wasser	['va sər]	Winter	['vɪn tər]
warum	[va 'rʊm]	Schwalbe	['ʃval bə]
Urwelt	['ur vɛlt]	Schafwolle	['ʃaf vɔ lə]
Volkswagen	['fɔlks va gən]	verwöhnen	[fɛr vø nən]

Practice speaking the following text with the sound of *w*.

Wie wär's wohl, wenn wir weilten
[vi vɛːrs vol vɛn vir 'vaɪltən]

Wo wogende Wellen weich winken?
[vo 'vogəndə 'vɛlːən vaɪç 'vɪŋkən]

Pronounce *x* as the combination [ks].

X

Note: The letter x acts as a double consonant and will cause the preceding vowel to be open in color.

Read aloud.

Hexe	['hɛ ksə]	Nixen	['nɪ ksən]
exakt	[ɛ 'ksakt]	existieren	[ɛ ksɪs 'ti rən]
Expreß	[ɛks 'prɛs]		

Pronounce *z*, *zz*, and the combination *tz* as a crisp [ts], clearly differentiated from the more gentle [s].

Z

Read aloud.

zart	[tsart]	Schmerzen	['ʃmɛr tsən]
Schatz	[ʃats]	zwei	[tsvaɪ]
zwischen	['tsvɪ ʃən]	intermezzo	[ɪn tər 'mɛ tso]

Z

When *t* ends one word element and *z* begins the next, prolong the sound of the *t*.

entzwei [ɛntː 'tsvaɪ]   entzücken [ɛntː 'tsʏ kən]

Practice speaking the following text with the sounds of *z* and *voiced s*.

Es zogen zwei Sänger zum säuselnden See,
[ɛs 'tsogən tsvaɪ 'zɛŋər tsʊm 'zɔʏzəlndən ze]

Zart sangen zur Zither sie Tänze;
[tsart 'zaŋən tsur 'tsɪtər zi 'tɛntsə]

Practice speaking the consonant cluster *tzt*.

Jetzt wetzt der Letzt', von Schmerz zersetzt -
[jɛtst vɛtst der lɛtst fɔn ʃmɛrts tsɛr'zɛtst]

French Diction

In all languages, there is an academic approach to presenting the content of the language — syllabification, stressing, etc —which is useful for organizing the information and returning to it later. This academic approach offers a whole picture, like a jigsaw puzzle, of how the language is put together. Yet, in French, perhaps a more useful way to begin is to pull out a few unusual pieces of the material and become familiar with their distinctiveness before placing them into the whole picture.

One unusual piece of French diction is that several letters are often pronounced as a single sound, as in the word *beaux* [bo], where the five letters *eaux* are pronounced simply as [o], or in the word *travaille* [tra 'vaj] where the four letters *ille* are pronounced as the single sound [j].

Also, many letters in French words are silent, particularly final consonants, final *mute e, h,* and the *m* and *n* that follow nasal vowels. There are sounds in French that do not exist in English. These include mixed vowels, nasal vowels, the enya [ɲ] and the glide [ɥ]. And there is a pattern of stressing in French that differs from other languages. You will find all of these usual "pieces" of French diction discussed in the" Special Features" section.

Your first challenge will be to learn how to group letters together. You will find the chart at the beginning of this chapter helpful because it displays the most common letter groupings. As you read through the text you will find exercises and word lists that will repetitively illustrate those same letter combinations. Finally, under the headings "French Vowels" and "French Consonants", you will find each spelling described in detail. By getting a handle on the letter groups, you will quickly become facile with French spelling and pronunciation.

176

Chart of French Sounds

The following chart lists the sounds of the French language in alphabetic order. Refer to this chart to quickly check the sound of a spelling. There are some special circumstances and exceptions to the sounds which cannot be presented easily in a simple chart. Detail is included in the discussion of the individual sounds.

French Letter & Position in Word			IPA	Example &	IPA	Page
a	a, à	usually	[a]	Paris, là	[pa 'ri], [la]	198
	a before *s* and *z*		[ɑ]	extase	[ɛk 'stɑ zə]	199
	a before final silent *s*		[ɑ]	bas	[bɑ]	199
	ai	usually	[ɛ]	mais	[mɛ]	199
	ai final		[e]	gai	[ge]	200
	aim & ain*		[ɛ̃]	faim, ainsi	[fɛ̃] [ɛ̃ 'si]	188, 200
	am & an*		[ɑ̃]	champ	[ʃɑ̃]	188, 201
				fumant	[fy 'mɑ̃]	
	au		[o]	chevaux	[ʃə 'vo]	201
	au before *r*		[ɔ]	Fauré	[fɔ 're]	201
	ay		[ɛj]	payer	[pɛ 'je]	201, 218
b	b		[b]	bois	['bwa]	219
	bb		[b]	abbesse	[a 'bɛ sə]	219
	b before *s* or *t*		[p]	absent	[ap 'sɑ̃]	219
c	c before *a, o, u* or a *consonant*		[k]	encore	[ɑ̃ 'kɔ rə]	219
	cc before *a, o, u* or a *consonant*		[k]	succulent	[sy ky 'lɑ̃]	220
	c before *e, i,* or *y*		[s]	cède	['sɛ də]	220
	cc before *e, i* or *y*		[ks]	accent	[ak 'sɑ̃]	220
	ç		[s]	garçon	[gar 'sõ]	220
	c final	usually	[k]	avec	[a 'vɛk]	220
	c final after *n*	usually	silent	blanc	[blɑ̃]	220
	ch	usually	[ʃ]	chemin	[ʃə 'mɛ̃]	221
	ct		silent	respect	[rɛs 'pɛ]	221
		or	[kt]	direct	[di 'rɛkt]	
d	d		[d]	diable	['dja blə]	221
	dd		[d]	addition	[a di 'sjõ]	221
	d final		silent	grand	[grɑ̃]	221
	d in liaison		[t]	quand‿un	[kɑ̃ tœ̃]	221
e	é		[e]	été	[e 'te]	202
	è, ê, & ë		[ɛ]	père	['pɛ rə]	202
				forêts	[fɔ 'rɛ]	
				Noël	[nɔ 'ɛl]	
	e before a *consonant* & a *vowel*		[ə]	cheval	[ʃə 'val]	202
	e before two *consonants*		[ɛ]	elle	['ɛ lə]	203

This letter combination can be nasal or non-nasal. See page 183 for full explanation.

French Letter & Position in Word			IPA	Example & IPA		Page
e *cont.*	e	before final pronounced *cons.*	[ɛ]	fer	[fɛr]	203
	e	before final silent *consonant* (except *s* or *t*, see below)	[e]	pied	[pje]	204
	er final	sometimes	[ɛr]	hiver	[i 'vɛr]	204
	er final in verb endings and	[e]		parler	[par 'le]	204
	some nouns and adjectives			boulanger	[bu lɑ̃ 'ze]	204
	es final		[ə]	parles	['par lə]	204
	es final in monosyllables		[e]	des	[de]	205
	et final		[ɛ]	filet	[fi 'lɛ]	205
	et (meaning *and*)		[e]	et	[e]	205
	e	final	*silent*	parle	[parl]	205
		or	[ə]	parle	['par lə]	
				je	[ʒə]	
	eau		[o]	beau	[bo]	205
	ei		[ɛ]	seize	['sɛ zə]	206
	eim & ein*		[ɛ̃]	plein	[plɛ̃]	188, 206
	em & en*		[ɑ̃]	ensemble	[ɑ̃ 'sɑ̃ blə]	188, 207
	en after *i*		[ɛ̃]	combien	[kɔ̃ 'bjɛ̃]	188, 207
	ent final in verb endings		[ə]	parlent	['par lə]	207
	ent final otherwise		[ɑ̃]	firmament	[fir ma 'mɑ̃]	207
	eu in the interior of a word		[œ]	heure	['œ rə]	185, 208
	eu before [z]		[ø]	creuse	['krø zə]	185, 208
	eu as final *sound*		[ø]	peu	[pø]	185, 208
f	f		[f]	foyer	[fwa 'je]	222
	ff		[f]	effort	[e 'fɔr]	222
	f	final usually	[f]	soif	[swaf]	222
	f	in liaison	[v]	neuf‿heures	[nœ vœ rə]	222
g	g	before *a, o, u* or a *consonant*	[g]	gant	[gɑ̃]	222
	gg	before *a, o, u* or a *consonant*	[g]	aggraver	[a gra 've]	223
	g	before *e, i* or *y*	[ʒ]	genou	[ʒə 'nu]	222
	gg	before *e, i* or *y*	[gʒ]	suggérer	[syg ʒe 're]	223
	g	final	*silent*	poing	[pwɛ̃]	223
	g	in liaison	[k]	sang‿impur	[sɑ̃ kɛ̃ pyr]	223
	ge	before *a* or *o*	[ʒ]	bourgeois	[bur 'ʒwa]	223
	gn	usually	[ɲ]	compagnon	[kɔ̃ pa 'ɲɔ̃]	223
	gu	before a *vowel*	[g]	fatiguer	[fa ti 'ge]	223
h	h		*silent*	heure	['œ rə]	192, 224
i	î, i final or before a *consonant*		[i]	île, finir	['i lə] [fi 'nir]	209
	i	before a stressed *vowel* usually	[j]	hier	[jɛr]	209
	i	before a *mute e*	[i]	partie	[par 'ti ə]	210

* This letter combination can be nasal or non-nasal. See page 183 for full explanation.

French Letter & Position in Word		IPA	Example	& IPA	Page
i ien*		[jɛ̃]	bien	[bjɛ̃]	188, 209
ient final, verb ending		[i] or [iə]	rient	[ri] or [ri ə]	210
il, ill, ille		[j]	soleil	[sɔ 'lɛj]	186, 210
		[j]	détaillant	[de ta 'jɑ̃]	
		[ij]	brille	['bri jə]	
im & in*		[ɛ̃]	timbre	['tɛ̃ brə]	211
j j		[ʒ]	Jean	[ʒɑ̃]	224
k k		[k]	kilo	[ki 'lo]	224
l l		[l]	larme	['lar mə]	225
l final		[l]	appel	[a 'pɛl]	225
ll		[l]	belle	['bɛ lə]	225
ll after *i* (see *ill* above)					
m m		[m]	marche	['mar ʃə]	225
m final		*silent*	parfum	[par 'fœ̃]	226
mm		[m]	comme	['kɔ mə]	225
n n		[n]	nous	[nu]	226
n final		*silent*	non	[nõ]	226
ng final		*silent*	poing	[pwɛ̃]	227
nn		[n]	donne	['dɔ nə]	226
o o	usually	[ɔ]	fort	[fɔr]	212
o before [z]		[o]	chose	['ʃo zə]	212
o as final *sound*		[o]	galop	[ga 'lo]	212
ô		[o]	vôtre	['vo trə]	213
oeu		[œ]	coeur	[kœr]	185, 213
oi		[wa]	vois	[vwa]	186, 213
oin*		[wɛ̃]	loin	[lwɛ̃]	186, 213
om & on*		[õ]	rond	[rõ]	188, 214
ou, où & oû		[u]	fou	[fu]	214
ou before a stressed *vowel*		[w]	oui	[wi]	186, 214
ou before *mute e*		[u]	dénouement	[de nuə 'mɑ̃]	186, 214
oy		[wa]	royal	[rwa 'jal]	186, 215
p p		[p]	pas	[pɑ]	227
pp		[p]	application	[ap li ka 'sjõ]	227
p final		*silent*	corp	[kɔr]	227
ph		[f]	morphine	[mɔr 'fi nə]	227
q q final		[k]	coq	[kɔk]	228
qu		[k]	quand	[kɑ̃]	227

* This letter combination can be nasal or non-nasal. See page 183 for full explanation.

French Letter & Position in Word			IPA	Example & IPA		Page
r	r		flipped [r]	ronde	['rɔ̃ də]	228
	rr		flipped [r]	terre	['tɛ rə]	228
	r	final	[r]	amour, professeur	[a 'mur], [prɔ fɛ 'sœr]	228
	r	as final -er in verb endings	silent	parler	[par 'le]	228
	r	as final -er, -ier & -yer in some nouns and adjectives	silent	boulanger	[bu lɑ̃ 'ʒe]	228
s	s	usually	[s]	sport	[spɔr]	228
	ss		[s]	tasse	['ta sə]	229
	s	between *vowels*	[z]	maison	[mɛ 'zɔ̃]	229
	s	final	silent	repos	[rə 'po]	229
	s	in liaison	[z]	puis‿il	[pɥi zil]	229
	sc	before *a, o, u*	[sk]	scandale	[skɑ̃ 'da lə]	229
	sc	before *e* or *i*	[s]	sceptre	['sɛp trə]	229
	sch	usually	[ʃ]	schema	['ʃe ma]	230
t	t		[t]	total	[tɔ 'tal]	230
	tt		[t]	quitter	[ki 'te]	230
	t	final	silent	saint	[sɛ̃]	230
	th		[t]	théâtre	[te 'ɑ trə]	230
	ti	in suffixes -tion, -tience	[sj]	élection	[e lɛk 'sjɔ̃]	230
	tie	final	[ti]	sortie	[sɔr 'ti ə]	230
u	u		[y]	une	['y nə]	184, 215
	u	final or before a *consonant*	[y]	subito	[sy bi 'to]	184, 216
	u	before a stressed *vowel*	[ɥ]	nuit	[nɥit]	187, 216
	u	before final *mute e*	[y]	revue	[rə 'vy ə]	184, 216
	u	after *g* and before a *vowel*	silent	guitare	[gi 'ta rə]	184, 223
	ue	before *il, ille*	[œ]	cercueil	[sɛr 'kœj]	185, 216
	um & un*		[œ̃]	parfum, chacun	[par 'fœ̃] [ʃa 'kœ̃]	188, 217
v	v		[v]	violon	[vjɔ 'lɔ̃]	231
w	w		[v]	wagon	[va 'gɔ̃]	231
x	x	before a *consonant*	[ks]	texte	['tɛk stə]	231
	x	before a *vowel* or *h* usually	[gz]	exile	[ɛg 'zi lə]	231
	x	final	silent	doux	[du]	231
	x	in liaison	[z]	deux‿ami	[dø za 'mi]	231
y	y	initial	[j]	yeux	[jø]	217
	y	before or after a *consonant*	[i]	lyre	['li rə]	218
	y	between two *vowels* = *ii*	[ij]	rayon	[rɛ 'jɔ̃]	218
	ym & yn*		[ɛ̃]	thym	[tɛ̃]	188, 218
z	z		[z]	Ézéchiel	[e ze 'kjɛl]	231
	z	final	silent	allez	[a 'le]	231

* This letter combination can be nasal or non-nasal. See page 183 for full explanation.

Syllabification

French is a language of long vowels! That is, when you are pronouncing correctly, you will elongate the French vowel to the greatest extent and then articulate the following consonant only at the beginning of the next note or the release of the note. Neither emphasize nor elongate a consonant in French, even when there is an orthographic doubling of the consonant. This differs from English, Italian and German where you would give considerable emphasis and prolongation to consonants.

The way a printed French word looks may not match the way it is pronounced. For example, in the text of a song, the word *connais* may be printed as *con-nais*; the first syllable is shown ending with *n*, ostensibly making it a closed syllable. The closed syllable implies that the first vowel has a short duration followed by a prolonged [n] in the same syllable. When singing, however, you will pronounce the word as *co-nnais* [kɔ 'nɛ], giving the first vowel long duration and putting the consonant [n] on the beginning of the second syllable.

In this text, we've divided syllables as they are printed in songs to keep the visual representation of words consistent with what you normally see. The IPA transcriptions will also follow that same syllable division to avoid confusion. You must remember, therefore, that *regardless of the printed syllabification, you must pronounce the vowels long and the consonants short.* The rhythm and flow of the French language is dependent upon keeping French a language of long vowels!

Many French words end with the letter *e*, which is silent in speech, and is referred to as the *mute e* . Composers will often give a note to a *mute e*, which will then be sung as schwa [ə]. The final *mute e* is so frequently sung in French songs that in this text we will treat it as a separate final syllable. For example, in this line it appears in all but one word.

> Toute fleurie semble ma destinée
> ['tutə flœ'riə 'sɑ̃blə ma dɛstin'eə]
> > from *Depuis le jour,* <u>Louise</u>, Charpentier

The rules on the following pages govern the division of French words into syllables.

Single Consonant

When a single consonant is between two vowel sounds, put the consonant with the second vowel sound.

re-ve-ler	[rə və 'le]	pi-co-ter	[pi kɔ 'te]
plai-sir	[plɛ 'zir]	na-tal	[na 'tal]
je-ter	[ʒə 'te]	fau-ves	['fo və]

Exception: When an *x* is between two vowels, put it with the first vowel sound.

ex-a-gé-rer [ɛg za ʒe 're]

Two Consonants

Divide double consonants.

con-nais	[kɔ 'nɛ]	glis-sant	[gli 'sɑ̃]
ver-meil-les	[vɛr 'mɛ jə]	ap-pel-lent	[a 'pɛ lə]
hom-mes	['ɔ mə]	sug-gé-rer	[syg ʒe 're]
ac-ci-dent	[ak si 'dɑ̃]	im-men-se	[i 'mɑ̃ sə]

Usually divide two different consonants.

par-ler	[par 'le]	en-fant	[ɑ̃ 'fɑ̃]
tan-te	['tɑ̃ tə]	im-por-te	[ɛ̃ 'pɔr tə]
ver-se	['vɛr sə]	lam-bris	[lɑ̃ 'bri]
an-ge	['ɑ̃ ʒə]	sem -ble	['sɑ̃ blə]

When a consonant is followed by *l* or *r*, put both consonants with the second syllable.

in-tri-gue	[ɛ̃ 'tri gə]	in-té-grant	[ɛ̃ te 'grɑ̃]
é-tran-gler	[e trɑ̃ 'gle]	ta-bleau	[ta 'blo]
rou-vrent	['ru vrə]	nu-clé-on	[ny kle 'õ]
dé-bris	[de 'bri]	dé-clas-ser	[de kla 'se]

When two consonants are digraphs, put them with the second syllable.

Note: Two consonants with a *single phonetic sound* such as *ch*, *th*, *ph*, and *gn* are called digraphs. They are treated as single consonants and join the second syllable.

ch: cher-cher	[ʃɛr 'ʃe]	*ph*: sy-phi-lis	[si fi 'lis]
th: mé-tho-de	[me 'tɔ də]	*gn*: mi-gnon	[mi 'ɲõ]

Three Consonants

Usually divide three consonants between the first and second letters.

souf-fler	[su 'fle]	sem-blaient	[sã 'blɛ ə]
en-clave	[ã 'kla və]	con-sti-tu-tion	[kõ sti ty 'sjõ]

Consecutive Vowels

Each syllable in French contains one, and only one, vowel sound. However, a single vowel sound may be indicated by multiple orthographic letters. In the word beauté [bo 'te], *for example, the three letters* eau *stand for the single vowel sound* [o].

Put consecutive vowels, which are pronounced as a *single vowel sound*, into a single syllable.

beau-coup	[bo 'ku]	vais-seaux	[vɛ 'so]
de-main	[də 'mɛ̃]	crain-dre	['krɛ̃ drə]
a-mour	[a 'mur]	cou-leur	[ku 'lœr]
tau-reau	[to 'ro]	re-viens	[rə 'vjɛ̃]

A syllable may contain a glide and a vowel, as in bien [bjɛ̃]. *A glide alone, however, cannot constitute a syllable. There are three glides in French,* [j], [w], *and* [ɥ].

Divide two consecutive vowels, with two dots over one of the vowels (called dieresis [daɪ 'ɛ rə sɪs]), into two syllables.

Noël	(No-el)	[nɔ 'ɛl]
haïr	(ha-ir)	[a 'ir]
Thaïs	(Tha-is)	[ta 'is]
Exception:	Saint-Saëns	[sɛ̃ 'sãs]

Occasionally divide two consecutive vowels into two syllables. Check a dictionary.

Two syllables:

cruel (cru-el)	[kry 'ɛl]
travailler (tra-va-iller)	[tra va 'je]
saillir (sa-illir)	[sa 'jir]
théâtre (thé-â-tre)	[te 'a trə]

Stress

In English, Italian, and German, you create strong and weak stress patterns in words by prominent changes in loudness and pitch on different syllables. Do not carry this practice into French, however; pronounce all syllables with almost equal emphasis. To pronounce a tonic syllable in French, say it with a *longer duration* than the other syllables.

The syllable which has the primary stress in a word is called the tonic *syllable.*

Final e is usually silent in French and is called mute e.

In French, the last syllable of a word is usually the tonic syllable. The only exception occurs in words ending with a *mute e*, when the second to last syllable is the tonic syllable. This pattern is so regular, that some texts do not even indicate the tonic syllable in IPA transcriptions.

To become more accustomed to this unfamiliar pattern of stress, listen to recordings of outstanding singers and speakers. Before you begin to sing a song, read aloud the lyrics to establish the pattern of stress.

The special rhythm of the French language is achieved by the prolonged duration of tonic syllables. This feature has considerable impact upon the melodic line of songs.

> Exercise: In the following list of words, the final syllable is the tonic syllable. Read aloud these words giving prolonged duration to the final syllable.

perdu	[pɛr 'dy]
liberté	[li bɛr 'te]
pensif	[pã 'sif]
occasion	[ɔ ka 'zjõ]
toujours	[tu 'ʒur]
wagon	[va 'gõ]
parler	[par 'le]

> In the two columns below, all of the words end with *mute e*, so the tonic syllable is the next to last syllable (the penultimate syllable). Pronounce the words in the first column of IPA transcriptions, omitting the final *mute e* as in spoken French. Then, pronounce the words in the second column, voicing the *mute e* as you would in singing. In both columns, as you pronounce the words, give prolonged duration to the penultimate syllable.

carte	[kart]	['kar tə]
charme	[ʃarm]	['ʃar mə]
quatre	[katr]	['ka trə]
école	[e 'kɔl]	[e 'kɔ lə]
flèche	[flɛʃ]	['flɛ ʃə]
écoute	[e 'kut]	[e 'ku tə]
théâtre	[te 'atr]	[te 'a trə]
impossible	[ɛ̃ pɔ 'sibl]	[ɛ̃ pɔ 'si blə]

> In short phrases, the primary stress, or longer duration, is reserved for the last syllable of the *phrase*. This gives French a very smooth rhythm. Read aloud the following short phrases and give the prolonged duration to the last syllable of the *phrase*.

de ta pensée	[də ta pã 'se ə]
au cri doux	[o kri 'du]
la vie importune	[la vi ɛ̃ pɔr 'ty nə]

Special Features of French Diction

The Mixed Vowels

Mixed vowels are those that combine, or mix, the articulation shape of a forward vowel with the articulation shape of a back vowel. For example, put your tongue in the forward arched position for *ee* [i] as in *beet*, *then without moving the tongue*, round your lips to the position of *oo* [u] as in *boot*. Add voice and you will hear the close mixed vowel [y], a blending of the forward sound of [i] and the back sound of [u].

Mixed vowels are not found in English, but the sound of reversed epsilon [ɜ] as in the word bird *when spoken with a dropped* r *as in a British accent,* [bɜd], *is very similar to open* [œ]. *The lips will be more rounded and the jaw dropped more for* [œ].

Of the four mixed vowels, only three are found in French. (All four are found in German).

The tongue and lip position for the three French mixed vowels are indicated on the following chart. For each mixed vowel, start with the high, forward tongue position suggested [i], [e], or [ɛ]. Then, *without moving the tongue*, round your lips for the back vowels [u], [o] or [ɔ]. Note that to produce the mixed vowel you do not glide from the forward vowel to the back vowel. Instead, you produce both vowels *simultaneously*. By combining the two sounds into a unified single vowel sound, you produce the mixed vowel.

Those people who know German often choose to refer to the mixed vowels as closed *umlauted* ü [y], *closed umlauted* ö [ø], *and* open *umlauted* ö [œ].

Chart of Tongue and Lip Positions for the Mixed Vowels

Tongue position		Lip position		Resulting mixed vowel
[i]	+	[u]	=	[y]
[e]	+	[o]	=	[ø]
[ɛ]	+	[ɔ]	=	[œ]

When reading IPA transcriptions aloud, refer to the mixed vowels by their sounds, or call them *closed* [y], *closed* [ø] and *open* [œ] to identify their method of production (from the most closed to most open).

In certain tenses of the verb avoir, eu *and* eû *are irregularly pronounced as* [y]. *(eu, eus, eûmes, eûtes, eurent, eusse, eusses, eût, eussions, eussiez, eussent)*

These are the usual spellings for [y]:

û and u when final, or before a consonant or a *mute e*

revue	[rə 'vy ə]	salut	[sa ly]
une	['y nə]	studio	[sty 'djɔ]
dû	[dy]	purée	[py 're ə]

These are the usual spellings for [ø]:

-eu or -oeu as final sound of a word (not necessarily the final
    letters of the word)

peu	[pø]	veut	[vø]
dieu	[djø]	peut	[pø]

-eu before [z]

creuse	['krø zə]	chanteuse	[ʃɑ̃ 'tø zə]

-eû

jeûne	['ʒø nə]

These are the usual spellings for [œ]:

-eu or -oeu when in the interior of a word

heure	['œ rə]	malheur	[ma 'lœr]
peuple	['pœ plə]	coeur	[kœr]

-ue when followed by -il or -ill

orgueil	[ɔr 'gœj]	écueil	[e 'kœj]

To familiarize yourself with the various spellings of [ø] and [œ],
    read the following lists of words. Recall the rule which
    governs the pronunciation of the underlined vowels.

Closed [ø]	Open [œ]
bleu	seul
harmonieux	heure
jeûne	jeunesse
mysterieux	demeure
cieux	fleurs
mieux	pleurent
malheureuse	malheureuse
amoureuse	boeuf

To familiarize yourself with the spellings of the mixed vowel [y],
    read through the following list, which includes words
    pronounced with the mixed vowel [y]. Recall the rule which
    governs the pronunciation of u as [y].

une	fumée
revue	lune
tu	perdu
importune	plus
ramures	pure
sur	vue
connu	salut

Glides

A glide is a speech sound characterized by a movement of the articulators from one position to another. Glides are classified as consonants, not vowels, because they do not form the core of a syllable. The glides in French, [j], [w], and [ɥ], are described below.

The glide [j], called *jot* [jɔt], is the sound of *y* in the English word *you* [ju].

> Pronounce the [j] sound by moving the blade of the tongue to a high, arched position, close to the hard palate, similar to the vowel [i], then quickly shifting to the vowel which follows.

The usual spellings that are pronounced as [j] are:

> *i* before a stressed vowel is [j]:
>
> | | | | |
> |---|---|---|---|
> | dieu | [djø] | nation | [nɑ 'sjõ] |
> | bien | [bjɛ̃] | premier | [prə 'mje] |
>
> *il, ill,* and *ille* are pronounced as [j] (See page 210):
>
> | | | | |
> |---|---|---|---|
> | soleil | [sɔ 'lɛj] | famille | [fa 'mi jə] |
>
> *y* is pronounced as [j] (see pages 217-218):
>
> | | | | |
> |---|---|---|---|
> | yeux | [jø] | payer | [pɛ 'je] |
> | rayon | [rɛ 'jõ] | ayant | [ɛ 'jɑ̃] |

The glide [w] is the sound of *w* in the English word *wear*.

> Pronounce the [w] sound by rounding your lips and raising the back of your tongue as if saying the vowel [u]. Then quickly shift to the vowel which follows.

The usual spellings which are pronounced as [w] are:

> *oi* is [wa]
>
> | | | |
> |---|---|---|
> | moi [mwa] | voix [vwa] | |
>
> *oin* is [wɛ̃]
>
> | | | |
> |---|---|---|
> | loin [lwɛ̃] | poindre ['pwɛ̃ drə] | |
>
> *oy* is [waj] (See page 215)
>
> | | |
> |---|---|
> | royal [rwa 'jal] | soyeux [swa 'jø] |
>
> *ou* is [w] when before a stressed vowel (a vowel other than a *mute e.*)
>
> | | |
> |---|---|
> | oui [wi] | ouest [wɛst] |

Note: In singing, if two notes are provided for a one syllable word like *jouer*, the *ou* will become [uw]: [ʒu-'we].

The glide [ɥ] has no equivalent sound in English. It is the gliding articulation of the mixed vowel [y]. The symbol [ɥ] is called by its sound.

Exercise: Discover the sound of the glide [ɥ] by first sustaining the mixed vowel [y]. Then speak the word *puis* [pɥi], shortening the duration of the first vowel until it becomes the glide [ɥ], a sound that is not sustained but rather moves quickly from one position to another.

The usual spelling of [ɥ] is *u* when before any vowel except [ə]:

lui	[lɥi]	nuage	['nɥa ʒə]
suis	[sɥi]	depuis	[də 'pɥi]
pluie	['plɥi ə]	suave	['sɥa və]

To familiarize yourself with the spellings of the glide [ɥ], read through this list. Recall the rule which governs the pronunciation of the underlined vowel.

nuit	luisant
bruit	luette
cuivre	enfuir
conduit	suivi
fruits	bruissant

[ɥ] must not sound like [w]. Your tongue should be more forward and your lips more tensely rounded for [ɥ].

When u is before a mute e, it is pronounced [y]. (See pages 184-85.)

In IPA transcriptions, the diacritical mark [~], called a tilde, indicates that the vowel is nasalized.

The four nasal vowels are listed in this order [ɛ̃], [ɑ̃], [õ], [œ̃] to indicate how the lips gradually increase their rounding and the jaw drops. This promotes more careful identification of the sounds.

Nasal Vowels

The following chart describes the four nasal vowels of French.

The Four French Nasal Vowels

The nasal vowel [ɛ̃] is nasalized *eh* as in *bet* [ɛ].
The nasal vowel [ɑ̃] is nasalized *ah* as in *father* [ɑ].
The nasal vowel [õ] is nasalized *o* as in *pole* [o].
The nasal vowel [œ̃] is nasalized *oeu* as in *coeur* [œ].

Produce the nasal vowels by slightly lowering your soft palate and permitting air to enter your nose. You must watch that the nasal vowels do not become so nasal as to be sharply twangy in quality. Listen to French singers and you will hear how beautifully these vowel sounds can be sung.

A vowel becomes nasalized in French under the following two conditions.

When a vowel precedes a final *m* or *n*, as in the word *son* [sõ], the letters *on* form a unit, which you pronounce as a single sound: the nasal vowel [õ]. Do not pronounce the *n;* it is silent.

When a vowel precedes an *m* or *n* that is followed by another consonant other than *m* or *n*, as in the word *songer* [sõ 'ʒe], the letters *on* form a unit, which you pronounce as [õ]. Do not pronounce the *n;* it is silent.

For clarification of the nasal sounds, you can refer to them as :

1st position   [ɛ̃]

2nd position   [ɑ̃]

3rd position   [õ]

4th position   [œ̃]

These are usual spellings of the nasal vowel [ɛ̃].

aim or *ain*

faim	[fɛ̃]	main	[mɛ̃]
sainte	['sɛ̃ tə]	daim	[dɛ̃]

eim or *ein*

Reims	[rɛ̃s]	teint	[tɛ̃]

im or *in*

simple	['sɛ̃ plə]	matin	[ma 'tɛ̃]

ym or *yn*

thym	[tɛ̃]	syndicat	[sɛ̃ di 'ka]

-ien

bien	[bjɛ̃]	reviens	[rə 'vjɛ̃]

These are usual spellings of the nasal vowel [ɑ̃].

am or *an*

champ	[ʃɑ̃]	dans	[dɑ̃]
grands	[grɑ̃]	devant	[də 'vɑ̃]

em or *en*

temps	[tɑ̃]	ensemble	[ɑ̃ 'sɑ̃ blə]
encor	[ɑ̃ 'kɔr]	prendre	['prɑ̃ drə]

Dictionaries often transcribe this nasal vowel as open [ɔ]. This sound is currently being identified in French speech as more closed [õ].

These are usual spellings of the nasal vowel [õ].

om and *on*

tombeau	[tõ 'bo]	son	[sõ]
ombre	['õ brə]	mon	[mõ]

These are usual spellings of the nasal vowel [œ̃].

um and *un*

parfum	[par 'fœ̃]	humble	['œ̃ blə]
un	[œ̃]	lundi	[lœ̃ 'di]

Do not nasalize a vowel followed by *m* or *n* under the following two conditions.

If a vowel precedes an *m* or *n* that is followed by another *m* or *n*, do not nasalize it.

comme	['kɔ mə]	donne	['dɔ nə]
tienne	['tjɛ nə]	connaître	[kɔ 'nɛ trə]
sonneé	[sɔ 'ne ə]	homme	['ɔ mə]

If a vowel precedes an *m or n* that is followed by a vowel, do not nasalize it.

émule	[e 'my lə]	timonier	[ti mɔ 'nje]
domaine	[dɔ 'mɛ nə]	image	[i 'ma ʒə]
sonore	[sɔ 'nɔ rə]	funeste	[fy 'nɛ stə]

In liaison, when you connect a final consonant to the initial vowel sound of the next word, you will pronounce the otherwise silent final *m* and *n*. The vowel retains its nasalization and you attach the final consonant to the initial vowel of the following word.

For a full discussion of liaison, see page 195.

en‿est fanée
[ãn‿ɛ fɑ 'ne ə]

qu'on‿aime
[kõn‿ɛ mə]

mon‿amour
[mõn‿a 'mur]

To familiarize yourself with the spellings of the nasal vowel [ɛ̃], read through this list. Recall the rule which governs the pronunciation of the underlined vowel.

soud<u>ain</u>	chem<u>in</u>
th<u>ym</u>	s<u>ein</u>
vi<u>en</u>dra	m<u>ain</u>
<u>in</u>visible	cr<u>ains</u>
chi<u>en</u>	pl<u>ein</u>
revi<u>en</u>s	v<u>ain</u>queur
v<u>in</u>gt	mat<u>in</u>
pr<u>in</u>temps	s<u>ain</u>te

To familiarize yourself with the various spellings of the nasal vowel [ɑ̃], read through this list. Recall the rules which govern the pronunciation of the underlined vowels.

qu<u>an</u>d	gr<u>an</u>d
fl<u>am</u>ber	élég<u>an</u>ce
h<u>an</u>che	bl<u>an</u>che
rep<u>an</u>d	r<u>en</u>ds
sil<u>en</u>ce	v<u>en</u>t
ch<u>am</u>ps	ch<u>am</u>ps
s<u>en</u>tier	naiss<u>an</u>t
couch<u>an</u>ts	t<u>em</u>ps
<u>em</u>brasse	dev<u>an</u>t
t<u>an</u>t	phal<u>an</u>ge
s<u>an</u>tal	charm<u>an</u>ts

To familiarize yourself with the various spellings of the nasal vowel [õ], read through this list. Recall the rules which govern the pronunciation of the underlined vowels.

r<u>on</u>	s<u>on</u>
m<u>on</u>	t<u>om</u>be
m<u>on</u>ter	<u>on</u>
prof<u>on</u>de	<u>om</u>bre
souff<u>on</u>	horiz<u>on</u>s
veni<u>on</u>s	m<u>on</u>ter
m<u>on</u>de	<u>om</u>brages
<u>om</u>breuse	

To familiarize yourself with the various spellings of the nasal vowel [œ̃], read through this list. Recall the rules which govern the pronunciation of the underlined vowels.

parf<u>um</u>s	<u>un</u>
h<u>um</u>ble	

Final *mute e*

The final *e*, called *mute e* in French words, is silent unless marked with an accent (é). Musical notation often requires the *mute e* to be sung in songs. When this occurs it is pronounced as *schwa* [ə].

The French *schwa* [ə] is a more forward and rounded sound than the *schwa* [ə] of English. It is more like the sound of the mixed vowel [ø] than that of the weakened, neutral vowel *uh* as in *about* [ə 'baʊt]. You must bring your lips forward into a more rounded position to achieve the French *schwa*.

French uses these accents:
    acute (é)
    grave (è)
    circumflex (ê)

Exercise: Read these words aloud to contrast the pronunciation final *mute e* and the accented *e*:

Final *mute e*		Final accented *é*	
marque	['mar kə]	marqué	[mar 'ke]
locale	[lɔ 'ka lə]	localité	[lɔ ka li 'te]
personne	[pɛr 'sɔ nə]	personalité	[pɛr sɔ na li 'te]

The Pure Vowels [e] and [o]

The vowels [e] and [o] are pure vowels in French, so you must never diphthongize them as in the English words *bait* [beɪt] and *boat* [boʊt]. Because American speakers consistently use the diphthongal forms of these vowels, you must be careful to identify and produce the pure vowel sounds that in English can only be found in a few unstressed syllables, as some people say [e] in *chaotic* [ke 'ɑ tɪk] and [o] in *obey* [o 'beɪ].

The French [e] is unlike English in a second way. The high point of the arch of the tongue of the French [e] is more forward and close to the alveolar ridge than in English. To American ears, the resulting [e] sounds almost like [i] as in *beet*.

The alveolar ridge, also called the teeth ridge, is the hard gum ridge behind the upper front teeth.

Read aloud these words using a pure [e].

fréter	[fre 'te]	fumer	[fy 'me]
détacher	[de ta 'ʃe]	manger	[mɑ̃ 'ʒe]
et	[e]	détirer	[de ti 're]

e before a final silent consonant is usually pronounced [e].

Read aloud these words using a pure [o].

faux	[fo]	baume	['bo mə]
chauffe	['ʃo fə]	repos	[rə 'po]
faute	['fo tə]	beau	[bo]

Mute and Aspirate *h*

The two kinds of *h* in French are mute and aspirate. Both are silent. The term aspirate indicates a special speech classification in French, it does not indicate that there is escaping air as you would generate with the *h* in English words <u>h</u>eat or <u>h</u>ome.

Liason is the linking of a normally silent final consonant to the initial vowel of the following word.

Elision is the omission of a sound, such as the dropping of the final mute e.

French pronunciation forbids the linking of words through liaison or elision with any word that begins with the initial *aspirate h*, while permitting the linking with a word with an inital *mute h* (see page 224), You should check the words in a dictionary to know whether a word begins with an aspirate or mute *h*. Often the dictionary will employ an asterick (*h) before the aspirate *h*.

Examples:

Mute h: Liaision and elision permitted.

heure	['œ rə]	quelle heure	[kɛl 'œrə]
herbe	['ɛr bə]	une herbe	[yn 'ɛr bə]

Aspirate h: Liaision and elision forbidden.

*haute	[ot]	voix/haute	[vwa ot]
*haine	[ɛ nə]	en/haine	[ɑ̃ ɛn]

The Enya

The sound of enya [ɲ] as in *bagne* is not found in English. It resembles the sound of [nj] in o<u>ni</u>on, but you form it with a single articulatory motion. The sound is much like the [n] except it is made with the blade of the tongue touching the boundary between the alveolar ridge and the hard palate instead of the tip of the tongue touching the alveolar ridge.

cognac	[kɔ 'ɲak]	poignet	[pwa 'ɲɛ]

Pronounced and Silent Consonants

Consonants in the interior of a word are usually pronounced.

ve-nais	[və 'nɛ]	e-xal-ter	[ɛg zal 'te]
jar-din	[zar 'dɛ̃]	ga-la	[ga 'la]

A medial consonant is one that is in the interior — the middle — of a word.

Note: Consonants before a final *mute e* are classified as medial in a word even when the *mute e* is silent and the consonant is the final sound.

po-se	['po zə]	or	[poz]
en-vo-les	[ɑ̃ 'vɔ lə]	or	[ɑ̃ 'vɔl]
le-vres	['lɛ vrə]	or	[lɛvr]
so-no-res	[sɔ 'nɔ rə]	or	[sɔ 'nɔr]
blan-che	['blɑ̃ ʃə]	or	[blɑ̃ʃ]

The final consonants *c, r, f, l,* and *q* are usually pronounced.

Final *c* is usually pronounced:

avec	[a 'vɛk]
lac	[lak]
parc	[park]

There is an old saying that the only final consonants which are pronounced in French are the ones in the word careful. *Final q is rarer.*

Final *r* is usually pronounced:

professeur	[prɔ fɛ 'sœr]	secteur	[sɛk 'tœr]
servir	[sɛr 'vir]	voir	[vwar]
soupir	[su 'pir]	tour	[tur]
hiver	[i 'vɛr]	car	[kar]

Note: Final *r* is sometimes silent: (See next paragraphs on Silent Consonants)

In spoken French, the uvula r [ʀ] *is commonly used in Paris and the Ile de France.. However, in singing, always use the tongue point r, either with a single flip — particularly between vowels — or two or three flaps.*

Final *f* is usually pronounced:

sauf	[sof]	vif	[vif]

Final *l* is usually pronounced:

idéal	[i de 'al]	racinal	[ra si 'nal]
vol	[vɔl]	bal	[bal]

Final *q* is pronounced:

coq	[kɔk]

For more information about final letters see The letter c, The letter r, The letter f, and The letter l, under French Consonants.

Otherwise, final consonants are usually silent.

Final *b* is silent:

plomb	[plõ]

Final *d* is silent:

regard	[rə 'gar]
pied	[pje]
pillard	[pi 'jar]

When r *precedes a final silent consonant, as the in the word* regard, *where the final* d *is silent, pronounce the* r. [rə 'gar]

Final *g* is silent:

sang	[sɑ̃]
poing	[pwɛ̃]

Final *m* is silent:

parfum	[par 'fœ̃]

Final *n* is silent:

chemin	[ʃə 'mɛ̃]
canon	[ka 'nõ]
refrain	[rə 'frɛ̃]

Final *p* is silent:

camp	[kɑ̃]
galop	[ga 'lo]

Final *r* is sometimes silent:
(See previous page under Final *r*).

Final *r* is silent in verb endings -*er* (first conjugation infinitives):

changer	[ʃɑ̃ 'ʒe]	chanter	[ʃɑ̃ 'te]
abuser	[a by 'ze]	regarder	[rə gar 'de]

Final *r* is usually silent in nouns and adjectives ending -*er*, -*ier*, and -*yer*:

boulanger	[bu lɑ̃ 'ʒe]	épicier	[e pi 'sje]
baiser (noun)	[bɛ 'ze]	danger	[dɑ̃ 'ʒe]
foyer	[fwa 'je]	premier	[prə 'mje]

There are a few common words in which the final s is pronounced: bis, hélas, Saint-Saëns and lis.

Final *s* is silent:

après	[a 'prɛ]	bas	[bɑ]
mais	[mɛ]	pas	[pɑ]

Note: The addition of a final *s* does not usually alter the pronunciation of the word. Treat the letter before the *s* as a final letter. The following examples show the identical pronunciations of the singular and plural forms of words.

baiser	[bɛ 'ze]	baisers	[bɛ 'ze]
noire	['nwa rə]	noires	['nwa rə]
branche	['brɑ̃ ʃə]	branches	['brɑ̃ ʃə]

Final *t* is silent:

bouquet	[bu 'kɛ]	tout	[tu]
secret	[sə 'krɛ]	port	[pɔr]

Final *t* frequently combines with other consonants:

Final *ct*: Sometimes both are silent, sometimes pronounced. Refer to a dictionary.

Silent:	aspect	[as 'pɛ]
Pronounced:	direct	[di 'rɛkt]

Final *st*: Sometimes both are silent, sometimes pronounced. Refer to a dictionary.

Silent:	est (*is*)	[ɛ]
Pronounced:	est (*east*)	[ɛst]

Final *gt*, *lt*, and *pt* are usually both silent:

doigt	[dwa]
prompt	[prõ]

Final *x* is silent:

> doux   [du]   prix   [pri]

Final *z* is silent:

> allez   [a 'le]   souffrez   [su 'fre]

Final silent consonants are often pronounced in liaison (see page 195):

pas	[pɑ]	=	pas a pas	[pɑ za pɑ]
est	[ɛ]	=	est un	[ɛ tœ̃]
faut	[fo]	=	faut il	[fo til]
suis	[sɥi]	=	suis heureuse	[sɥi zœ rø zə]
leurs	[lœr]	=	leurs ébats	[lœr ze ba]
sentais	[sɑ̃ 'tɛ]	=	sentais en	[sɑ̃ tɛ zɑ̃]

Liaison and Elision

French is a legato language. Its smooth flow results from the generous linking together of words.

The linking of most concern to you is that which is done through liaison and elision. The terms liaison and elision have been poorly defined in some diction texts, and are often mistakenly used interchangably. *Liaison* [li ɛ 'zɔ̃] is the pronunciation of a normally silent final consonant at the end of a word to link with the next word beginning with a vowel, a glide, or *mute h. Elision* is the omission of a sound, such as the dropping of the *mute e.*

Exercise: Read aloud these words, linking the normally silent consonant to the initial vowel of the next word. This liaison is indicated by the curved line between the words.

> après un   [a prɛ zœ̃]
> revient un   [rə vjɛ̃ tœ̃]
> des oiseaux [de zwa zo]
> ton âme   [tɔ̃ nɑ mə]

Exercise: Read aloud these words which elide the *mute e.* Link the preceding consonant to the initial vowel of the next word.

> âme en   [a mɑ̃]
> rose et   [ro ze]
> notre amour [nɔ tra mur]

Rules for Liaison and Elision

Liaison and elision occur more frequently in singing than in speech and deciding which words can be appropriately connected in singing is a somewhat complex subject and requires understanding of the grammatical structure of the language. There are times when linking is compulsory, when it is optional, and when it is forbidden. Listening to recordings of leading French singers can help you build good discernment about the principles of liaison and elision. Meanwhile, these simplified rules can guide you into reasonable choices.

You may link a word ending in a normally silent final consonant sound to a following word beginning with a vowel, a glide or a mute *h*. The words should be closely connected (as an article connects to an adjective or noun, an adjective to a noun, or a personal pronoun to a verb.)

The following list of books offer excellent sources for further study of liaison.
The Interpretation of French Song,
Singing in French,
Phonetic Readings of Songs and Arias
See bibliography.

un‿enfant	[œ̃ nɑ̃ 'fɑ̃]
un‿ami	[œ̃ na 'mi]
bien‿aimée	[bjɛ̃ nɛ 'me ə]
puis‿il revient	[pɥi zil rə 'vjɛ̃]

Some consonants take on a different sound in liaison.

s will sound like [z]:

Dans‿un sommeil	[dɑ̃ zœ̃ sɔ 'mɛj]
De tes traitres‿yeux	[də te trɛ trə 'zjø]

x will sound like [z]:

deux‿ami	[dø za 'mi]
aux‿aurores	[o zo 'rɔ rə]

d will sound like [t]:

de pied‿en cap	[də pje tɑ̃ 'kap]
grand‿arbre	[grɑ̃ 'tar brə]

g will sound like [k]:

long hiver	[lõ ki 'vɛr]

Y̶ou may elide the final *mute e* to permit the preceding consonant to
be linked to the next word.

l'herbe‿agitée	[lɛr ba ʒi 'te ə]
Je rêve‿aux baisers	[ʒə rɛ vo bɛ 'ze]
la fille‿en rose	[la fi jã 'ro zə]

D̶o not link in these situations:

Do not link words where a separation is needed to support the
meaning of the text.

Tu m'appelais, | et je quittais las terre
[tu ma pə lɛ e jə ki te la tɛ rə]

si tu le veux, | o mon‿amour
[si tu lə vø   o mõ na mur]

mais, | o mon bien-aimé,
[mɛ o mõ bjɛ̃ nɛ me]

Do not link the word *et* (and) to the next word.

et alors	[e ɑ 'lɔr]
et aussi	[e o 'si]

Do not link a final consonant to a word that begins with an
aspirate *h*.

des haies	[de ɛ]
des hérauts	[de e ro]

Do not link into *oui* (yes).

mais oui	[mɛ wi]

In words ending with *rd*, *rs*, or *rt*, usually link the *r* instead of the
final silent consonant.

sur le bord‿arrivée	[syr lə bɔ ra ri 've ə]
mort‿exquise	[mɔ rɛk ski zə]
me penchant vers‿elle	[mə pã ʃã vɛ rɛ lə]

Exception: When final -*rs* indicates pluralization,
link the *s*.
Si mes vers‿aváient des ailes [si me vɛr za de zɛ lə]

French Vowels in Detail

The letter

The letter *a* in French has a variety of pronunciations, depending upon the following qualifiers. To determine the pronunciation of *a*, ask yourself these four questions.

1. Is there an accent mark over the *a*?

2. What letters follow the *a*?

3. Is the letter *a* found as a single letter, or is it part of a letter group?

4. What is the position of *a* in the word? Is it initial, medial, or final?

The pronunciation rules below will help you determine the answers to these questions.

The single letter a

The letter *a* in French is almost always pronounced as [a]. And when *à* has a grave accent, it is *always* [a].

Note: *Bright* [a] is more frequently used in the French language than *dark* [ɑ] as in the English word *father*. *Bright* [a] is not used in isolation in English, but can be heard in the first part of the diphthong in the words *I* [aɪ], *by* [baɪ], and *might* [maɪt], or as Bostonians say "*pahk the cah*" (*park the car*). *Bright* [a] is a more forward vowel than the *dark* [ɑ]. On the vowel chart it is found between [ɑ] and [æ] as in *c*a*t*. Americans must be careful not to produce the *bright* [a] as [æ].

Read aloud:

Paris	[pa 'ri]	chapelle	[ʃa 'pɛ lə]
chalet	[ʃa 'lɛ]	nativité	[na ti vi 'te]
pardon	[par dõ]	caviar	[ka 'vjar]
harpe	['ar pə]	dame	['da mə]
là	[la]	voilà	[vwa 'la]
ami	[a 'mi]	bagatelle	[ba ga 'tɛ lə]

The following spellings are exceptions to the above rule.

1. The letter *a* before the sounds [s] or [z] is sometimes [ɑ].

Note: The *sounds* [s] or [z] can be spelled by several orthographic letters, such as *c* in *lacer,* where the letter c is pronounced [s].

Read aloud:

passer	[pɑ 'se]	occasion	[ɔ kɑ 'sjõ]
lacer	[lɑ 'se]	extase	[ɛk 'stɑ zə]
rasade	[rɑ 'za də]	razer	[rɑ 'ze]

2. The letter *a* before final silent *s* usually [ɑ].

Read aloud:

pas	[pɑ]	trépas	[tre 'pɑ]
las	[lɑ]	bas	[bɑ]

3. The letter *â* is always [ɑ].

Read aloud.

aĝe	['ɑ ʒə]	âme	['ɑ mə]
pâle	['pɑ lə]	mâle	['mɑ lə]

4. The letter *a* in a few other words is pronounced as [ɑ]. Refer to a dictionary.

Read aloud.

miracle	[mi 'rɑ klə]	diable	['djɑ blə]
espace	[ɛs 'pɑ sə]	esclave	[ɛs 'klɑ və]
flamme	['flɑ mə]	proclamer	[prɔ klɑ 'me]

a

The letter group ai

When *ai* is in the interior of a word, the letters are pronounced [ɛ].

Note: The spellings *aî, aie, ais, ait, aient* are also pronounced [ɛ].

Read aloud.

mais	[mɛ]	malais	[ma 'lɛ]
serait	[sə 'rɛ]	malâise	[ma 'lɛ zə]
faite	['fɛ tə]	comparaî tre	[kom pa 'rɛ trə]

Note: *ai* is irregularly pronounced as schwa [ə] in some forms of the verb *faire* [fɛ rə] (*to do*), when *ai* is before [z].

faisais	[fə 'zɛ]	faisant	[fə 'zã]

a
cont.

When *ai* is final in a word, the letters are pronounced [e].

Note: To be pronounced as [e], *ai* must be the final *letters* of the word, as in the following words. When a silent consonant follows *ai*, as in the word *mais*, *ai* is pronounced with the open vowel [mɛ].

Read aloud.

gai   [ge]   serai   [sə 're]

The letters *ail*, *aill*, & *aille* are pronounced [aj]

Note: The letters *ail*, *aill*, and *aille* are composed of the single letter *a* followed by the digraphs *il*, *ill*, and *ille*, which are pronounced as [j]. When you look at the word *travail*, it may appear that the *ai* forms the vowel unit. However, it doesn't: the *il* actually forms the unit — pronounced as [j] — and the *a* is separate. The word *travail*, for example, is pronounced as [tra 'vaj]. See The letter i for more listings with -*il*, -*ill*, -*ille*.

Read aloud.

travail   [tra 'vaj]   cailloux   [ka 'ju]

The letter group aim & ain

When the letters *aim* & *ain* are final or before another consonant, pronounce them as the nasal vowel [ɛ̃]. Do not pronounce the *m* and *n* consonants unless in liaison.

Read aloud.

faim	[fɛ̃]	ainsi	[ɛ̃ 'si]
daim	[dɛ̃]	grain	[grɛ̃]

When the letters *aim* & *ain* are followed by a vowel or another *m* or *n*, do not nasalize them, but pronounce them as [ɛm] and [ɛn].

Read aloud.

haine	['ɛ nə]	plaine	['plɛ nə]
je t'aime	[ʒə 'tɛ mə]	graine	['grɛ nə]

The letter group am & an

When the letters *am* & *an* are final or before another consonant, pronounce them as the nasal vowel [ã]. Do not pronounce the *m* and *n* consonants unless in liaison.

Read aloud.

champ	[ʃã]	grand	[grã]
chantant	[ʃã 'tã]	cependant	[sə pã 'dã]
secouant	[sə ku 'ã]	ambigu	[ã bi 'gy]
galant	[ga 'lã]	an	[ã]

When the letters *am* & *an* are followed by a vowel or another *m* or *n*, do no nasalize them, but pronounce them as [am] and [an].

Read aloud.

tamis	[ta 'mi]	mannifest	[ma ni 'fɛ stə]
damne	['da nə]	animer	[a ni 'me]

cont.

The letter group au

The letters *au* and *aux* are usually pronounced as closed [o].

Read aloud.

au	[o]	Renault	[rə 'no]
chevaux	[ʃə 'fo]	sauve	['so və]

There is one exception to this rule: *au* before *r* is open [ɔ].

Fauré	['fɔ re]	aurai	[ɔ 're]
restaurant	[rɛ stɔ 'rã]		

The letter group ay

The letters *ay* are pronounced as [ɛj]. The sound of [ɛj] is similar to the sound of the letters *ay* in the English word *say* [seɪ].

payer	[pɛ 'je]	payement	[pɛ yə 'mã]

Note: *pays* [pɛ 'i] is an exception to this rule.

The letter

The letter *e* in French has a variety of pronunciations, depending upon the following qualifiers. To determine the pronunciation of *e*, ask yourself these four questions.

1. Is there an accent mark over the *e*?

2. What letters follow the *e*?

3. Is the letter *e* found as a single letter, or is it part of a letter group?

4. What is the position of *e* in the word? Is it initial, medial, or final?

The pronunciation rules below will help you determine the answers to these questions.

The single letter e

Pronounce *é* as [e].

Read aloud.

été	[e 'te]	défaut	[de 'fo]
dictée	[dik 'te ə]	élément	[e le 'mã]

Pronounce *è, ê, & ë* as [ɛ].

Read aloud.

père	['pɛ rə]	forêts	[fɔ 'rɛ]
sortilège	[sɔr ti 'lɛ ʒə]	après	[a 'prɛ]
Noël	[nɔ ɛl]	rêver	[rɛ 've]

Exception: Saints-Saëns [sɛ̃ 'sãs]

When *e* is before a single consonant followed by a vowel, it is pronounced as [ə].

Read aloud.

cheval	[ʃə 'val]	banderilles	[bã də 'ri jə]
premier	[prə 'mje]	venez	[və 'ne]
demain	[də 'mɛ̃]	cheveux	[ʃə 'vø]
jeter	[ʒə 'te]	rayonnement	[rɛ jɔ nə 'mã]

Note: *e* after another vowel or glide is usually silent.

gaie-ment [gɛ 'mã]   paye-ment [pɛj 'mã]

When *e* is before two or more consonants, it is pronounced as [ɛ].

Read aloud.

esprit	[ɛs 'pri]	permettre	[pɛr 'mɛ trə]
elle	['ɛ lə]	nerveux	[nɛr 'vø]
est	[ɛ]	servir	[sɛr 'vir]
esclave	[ɛs 'kla və]	verse	['vɛr sə]
exile	[ɛg 'zi lə]	geste	['ʒɛs tə]
expert	[ɛk 'spɛr]	soutanelle	[su ta 'nɛ lə]

Note: *e* is pronounced as [ɛ] before the letter *x* which has two *phonetic* consonant sounds, [ks] or [gz].

There are three exceptions to this rule:

1. *e* before *ss* or *ff* is closed [e]
   essor [e 'sɔr]   effort [e 'fɔr]

2. *e* in the prefix *re-* is schwa [ə]
   re-frain [rə 'frɛ̃]   re-flux [rə 'fly]

3. *e* when followed by *m* or *n* and another consonant is [ɑ̃]
   (See Letter *e*: *em* and *en*.)
   emporte [ɑ̃ 'pɔr tə] enrobe [ɑ̃ 'rɔ bə]

When *e* is before a *final pronounced consonant,* it is pronounced as [ɛ].

Read aloud.

avec	[a 'vɛk]	hôtel	[ɔ 'tɛl]
chef	[ʃɛf]	rappel	[ra 'pɛl]

Note: Usually *r* is a *final pronounced consonant.* However, after *e*, it is sometimes pronounced, sometimes not. You may need to consult a dictionary. There is only one clear and easy rule: When *er* is a verb ending, pronounce it as [e].

These words end in final pronounced *r*.

Read aloud.

hiver	[i 'vɛr]	cher	[ʃɛr]
mer	[mɛr]	ver	[vɛr]

e

cont.

When *e* is before a *final silent consonant*, it is [e], [ə], or silent. (For a discussion of Pronounced and Silent Consonants, see page 192).

1. When *e* is before a *final silent consonant*, it is usually [e].

Read aloud.

pied   [pje]   allez   [a 'le]

Note: It is helpful to think of final *er, es,* and *et* as units by themselves.

2. Final *er*

a. Pronounce *er* as in verb endings (first conjugation infinitives) as [e] .

Read aloud.

chanter	[ʃɑ̃ 'te]	chercher	[ʃɛr 'ʃe]
importer	[ɛ̃ pɔr 'te]	donner	[dɔ 'ne]
rêver	[rɛ 've]	danser	[dɑ̃ 'se]
monter	[mõ 'te]	refuser	[rə fy 'ze]
aller	[a 'le]	écouter	[e ku 'te]
tier	[ti 're]	bouler	[bu 'le]
doubler	[du 'ble]	charger	[ʃar 'ʒe]

b. When final *er* occurs in nouns and adjectives, it is sometimes [ɛr] but usually [e]. In endings *ier* and *yer*, the *er* is pronounced as [e].

Read aloud.

guerrier	[gɛ 'rje]	danger	[dɑ̃ ʒe]
premier	[prə 'mje]	léger	[le 'ʒe]
berger	[bɛr ʒe]	foyer	[fwa 'je]
étranger	[e trɑ̃ 'ʒe]	portier	[pɔr 'tje]
boulanger	[bu lɑ̃ 'ʒe]	épicier	[e pi 'sje]

3. Final *es*

a. Final *es* in a *polysyllable* is silent or schwa [ə], depending on the number of notes provided in the melody. Final *es* as a pluralization occurs frequently in French.

Read aloud.

parles	['par lə]	elles	['ɛ lə]
lettres	['lɛ trə]	belles	['bɛ lə]
écloses	[e 'klɔ zə]	noires	['nwa rə]

b. Final *es* in a *monosyllable* is pronounced [e].

Read aloud.

des	[de]	les	[le]
tes	[te]	mes	[me]

Note: Some diction books transcribe final *es* in mono-syllables as [e] and others transcribe these letters as [ɛ]. Actually the vowel sound in these monosyllables might be described as a sound *between* the very closed French [e] and the open [ɛ].

4. Final *et*

a. Final *et* is pronounced [ɛ].

Read aloud.

goulet	[gu 'lɛ]	filet	[fi 'lɛ]
flanchet	[flɑ̃ 'ʃɛ]	bouquet	[bu 'kɛ]

b. An important exception is the monosyllable *et*, meaning *and*, which is pronounced closed [e]

e

cont.

Final *e* without an accent is silent or schwa [ə]. Final *e* in mono-syllables is schwa [ə].

Note: Final *e* in polysyllables, normally silent in spoken French, is pronounced *schwa* in singing when a note in the music is provided. Also see section on Liaison and Elision, page 195.

Read aloud.

le	[lə]	parle	['par lə]
je	[ʒə]	image	[i 'ma ʒə]
fumée	[fy 'me ə]	embrumée	[ɑ̃ bry 'me ə]

The letter group eau

Pronounce *eau* (or *eaux*) as [o].

Read aloud.

beau	[bo]	beaux	[bo]
l'eau	[lo]	ruisseaux	[rɥi 'so]
tombeau	[tõ 'bo]	nouveau	[nu 'vo]

The letter group ei

e

cont.

Pronounce *ei* as [ε].

Read aloud.

seine	['sε nə]	geignard	[ʒε 'ɲar]
seize	['sε zə]	cheik	[ʃεk]

Pronounce *eil. eill, & eille* as [εj].

The letters *il, ill,* and *ille* are pronounced as [j]. When *e* is before these letters, it is pronounced as open [ε]. The symbols sound very similar to the *ay* in the English word *say* [seɪ].

soleil	[sɔ 'lεj]	appareilles	[a pa 'rε jə]
vermeil	[vεr 'mεj]	meilleur	[mε 'jœr]
veille	['vε jə]	sommeil	[sɔ 'mεj]

The letter group eim & ein

When the letters *eim & ein* are final or before another consonant, pronounce them as the nasal vowel [ɛ̃]. Do not pronounce the *m* and *n* consonants unless in liason.

Read aloud.

Reims	[rɛ̃s]	plein	[plɛ̃]
teint	[tɛ̃]	peindre	['pɛ̃ drə]

When the letters *eim & ein* are followed by a vowel or another *m* or *n*, do not nasalize them, but pronounce them as [εm] and [εn].

Read aloud.

reine	['rε nə]	seine	['sε nə]

The letter group em & en

When the letters *em* & *en* are final or before another consonant, pronounce them as the nasal vowel [ã]. Do not pronounce the *m* and *n* consonants unless in liason.

Read aloud.

temps	[tã]	enfant	[ã 'fã]
ensemble	[ã 'sã blə]	encor	[ã 'kɔr]

The letters *en* after *i* are pronounced as [ɛ̃]. Do not pronounce the *n* unless in liaison.

Read aloud.

bien	[bjɛ̃]	combien	[kõ 'bjɛ̃]
rien	[rjɛ̃]	reviens	[rə 'vjɛ̃]

When the letters *em* & *en* are followed by a vowel or another *m* or *n*, do not nasalize them.

Read aloud.

émmission	[e mi 'sjõ]	émule	[e 'my lə]
énervant	[e nɛr 'vã]	cène	['sɛ nə]
tenir	[tə nir]	tennis	[tɛ 'nis]

Exception: Initial *emm* is nasalized:

emmancher	[ã mã 'ʃe]
emmèler	[ã mɛ 'le]

Exception: The word *femme* is irregularly pronounced as ['fa mə].

The final letters *ent*

a. Final *ent* in verbs (third person plural) is silent or schwa [ə], depending on the number of notes in the music.

Read aloud.

parlent	['par lə]	parlaient	[par 'lɛ ə]
semblent	['sã blə]	donnent	['dɔ nə]
avaient	[a 've ə]	envolent	[ã 'vɔ lə]
songent	['sõ ʒə]	plaignent	['plɛ ɲə]
tournent	['tur nə]	échangent	[e 'ʃã ʒə]
tombent	['tõ bə]	disent	['di sə]

b. Otherwise, *ent* is pronounced as [ã],

Read aloud.

firmament	[fir ma 'mã]	apaisement	[a pɛ zə 'mã]
excellent	[ɛk sɛ 'lã]	emplacement	[ã plas 'mã]

e

cont.

The letter group eu

e

cont.

When the letters *eu* are in the interior of a word, they are usually pronounced as [œ].

Read aloud.

peuple	['pœ plə]	jeune	[ʒœ 'nə]
heure	['œ rə]	malheur	[ma 'lœr]
seigneur	[sɛ 'ɲœr]	monseineur	[mõ sɛ 'ɲœr]

There are two exceptions to this rule.

a. *eu* before the sound of [z] is [ø].

Read aloud.

creuset	[krø 'zɛ]	malheureuse	[ma lœ 'rø zə]

b. *eû* is [ø].

Read aloud.
jeûner   [ʒø 'ne]

Note: *eu* and *eû* in certain tenses of the verb *avoir* are [y].
eu [y], *eût* [y], *eusse* ['y sə]

When *eu* is the final sound of the word (not necessarily the final letters), pronounce it as [ø].

Read aloud.

peu	[pø]	honteux	[õ 'tø]
veut	[vø]	malheureux	[ma lœ 'rø]
jeu	[ʒø]	joyeux	[ʒwa 'jø]
queue	[kø] or [kø ə]	bleu, bleue, bleues	[blø] [blø ə]

Note: Final -*r* and -*rs* are silent in these two words:

monsieur (singular)	[mə 'sjø]
messieurs (plural)	[mɛ 'sjø]

Note: When the normally silent final consonant is pronounced in liaison, it does not change the preceding vowel sound.

peut‿être   [pø 'tɛ trə]

The letter

The letter *i* in French has a variety of pronunciations, depending upon the following qualifiers. To determine the pronunciation of *i*, ask yourself these four questions.

1. Is there an accent mark over the *i*?

2. What letters follow the *i*?

3. Is the letter *i* found as a single letter, or is it part of a letter group?

4. What is the position of *i* in the word? Is it initial, medial, or final?

The pronunciation rules below will help you determine the answers to these questions.

The single letter i

When the single letter *î* or *i* is final or before a consonant, it is pronounced [i].

Note: The letter *i* has two pronunciations in French: as [i] in *beet* [bit] and as [j] in *you* [ju]. The French letter *i* is never pronounced as Americans say *ih* [ɪ] as in *bit* [bɪt].

Read aloud.

dîner	[di 'ne]	île	['i lə]
ici	[i 'si]	divisible	[di vi 'zi blə]
finir	[fi 'nir]	puisque	['pɥis kə]

When *i* precedes any stressed vowel, it is pronounced as the glide [j].

Read aloud.

ie:	hier	[jɛr]		
	pieds	[pje]	Charpentier	[ʃar pɑ̃ 'tje]
ieu:	dieu	[djø]		
	cieux	[sjø]		
ien:	bien	[bjɛ̃]	vient	[vjɛ̃]
	rien	[rjɛ̃]	reviens	[rə 'vjɛ̃]
ion:	nation	[nɑ 'sjõ]		

There is one exception to this rule: When *i* follows *l* or *r*, pronounce it as [ij].

oublion [u bli 'jõ]   prier   [pri 'je]

i

When the single letter *i* precedes *mute e*, it is pronounced as [i].

> Note: French speakers do not pronounce the *mute e*. Singers, however, will pronounce *mute e* as *schwa* [ə] when there is a note provided in the melody.

1. When *ie(s)* is final in a word or syllable, pronounce it as [i] or [iə] depending on the number of notes.

sortie	[sɔr 'ti ə]	partie	[par 'ti ə]
Italie	[i ta 'li ə]	philosophie	[fi lɔ zɔ 'fi ə]
ranie-ment	[ra ni (ə) 'mã]	vie, vies	['vi ə]

2. When *ient* is final in 3rd person plural verb endings, pronounce it as [i] or [iə], again depending upon number of notes.

rient   [ri] or [ri ə]

The letter groups il, ill, & ille

There are several pronunciations for these letters as you will see below. The most common spelling and pronunciation is described under the first listing.

1. In French, final *il* and *ille*, and medial *ill* are digraphs, pronounced as the single sound [j]. These letters normally follow another vowel as in the word *ailles*, where *ille* follows the letter *a*.

When a word has *ail* as part of the spelling, as in *travail*, the vowels *ai* do not pair up to form a unit. Instead, the *il* forms a unit and *a* is by itself resulting in the sound of: [a] followed by the glide [j]. The word *travail*, for example, is pronounced as [tra 'vaj] or [tra 'va jə]., depending upon the number of notes.

In each of the following words, *il*, *ill*, and *ille*, pronounced as [j] follows the underlined vowel.

Read aloud.

deuil	[dœj]	co-rail	[kɔ 'raj]
détaillant	[de ta 'jã]	tra-vail-le	[tra 'va jə]
a-beille	[a 'bɛ jə]	grenouille	[grə 'nu jə]
aille	['a jə]	cailloux	[ka 'ju]

> Note: Final *-ile* is not included in this rule. The word *aile* forms two syllables, *ai-le* ['ɛ lə].

2. When the syllable does not contain another vowel, pronounce *ill*, and *ille* as [ij].

> Read aloud.
> | | | | |
> |---|---|---|---|
> | gentille | [ʒɑ̃ 'ti jə] | grilles | ['gri jə] |
> | charmille | [ʃar 'mi jə] | brilliant | [bri 'jɑ̃] |
> | brille | ['bri jə] | fille | ['fi jə] |
> | papillons | [pa pi 'jõ] | famille | [fa 'mi jə] |
>
> Note: Final *-il* is not included in this rule. The word *profil* is [prɔ 'fil].

3. In the three words *mille, tranquille,* and *ville,* and their derivatives, the letter groups *ill* and *ille* are pronounced as [il]. A memory "tickler" is to recall the sentence a "million tranquil villages."

> Read aloud.
> | | | | |
> |---|---|---|---|
> | ville | ['vi 'lə] | village | [vi 'la ʒə] |
> | villa | [vi 'la] | mille | ['mi lə] |
> | tranquille | [trɑ̃ 'ki lə] | million | [mi 'ljõ] |

4. When *il* is initial in the word, it is pronounced as [il].

> Read aloud.
> | | | | |
> |---|---|---|---|
> | illusion | [il ly 'zjɑ̃] | ils | [il] |
> | illicite | [il li 'si tə] | il | [il] |

The letter groups im & in

When the letters *im* & *in* are final or before another consonant, pronounce them as the nasal vowel [ɛ̃]. Do not pronounce the *m* and *n* consonants unless in liaison.

> Read aloud.
> | | | | |
> |---|---|---|---|
> | importune | [ɛ̃ pɔr 'ty nə] | vin | [vɛ̃] |
> | timbre | ['tɛ̃ brə] | inviter | [ɛ̃ vi 'te] |

When the letters *im* & *in* are followed by a vowel or another *m* or *n*, do no nasalize them, but pronounce them as [im] and [in].

> Read aloud.
> | | | | |
> |---|---|---|---|
> | timonier | [ti nɔ 'nje] | tinette | [ti 'nɛ tə] |
> | image | [i 'ma ʒə] | innocent | [in ɔ 'sɑ̃] |
> | inimitable | [i ni mi 'ta blə] | immobile | [im mɔ 'bi lə] |

The letter

The letter *o* in French has a variety of pronunciations, depending upon the following qualifiers. To determine the pronunciation of *o*, ask yourself these four questions.

1. Is there an accent mark over the *o*?

2. What letters follow the *o*?

3. Is the letter *o* found as a single letter, or is it part of a letter group?

4. What is the position of *o* in the word? Is it initial, medial, or final?

The pronunciation rules below will help you determine the answers to these questions.

The single letter o

The letter o is usually pronounced [ɔ].

Read aloud.

comme	['kɔ mə]	cloches	['klɔ ʃə]
bonne	['bɔ nə]	gorge	['ʒɔr ʒə]
potager	[pɔ ta 'ʒe]	fort	[fɔr]
soleil	[sɔ 'lɛj]	Toréador	[tɔ re a 'dɔr]

There are three major exceptions to this rule:

1. *o* before [z] is closed [o].

Read aloud.

rose	['ro zə]
poser	[po 'ze]
chose	['ʃo zə]

2. *o* as the final sound of a word is closed [o].

Read aloud.

galop	[ga 'lo]	écho	[e 'ko]
sanglot	[sɑ̃ 'glo]	pierrot	[pjɛ 'ro]
kilo	[ki 'lo]	flot	[flo]

3. *ô* is pronounced as closed [o].

Read aloud.

tôt	[to]	nôtre	['no trə]
drôle	['dro lə]	vôtre	['vo trə]

One exception: *hôtel* is [ɔ 'tɛl]

O

The letter group oeu

The letters *oeu* are usually pronounced [œ].

Read aloud.

coeur	[kœr]	boeuf	[bœf]
oeuf	[œf]	oeillet	[œ 'jɛ]

The letter group oi

The letters *oi* are usually pronounced [wa].

Read aloud.

toi	[twa]	droit	[drwa]
noir	[nwar]	crois	[krwa]
voici	[vwa 'si]	doigts	[dwa]
vois	[vwa]	voix	[vwa]

Exception: *trois* is [twɑ]

The letter group oin

When the letters *oin* are final or before another consonant, pronounce them as [wɛ̃]. Do not pronounce the *m* and *n* consonants unless in liaison.

Read aloud.

loin	[lwɛ̃]	besoin	[bə 'zwɛ̃]

The letter groups om & on

cont.

When the letters *om* & *on* are final or before another consonant, pronounce them as [õ]. Do not pronounce the *m* and *n* consonants unless in liaison.

Read aloud.

gondole	[gõ 'dɔ lə]	donc	[dõ] or [dõk]
maison	[mɛ 'zõ]	rond	[rõ]
pompe	['põ pə]	nom	[nõ]

Exceptions: The word *monsieur* is pronounced [mə 'sjø] and *bonheur* is [bɔ 'nœr].

When the letters *om* & *on* are followed by a vowel or another *m* or *n*, do no nasalize them, but pronounce them as [ɔm] and [ɔn].

Read aloud.

homme	['ɔ mə]	honorer	[ɔ nɔ 're]
donne	['ɔ nə]	domaine	[dɔ 'mɛ nə]
madone	[ma 'dɔ nə]	automne	[o 'tɔ nə]

The letter group ou

The letters *ou*, *où* & *oû* are usually pronounced [u].

Read aloud.

où	[u]	goût	[gu]
fou	[fu]	loup	[lu]
doux	[du]	tout	[tu]
coup	[ku]	nouvelle	[nu 'vɛ lə]
pour	[pur]	court	[kur]
sourd	[sur]	toujours	[tu 'ʒur]
souche	['su ʃə]	sourire	[su 'ri rə]

When the letters *ou* is before a stressed vowel (a vowel other than *mute e*), they are usually pronounced as the glide [w] as in the word *oui*, [wi] which means *yes*.

Read aloud.

oui	[wi]	ouest	[wɛst]

When the letters *ou* are before a *mute e*, they are pronounced as [u] or [uə] depending on the number of notes.

Read aloud.

dénouement	[de nu (ə) 'mã]

The letter group oy

The letters *oy* are pronounced [waj].

> Note: For a full discussion of *y* occuring between two vowels see the listing for <u>The letter y</u>, page 218.

> Read aloud.
>
> | | | | |
> |---|---|---|---|
> | noyée | [nwa ˈje ə] | royal | [rwa ˈjal] |
> | foyer | [fwa ˈje] | | |

The letter u

The letter *u* in French has a variety of pronunciations, depending upon the following qualifiers. To determine the pronunciation of *u*, ask yourself these four questions.

1. Is there an accent mark over the *u*?

2. What letters follow the *u*?

3. Is the letter *u* found as a single letter, or is it part of a letter group?

4. What is the position of *u* in the word? Is it initial, medial, or final?

The pronunciation rules below will help you determine the answers to these questions.

The single letter u

The French letter *u* is pronounced as the mixed vowel [y]. It is never pronounced [u] as in the English word *boot* nor [ju] as in the word *use*. The letter *u* in French is often used in the vowel combinations of *eu*, *oeu*, *ou*, and *ue*, each of which has its own pronunciation. See the alphabetical listings for combined spellings with *u*.

> Note: See Mixed Vowels page 184 for full description of the sound [y] which is formed with tongue in [i] position and lips in the [u] position.

u

cont.

The letter *û* is pronounced [y].

Read aloud.

dû   [dy]

The letter *u* final or before a consonant is [y].

Read aloud.

une	['y nə]	inutile	[i ny 'ti lə]
salut	[sa 'ly]	connu	[kɔ 'ny]
murmure	[myr 'my rə]	union	[y 'njõn]
sud	[syd]	studio	[sty 'djɔ]

The letter *u* before a stressed vowel (a vowel other than *mute e*) is usually the glide [ɥ].

Note: The sound of the glide [ɥ] is produced by quickly moving over the pronunciation of [y]. Be careful never to pronounce the glide [ɥ] as [w] or [u]. See Glides, page 186.

Read aloud.

nuit	[nɥit]	puisque	['pɥis kə]
suave	['sɥa və]	bruit	[brɥi]
lueur	[lɥœr]	suis	[sɥi]

Exception: Some words are pronounced as two syllables: as *cruelle* [kry 'ɛl] and *fluide* [fly 'i də].

The letter *u* before a final *mute e* is usually pronounced [y]. (Exceptions: see below and The letter group ue.)

revue	[rə 'vy ə]	vue	[vy ə]

The letter *u* after *g* and before a vowel is silent.

guitare	[gi 'tɑ rə]	guet	[gɛ]

The letter group ue

When the letters *ue* are followed by *il, ill,* or *ille,* they are pronounced as open [œ]. (See mixed Vowels, page 184, for a description of the sound [œ].

Read aloud.

cercueil	[sɛr 'kœj]	orgueil	[ɔr 'gœj]

The letter groups um & un

When the letters *um* & *un* are final or before another consonant, pronounce them as [œ̃]. Do not pronounce the *m* and *n* consonants unless in liaison.

Read aloud.

parfum	[par 'fœ̃]	chacun	[ʃa 'kœ̃]
humble	['œ̃ blə]	un	[œ̃]

When the letters *um* & *un* are followed by a vowel or another *m* or *n*, do no nasalize them, but pronounce them as [ym] and [yn].

Read aloud.

une	['y nə]	plume	['ply mə]

The letter y

The letter *y* in French has a variety of pronunciations, depending upon the following qualifiers. To determine the pronunciation of *y*, ask yourself these three questions.

1. What letters follow the *y*?

2. Is the letter *y* found as a single letter, or is it part of a letter group?

3. What is the position of *y* in the word? Is it initial, medial, or final?

The pronunciation rules below will help you determine the answers to these questions.

The single letter y

When the letter *y* is initial in a word, it is pronounced as [j].

Read aloud.

yeux	[jø]	yeuse	['jø zə]

When the letter *y* is before or after a consonant, it is pronounced as [i].

Read aloud.

lyre	['li rə]	martyr	[mar 'tir]
style	['sti lə]	lycée	[li 'se ə]

When the letter *y* is between two vowels, it becomes double *ii*.

Note: The first *i* combines with the preceding vowels and the second *i* becomes [j] which joins the next syllable. In the word *rayon*, for example, the syllables are spelled as *rai-ion* [rɛ - jõ].

Read aloud.

royal = roi-ial	[rwa 'jal]
fuyard= fui-iard	[fyi 'jar]

The letter group ym & yn

When the letters *ym* and *yn* are final or followed by another consonant, pronounce them as the nasal vowel [ɛ̃]. Do not pronounce the *m* and *n* consonants unless in liason.

Read aloud.

thym	[tɛ̃]	syndicat	[sɛ̃ di 'ka]
symbole	[sɛ̃ 'bɔ lə]	symphonie	[sɛ̃ fɔ 'ni ə]
synthèse	[sɛ̃ 'tɛ zə]		

When the letters *ym* and *yn* are followed by a vowel or another *m* or *n*, do not nasalize them, but pronounce them as [im] and [in].

Read aloud.

hymne	['i mə]

French Consonants in Detail

b

Pronounce the letters *b* or *bb* as [b].

Read aloud.

beau	[bo]	ballades	[ba 'la də]
blanc	[blɑ̃]	oublier	[u bli 'e]
baiser	[bɛ 'ze]	arbres	['ar brə]
belles	['bɛ lə]	double	['du blə]
abbesse	[a 'bɛ sə]	gabbro	[ga 'bro]

When *b* is final, pronounce it sometimes as [b].

Read aloud.

club	[klyb]	snob	[snɔb]

When *b* is final and after a nasal consonant, do not pronounce it. It is silent.

Read aloud.

plomb   [plɔ̃]

When *b* is followed by *s* or *t*, pronounce it as unvoiced [p].

Note: The voiced *b* becomes unvoiced [p] when before *s* or *t* .

Read aloud.

absent	[ap 'sɑ̃]	obtus	[ɔp 'ty]
absorber	[ap sɔr 'be]	obtenir	[ɔp tə 'nir]

C

When *c* is followed by *a, o, u,* or a *consonant*, pronounce it as [k].

Read aloud.

académie	[a ka de 'mi ə]	composer	[kɔ̃ pɔ 'ze]
cause	['ko zə]	encore	[ɑ̃ 'kɔ rə]
catholique	[ka tɔ 'li kə]	conduit	[kɔ̃ 'dɥi]
captivité	[kap ti vi 'te]	cuisine	[kɥi 'zi nə]
âcre	['a krə]	cueillir	[kœ 'jir]
action	[ak 'sjɔ̃]	sacre	['sa krə]
contacteur	[kɔ̃ tak 'tœr]	octavo	[ɔk ta 'vɔ]

C

When *c* is followed by *e, i,* or *y,* pronounce it as [s].

Read aloud.

cède	['sɛ də]	pièce	['pjɛ sə]
cieux	[sjø]	licence	[li 'sã sə]
ciel	[sjɛl]	facile	[fa 'si lə]
cigarette	[si ga 'rɛ tə]	cygne	['si ɲə]
concierge	[kõ 'sjɛ ʒə]	radience	[ra 'djã sə]

When *c* is final, pronounce it as [k].

Read aloud.

parc	[park]	lac	[lak]
avec	[a 'vɛk]	Poulenc	[pu 'lɛ̃k]

Note: In the composer's name, *Poulenc,* the *en* is irregularly pronounced [ɛ̃].

When *c* is final and after *n,* it is usually silent.

Read aloud.

jonc	[ʒõ]	blanc	[blã]
donc	[dõ]		

Note: When spoken with emphasis, the final *c* is pronounced in the word *donc* [dõk].

When *cc* is followed by *a, o, u,* or a *consonant,* pronounce it as [k].

Read aloud.

succulent	[sy ky 'lã]	accabarant [a ka ba 'rã]

When *cc* is followed by *e, i,* or *y,* pronounce it as [ks].

Read aloud.

succès	[syk 'sɛ]	accent	[ak 'sã]
accélérer	[ak se le 're]	accident	[ak si 'dã]

Pronounce *ç* as [s].

The hooked diacritical mark under the *c* is called a *çàdille* [sɛ 'di jə].

Read aloud.

suçon	[sy 'sõ]	deça	[də 'sa]
garçon	[gar 'sõ]	façon	[fa 'sõ]

Pronounce *ch* as [ʃ].

The IPA symbol [ʃ] is the sound of *sh* as in *she*. It is called *esh* [ʃ].

Read aloud.

chose	['ʃo zə]	floche	['flɔ ʃə]
échotier	[e ʃɔ 'tje]	faucher	[fo 'ʃe]
chemin	[ʃə 'mɛ̃]	chacun	[ʃa 'kœ̃]

Exception: In a few words of Greek derivation, *ch* is [k].

Read aloud.

Christ	[krist]	orchestre	[ɔr 'kɛs trə]
écho	[e 'ko]	choeur	[kœr]

Pronounce *cqu* as [k].

Read aloud.

acquisition	[a ki zi 'sjõ]
acquérir	[a ke 'rir]
acquitter	[a ki 'te]

When *ct* is final, pronounce it as [kt] or silent. Refer to a dictionary for the pronunciation of final *ct*.

Read aloud.

[kt]		silent	
direct	[di 'rɛkt]	respect	[rɛs 'pɛ]
infect	[ɛ̃ 'fɛkt]	aspect	[as 'pɛ]
		instinct	[ɛ̃s 'tɛ̃]

d

Pronounce *d* or *dd* as [d].

Read aloud.

diable	['dja blə]	admirable	[ad mi 'ra blə]
désoler	[de zo 'le]	addition	[a di 'sjõ]

When *d* is final, it is usually silent.

Read aloud.

pied	[pje]	pillard	[pi 'jar]

When *d* is in liason, pronounce it as [t] or silent.

grand arbre	[grã tar brə]

f

Pronounce *f* or *ff* as [f].

Read aloud.

foyer	[fwa 'je]	enfant	[ã 'fã]
flambeau	[flã 'bo]	référence	[re fe 'rã sə]
officer	[ɔ fi 'sje]	affection	[a fɛk 'sjõ]

Note: *e* before *ff* is pronounced closed [e].

effort	[e 'fɔr]	effroi	[e 'frwa]

When *f* is final, usually pronounce it as [f].

Read aloud.

soif	[swaf]	chef	[ʃɛf]
neuf	[nœf]	subjectif	[syb ʒɛk 'tif]
décisif	[de si 'zif]	comparatif	[kõ pa ra 'tif]

When *f* is in liason, pronounce it as [v].

Read aloud.

neuf_heures	[nœ vœ rə]

g

When *g* is followed by *a, o, u,* or a *consonant*, pronounce it as [g].

Note: *g* pronounced as [g] is called hard *g*.

Read aloud.

goût	[gu]	grève	['grɛ və]
gant	[gã]	glotte	['glɔ tə]
guerre	['gɛ rə]	navigateur	[na vi ga 'tœr]

When *g* is followed by *e, i,* or *y*, pronounce it as [ʒ].

Note: *g* pronounced as [ʒ] is called soft *g*.

The symbol [ʒ] represents the sound in the English words *vision* ['vɪ ʒən] and *azure* ['æ ʒʊr].

Read aloud.

gentille	[ʒã 'tij]	gypse	['ʒip sə]
girafe	[ʒi 'ra fə]	geste	['ʒɛs tə]
courage	[ku 'ra ʒə]	partage	[par 'ta ʒə]
sabotage	[sa bɔ 'ta ʒə]	énergie	[e nɛr 'ʒi ə]

When *g* is final, it is usually silent.

Read aloud.

sang	[sã]	long	[lõ]
poing	[pwɛ̃]	seing	[lɛ̃]

When *g* is in liason, pronounce it as [k].

Read aloud.

suer sang͜ et eau   [sɥe sɑ̃k͜ e o] (*to sweat blood*)

g

When *ge* is followed by *a* or *o*, pronounce it as [ʒ].

Read aloud.

pigeon	[pi 'ʒõ]	nageoire	[na 'ʒwɑ rə]
égrugeoir	[e gry 'ʒwar]	bourgeois	[bur 'ʒwa]

When *gg* is followed by *a, o, u,* or a *consonant*, pronounce it as [g].

Read aloud.

aggraver [a gra 've]

When *gg* is followed by *e, i,* or *y,* pronounce it as [gʒ].

Read aloud.

suggérer [syg ʒe 're]   suggestion [syg ʒɛs 'tjõ]

Pronounce *gn* as [ɲ].

The sound of enya [ɲ] does not exist in English. It is similar to the [nj] in the English word *onion.* See page 192 for a full discussion of this sound.

Read aloud.

consigner	[kõ si 'ɲe]	peigner	[pɛ' ɲe]
compagnon	[kõ pa 'ɲõ]	montagne	[mõ 'ta ɲə]

The letters *gt* are silent.

Read aloud.

doigt [dwa]

When *gu* is followed by a *vowel,* pronounce it as [g].

Read aloud.

gigue ['ʒi gə]   fatiguer [fa ti 'ge]

h

In French there are two classifications of *h*, mute and aspirate. Both classifications are silent, except during expressions of great intensity.

The mute *h* and aspirate *h* classifications become significant when words are linked: liaison and elision are permitted with mute *h*, but forbidden with aspirate *h*.

To identify aspirate *h*, refer to a dictionary, where you will find it indicated by a diacritical mark, usually an astrisk (*).

Read aloud.

mute h		*aspirate h	
hélas	[e 'las]	*haut	[o]
heure	['œ rə]	*habler	[a 'ble]
herbe	['ɛr bə]	*halte	['al tə]
inhabité	[i na bi 'te]	*hideuse	[i 'dø zə]

Note: In words such as *inhabité*, the *in* before *h* is not nasalized.

Read aloud.

des_hirondelles	[de zi rõ dɛ lə]
votre_horizon	[vɔ trɔ ri zõ]
la gerbe_hélas	[la ʒɛr be las]

j

Pronounce *j* as [ʒ].

Read aloud.

jouer	[ʒu 'e]	jouir	[ʒu 'ir]
jeune	['ʒœ nə]	jet	[ʒɛ]
je	[ʒə]	joie	['ʒwa ə]
Jean	[ʒɑ̃]	jardin	[ʒar 'dɛ̃]

k

Pronounce *k* as [k].

Read aloud.

kimono	[ki mɔ 'nɔ]	kiosque	['kjɔs kə]
kilo	[ki 'lɔ]	kaki	[ka 'ki]

l

Pronounce *l* as [l].

Read aloud.

larme ['lar mə]   lecture [lɛk 'ty rə]
Napoléon [na pɔ le 'õ]   nominal [nɔ mi 'nal]

When *l* is final, usually pronounce it as [l].

Read aloud.

ideal [i de 'al]   mal [mal]
nominal [nɔ mi 'nal]   appel [a 'pɛl]
fil [fil]   profil [pro 'fil]

Pronounce *ll* as [l].

Read aloud.

pelle ['pɛ lə]   follet [fɔ 'lɛ]
ballet [ba 'lɛ]   tulle ['ty lə]
calleuse [ka 'lø zə] selle ['sɛ lə]

Exceptions: When *ll* follows the letter *i*, the letter group is usually pronounced [j] as in *fouiller* [fu 'je] or *cailloux* [ka 'ju]. (See listing in <u>The Letter i</u> , the listings *il, ill, ille*).

mille ['mi lə]   ville ['vi lə]
tranquille [trã 'ki lə] village [vi 'la ʒə]

Note: The word *fils* (meaning *son*) is irregularly pronounced [fis].

m

Pronounce *m* as [m].

Read aloud.

malheur [ma 'lœr]   estime [ɛs 'ti mə]
moduler [mɔ 'dy lə] limite [li 'mi tə]
timidie [ti mi 'di ə] gémir [ʒe 'mir]

Pronounce *mm* as [m].

Read aloud.

comme ['kɔ mə]   commerce [kɔ 'mɛr sə]
nommer [nɔ 'me]

m

When *m* is combined with a nasal vowel, it is silent.

m, final or after a vowel and before a consonant other than *m* or *n*, is silent. (See Nasal Vowels in section entitled Special Features of French)

Read aloud.

parfum	[par 'fœ̃]	timbre	['tɛ̃ brə]
combat	[kõ 'ba]	humble	['œ blə]
impayable	[ɛ̃ pɛ 'ja blə]	champs	[ʃɑ̃]

When *m* is in liason, pronounce it as [m].

The silent *m* that follows a nasal vowel is pronounced in liaison.

Read aloud.

nom ‿ à tiroirs   [nõ ma ti 'rwar]

n

Pronounce *n* as [n].

Read aloud.

neige	['nɛ ʒə]	nez	[ne]
raffine	[ra 'fi nə]	nombre	['nõ brə]

Pronounce *nn* as [n].

Read aloud.

donne	['dɔ nə]	abonne	[a 'bɔ nə]

When *n* is followed by a nasal vowel, it is silent.

n, final or after a vowel and before a consonant other than *n* or *m*, is silent. (See Nasal Vowels in section entitled Special Features of French)

Read aloud.

non	[nõ]	bon	[bõ]
craindre	['krɛ̃ drə]	grand	[grɑ̃]
ensemble	[ɑ̃ 'sa blə]	montre	['mõ trə]

When *n* is in liason, pronounce it as [n].

A silent *n* that follows a nasal vowel is pronounced in liaison.

Read aloud.

en ‿ aimant	[ɛ̃n ɛ mɑ̃]
son ‿ âme	[sõ na mə]

When *ng* is final, it is silent.

> Read aloud.
>
> poing [pwɛ̃]

Pronounce *p* as [p].

> Read aloud.
>
> père [pɛ rə] impression [ɛ̃ prɛ sjõ]
> pas [pɑ] spirtuelle [spir 'tyɛ lə]
> opéra [ɔ pe 'ra] plain [plɛ̃]

When *p* is final, it is usually silent.

> Read aloud.
>
> trop [tro] beaucoup [bo 'ku]
> corp [kɔr] loup [lu]

The *p* in the letter group *mpt* is silent.

> Read aloud.
>
> compter [kõ 'te] compte [kõ 'tə]
> escompt [ɛs 'kõt] exempt [eg 'zɑ̃]

Pronounce *ph* as [f].

> Read aloud.
>
> Joseph [ʒɔ 'zɛf] morphine [mɔr 'fi nə]
> phrase ['fra zə] colophane [kɔ lɔ 'fa nə]

Pronounce *pp* as [p].

> Read aloud.
>
> application [a pli ka 'sjõ] support [sy 'pɔr]

p

Pronounce *qu* as [k].

> Read aloud.
>
> quand [kɑ̃] qualité [ka li 'te]
> liqueur [li 'kœr] musique [my 'zi kə]
> que [kə] lorsque ['lɔr skə]
> croquet [krɔ 'kɛ] aquis [a 'ki]

q

When *q* is final, pronounce it as [k].

Read aloud.

coq	[kɔk]	cinq	[sɛ̃k]

r

When singing French, pronounce the letter r as a flipped [ɾ] or trilled [r̄]. Although in speaking French, you may use a uvula [ʀ], which is a standard pronunciation in the vicinity of Paris, do not use a uvula [ʀ] in singing. A single flip or two or three flaps of the tip of the tongue is preferable. This chapter uses the symbol [r] to represent the tongue tip r.

Pronounce *r* as [r].

Read aloud.

regard	[rə 'gar]	régale	[re 'ga lə]
refuser	[rə fy 'ze]	ronde	['rõ də]
tremble	['trɑ̃ blə]	timbre	['tɛ̃ brə]

Pronounce *rr* as [r].

Read aloud.

terre	['tɛ rə]	terrible	[tɛ 'ri blə]

When *r* is final, usually pronounce it as [r].

Read aloud.

espoir	[ɛs 'pwar]	pour	[pur]
miroir	[mi 'rwar]	coeur	[kœr]
enfer	[ɑ̃ 'fɛr]	amour	[a 'mur]
or	[ɔr]	hiver	[i 'vɛr]

When *r* is in final *er, ier,* or *yer* in some nouns, it is silent.

Read aloud.

routier	[ru 'tje]	communier	[kɔ my 'nje]
foyer	[frwa 'je]	léger	[le 'ʒe]

When *r* is in final *er* in verbs, it is silent.

Read aloud.

chanter	[ʃan 'te]	baiser	[bɛ 'ze]
parler	[par 'le]	manger	[mɑ̃ 'ʒe]

s

Usually pronounce *s* as [s].

Read aloud.

saucée	[so 'se ə]	séance	[se 'ɑ̃ sə]
sport	[spɔr]	sensualité	[sɛn sɥa li 'te]
posture	[pɔs 'ty rə]	escorte	[ɛs 'kɔr tə]

Pronounce *ss* as [s].

Read aloud.

défausser	[de fo 'se]	florissant	[flɔ ri 'sɑ̃]
tasse	['tɑ sə]	assimiler	[a si mi 'le]

When *s* is between vowels, pronounce it as [z].

Read aloud.

malheureuse	[ma lœ 'rø zə]	honteuse	[õ 'tø zə]
fusant	[fy 'zɑ̃]	maison	[mɛ 'zõ]

When *s* is final, it is silent.

Read aloud.

tous	[tu]	las	[la]
repos	[ra 'po]	des	[de]
pas	[pɑ]	déclos	[de 'klo]

An *s* may be added to a word for plurization, as in English, but it is silent and does not change the pronounciation of the word.

belle   ['bɛ lə]   belles   ['bɛ lə]

When *s* is in liason, pronounce it as [z].

Read aloud.

sans͜ amour   [sɑ̃ za mur]
prends͜ un   [prɑ̃ zœ̃]

When *sc* is followed by *a, o, u,* or a *consonant*, pronounce it as [sk].

Read aloud.

scandale	[skɑ̃ da lə]	scolastique	[skɔ lɑs 'ti kə]
sculpture	[skyl 'ty rə]	scruter	[skry 'te]

When *sc* is followed by *e* or *i*, pronounce it as [s].

Read aloud.

sciant	[sjɑ̃]	sceptre	['sɛp trə]
science	['sjɑ̃ sə]	adolescent	[a dɔ lɛ 'sɑ̃]
scintillant	[sɛ̃ ti 'jɑ̃]	scion	[sjõ]
sceau	[so]	descendre	[de 'sɑ̃ drə]

S

Pronounce *sch* as [ʃ].

The symbol *esh* [ʃ] represents the sound of *sh* as in *she*.

Read aloud.

schéma	['ʃe ma]	schisme	['ʃis mə]

t

Pronounce *t* as [t].

Read aloud.

tout	[tu]	spectacle	[spɛk 'tak lə]
total	[tɔ 'tal]	tension	[tɑ̃ 'sjõ]
tendre	['tɑ̃ drə]	compte	['kõ tə]

Pronounce *tt* as [t].

Read aloud.

quitter	[ki 'te]	flottille	[flɔ 'ti jə]

When *t* is final, it is silent.

Read aloud.

et	[e]	esprit	[ɛs 'pri]
saint	[sɛ̃]	enfant	[ɑ̃ 'fɑ̃]
trait	[trɛ]	complet	[kõ 'plɛ]

Pronounce *th* as [t].

Read aloud.

théâtre	[te 'a trə]	éthéré	[e te 're]

When *ti* is before a vowel in noun endings *-tion* or *-tience*, pronounce it as [sj].

Read aloud.

traction	[trak 'sjõ]	élection	[e lɛk 'sjõ]
location	[lɔ ka 'sjõ]	conviction	[kõ vik 'sjõ]
patience	[pa 'sjɑ̃ sə]		

When *tie* is final, pronounce it as [ti ə].

Read aloud.

sortie	[sɔr 'ti ə]	partie	[par 'ti ə]

Pronounce *v* as [v].

Read aloud.

vie	['vi ə]	esclave	[ɛs 'kla və]
vieux	[vjø]	livre	['li vrə]
vingt	[vɛ̃]	souvenir	[su vɛ 'nir]
violon	[vjɔ 'lõ]	voix	[vwa]

V

Usually pronounce *w* as [v].

Read aloud.

Wagnérien [vag ne 'rjɛ̃]   wagon [va 'gõ]

W

When *x* is followed by a consonant, pronounce it as [ks].

Read aloud.

texte	['tɛk stə]	expose	[ɛk 'spɔ zə]
externe	[ɛk 'stɛr nə]	extra	[ɛk 'stra]
extase	[ɛk 'sta zə]	expansif	[ɛk spã 'sif]

When *x* is followed by a vowel or *h*, pronounce it as [gz].

Read aloud.

exhibition	[ɛg zi bi 'sjõ]	exilé	[ɛg zi 'le]
exulter	[ɛg zyl 'te]	exode	[ɛg 'zɔ də]
exasperer	[ɛg zɑs pe 're]	exemple	[ɛg 'zã plə]

Exceptions: *x* in these words is pronounced [z].
Read aloud.

deuxieme	[dø 'zjɛ mə]
sixieme	[si 'zjɛ mə]
dixieme	[di 'zjɛ mə]

When *x* is final, it is silent.

Read aloud.

deux	[dø]	prix	[pri]
croix	[krwa]	voix	[vwa]

When *x* is in liason, pronounce it as [z].

Read aloud.

deux‿enfants   [døz‿ã fã]

X

Pronounce *z* as [z].

Ézéchiel [e ze kjɛl]   seizième [se 'zjɛ mɛ]

When *z* is final, it is silent.

allez	[a 'le]	dépechez	[de pɛ 'ʃe]
chez	[ʃe]	dormez	[dɔr 'me]

However, Berlioz [bɛr 'ljɔz]

Z

Spanish Diction

As a singer, you need to include Spanish in your arsenal of pronunciation skills. During the last twenty years songs from Spain and South America have slipped into the standard vocal literature.

You will meet several new ideas as you learn to pronounce Spanish, particularly the <u>breath phrase:</u> between breaths all words are run together and pronounced as a stream of even-length syllables. You will hear the word boundaries disappear within the breath phrase, which essentially causes the words to sound like one long word. You will also find that consonants are pronounced differently depending on their position in a word or breath phrase. You will see how vowels change at word boundaries. And finally, you will encounter the special way Spanish syllables are stressed, which, together with the other features mentioned above, gives Spanish its distinct staccato rhythm.

234

Chart of Spanish Sounds

The following chart lists the sounds of the Spanish language in alphabetic order. Refer to this chart to quickly check the sound of a spelling. There are some special circumstances and exceptions to the sounds that cannot be presented easily in a simple chart. Detail is included in the discussion of the individual sounds.

Spanish Letter & Position in Word			IPA	Example & IPA		Page
a	a	syllable initial	[a]	atrás, agua	[a tras] [a ɣua]	252
		syllable final	[a]	mano, taza	[ma no] [ta sa]	252
	ay	syllable final	[ai]	hay, ay	[ai] [ai]	252
	ai	syllable final	[ai]	paila, vainita	[pai la] [bai ni ta]	252
	aí	syllable final	[ai]	país, raíz	[pa is] [ra is]	252
	au	syllable final	[au]	causa, jaula	[kau sa] [xau la]	253
b	b	syllable initial	[b]	bala, bono	[ba la] [bo no]	258
		between vowels	[β]	tubo, haba	[tu βo] [a βa]	258
		following s, r	[β]	esbelto, hierba	[ez βel to] [jer βa]	258
		syllable final	[β]	obscuro	[oβs ku ro]	258
				submarino	[suβma ri no]	
c	c	before a, o, u	[k]	casa, cosa, cuna	[ka sa] [ko sa] [ku na]	258
		before e, i	[s]	cesar, cima	[se sar] [si ma]	258
	cc	across syllables	[ks]	accion, ficción	[ak sjon] [fik sjon]	258
ch	ch	syllable initial	[ʧ]	choza, mucho	[ʧo sa] [mu ʧo]	259
d	d	syllable initial	[d]	danza, discreto	[dan sa] [dis kre to]	259
		between vowels	[ð]	hada, mido	[a ða] [mi ðo]	260
		after s, r	[ð]	desde	[dez ðe]	260
		syllable final	[ð]	verdad, usted	[ber ðað] [us teð]	260
e	e	syllable initial	[e]	elegante, echar	[e le ɣan te] [e ʧar]	253
		syllable final	[e]	mesa, puse	[me sa] [pu se]	253
	ey	syllable final	[ei]	rey	[rei]	254
	ei	syllable final	[ei]	reina, peine	[rei na] [pei ne]	254
	eu	syllable final	[eu]	deuda, feudal	[deu ða] [feu ðal]	254
f	f	syllable initial	[f]	fácil, afanar	[fa sil] [a fan ar]	260
g	g	before a, o, u	[g]	gato, gota,	[ga to] [go ta]	261
		before e, i	[x]	gente, gimnasia	[xen te] [xim na sia]	261
		between vowels	[ɣ]	haga, miga	[a ɣa] [mi ɣa]	261
		after s	[ɣ]	desgana	[dez ɣa na]	261
				desgarra	[dez ɣa ra]	

These g's are pronounced [ɣ] because they are between vowels.

Spanish Letter & Position in Word			IPA	Example & IPA		Page
g *cont.*	gua	syllable initial	[gua]	agua, fraguar	[a ɣua] [fra ɣuaɾ]*	261
	gue	syllable initial	[ge]	guerra, guerrilla	[ge Ťa] [ge Ťi ʎa]	261
	gui	syllable initial	[gi]	guitarra, guiso	[gi ta Ťa] [gi so]	261
	güi	syllable initial	[gwi]	lingüística	[liŋ gwis ti ka]	261
	güe	syllable initial	[gwe]	averigüe	[a βe ɾi ɣwe]	261
h	h	syllable initial	silent	hogar, ahorrar	[o ɣaɾ] [a o Ťaɾ]	262
				hielo, huerta	[ie lo] [uer ta]	
i *	i	syllable initial	[i]	imagen, isla	[i ma xen] [iz la]	255
		syllable final	[i]	piso, mi	[pi so] [mi]	255
	ia	syllable final	[ja]	hacia, piano	[a sja] [pja no]	255
	ie	syllable final	[je]	tiene, viene	[tje ne] [bje ne]	255
	iu	syllable final	[ju]	viuda, ciudad	[bju ða] [sju ðað]	255
	io	syllable final	[jo]	adiós, amplio	[a ðjos] [am pljo]	255
j	j	syllable initial	[x]	joven	['xo βen]	262
				jaula	[xau la]	262
				ajustar	[a xus taɾ]	262
k	k	syllable initial	[k]	kilogramo	[ki lo gra mo]	262
				kibutz	[ki βuts]	
l	l	syllable initial	[l]	litro, palo	[li tro] [pa lo]	263
		syllable final	[l]	mil, vil, alto	[mil] [bil] [al to]	263
ll	ll	syllable initial	[ʎ] or [j]	lleno, cabello	[ʎe no] [ka βe ʎo]	242, 263
m	m	syllable initial	[m]	mano, amasar	[ma no] [a ma saɾ]	263
n	n	syllable initial	[n]	nene, nido	[ne ne] [ni ðo]	264
		before *m*	[mː]	inmenso	[i mːen so]	264
				inmejorable	[i mːe xo ɾa ble]	
		before [k] [g]	[ŋ]	incubar, ingrato	[iŋ ku βaɾ] [iŋ gra to]	264
				ingle, incoherente	[iŋ gle] [iŋ ko e ɾen te]	
ñ	ñ	syllable initial	[ɲ]	ñuto, puño	[ɲu to] [pu ɲo]	242, 264
o	o	syllable initial	[o]	oro, ocaso	[o ɾo] [o ka so]	256
	oy	syllable final	[oi]	voy, hoy	[boi] [oi]	256
	oi	syllable final	[oi]	heroico, estoico	[e ɾoi ko] [es toi ko]	256
	oí	across syllables	[oi]	egoísta, boína	[e ɣo is ta] [bo i na]	256

* When a written stress is placed over the *i*, the *i* is no longer a glide and the two vowels are pronounced in separate syllables. (See page 255.)

Spanish Letter & Position in Word			IPA	Example & IPA		Page
p	p	syllable initial	[p]	peso, apostar	[pe so] [a pos tar]	264
		syllable final	[p]	optar, captar	[op tar] [kap tar]	264
q	que		[ke]	queso, quedar	[ke so] [ke dar]	265
	qui		[ki]	quitar, quiso	[ki tar] [ki so]	265
r	r	word initial	[r̄]	rosa, rana	[r̄o sa] [r̄a na]	265
		syllable initial	[r]	pero, apuro	[pe ro] [a pu ro]	265
		syllable final	[r] or [r̄]	ir, cesar	[ir] [se sar]	265
		after s, n	[r]	Israel, enredar	[iz r̄a el] [en r̄e ðar]	265
rr	rr	between vowels	[r̄]	perro, carro	[pe r̄o] [ka r̄o]	265
s	s	syllable intial	[s]	sala, aseo	[sa la] [a se ɵ]	266
		between vowels	[s]	oso, pasa	[o so] [pa sa]	266
		before voiced consonants	[z]	desde, musgo	[dez ðe] [muz ɣo]	266
		syllable final	[s]	los, niños	[los] [ni ɲos]	266
t	t	syllable initial	[t]	tina, untar	[ti na] [un tar]	267
		syllable final	[t]	atlas, atmósfera	[at las] [at mos fe ra]	267
u	u	syllable initial	[u]	uso, usual	[u so] [u swal]	256
		syllable final	[u]	nuca, confuso	[nu ka] [kon fu so]	256
	ua	syllable final	[wa]	suave, cuarto	[swa βe] [kwar to]	245
	ue	syllable final	[wɛ]	cuerda, puesta	[kwer ða] [pwes ta]	245
	ui	syllable final	[wi]	cuidar, buitre	[kwi ðar] [bwi tre]	245, 257
	ui	syllable final	[wi]	cuidado	[kwi ða ðo]	245, 257
	uy	syllable final	[wi]	muy	[mwi]	245
v	v	syllable initial	[b]	vaca, vengo	[ba ka] [beŋ go]	267
		between vowels	[β]	uva, tuvo	[u βa] [tu βo]	267
w[*]	w	syllable initial	[w]	whisky	[wis ki]	268
x	x	word initial	[s]	Xenofobia	[se no fo βja]	268
				Xerocopiax	[se ro ko pja]	
		syllable initial	[ks]	exámen	[ek sa men]	268
				exoneración	[ek so ne ra sjon]	
y	y	syllable initial	[j]	yeso, yegua	[ye so] [je ɣwa]	257
z	z	syllable initial	[s] or [θ]**	zapato, zar	[sa pa to] [sar]	268
		syllable final	[s]	tez, nariz	[tes] [na ris]	268
		before a voiced consonant	[z]	hazlo, pazmado	[az lo] [paz ma ðo]	268

*Not a letter of the Spanish alphabet; only appears in borrowed words.
**Castilian Spanish.

Special Features of Spanish Diction

Alphabet—Sound Correspondences

In contrast to English, Spanish is virtually pronounced as it is written. The alphabet-sound correspondences charted in the previous section hold true in all instances.

Syllabification

The division of Spanish words into syllables is quite straightforward and follows clear rules. The correct division is important since it often determines how a sound is pronounced. Certain consonant sounds [p t k b d g] are pronounced differently if they occur at the beginning of a syllable or at the end. (See page 258 Spanish Consonants in Detail for more detailed explanations.)

Examples:

cac-tus: c initial [k]

               c final [ɣ]

denso: d initial[d]

verdad: d final [ð]

See page 239 for a description of the fricative g [ɣ].

Single Consonant

A single consonant starts a new syllable when it occurs between vowels.

    ma-ma [mɑ mɑ] ca-sa [kɑ sɑ]   to-ma [to mɑ]

The letters *ch, ll,* and *rr* represent one sound and are treated as a single consonant; therefore, they are not divided.

    mu-cho [mu ʧo] ca-lle [kɑ ʎe]   pe-rro [pe ɾo]

Double Consonants

Two consonants together may or may not be divided.

Note: A rule of thumb is that if the two consonants can occur at the beginning of a word, they form a cluster and will always be in the same syllable.

blanco   blan - co
ablandar   a - blan - dar
(*bl* can occur at the beginning of a word)

calma   cal - ma
(*lm* cannot occur at the beginning of a word, so you must divide it into separate syllables)

There are 12 clusters that can go together in the same syllable. They are:

bl br   cl cr   dr   fl fr
gl gr   pl pr   tr

Three Consonants

Three consonants are always divided. The rule above will help you to decide where to divide them. If the last two consonants form one of the twelve indivisible clusters, you must keep them in the same syllable.

siem-pre   hom-bre   am-pliar

However, if the last two consonants are not one of the twelve, you make the division between the second and third consonant.

ins-pi-rar   cons-tar

Four Consonants

Four consonants are rare. When they do occur, divide them in the middle.

obs-truc-ción

Two Vowels

Two vowels together can be divided in two ways. If one of the vowels is an unstressed *i* or *u*, the two vowels occur in the same syllable.

cau-sa cai-go cie-lo pies

A written accent mark over a vowel means that it is stressed. The stress mark over the i in the word raíz, for example, means that the i is stressed.

In all other cases, two vowels together are divided into separate syllables.

le-ón   ca-er   le-er   ra-íz   ba-úl

Exercise:

Divide the words into syllables:

quieto	poeta	caido
allá	pasilo	carro
exponer	deuda	subyacente
paisaje	airoso	isla
hombre	dialecto	transportar

Breath Phrases

Word boundaries are, for the most part, ignored when speaking Spanish. Between breath pauses, whatever words are being spoken are run together and pronounced as one word. The phrase "Tómas anduvo con Ana" (Thomas walked with Ann) would be pronounced like this: [to ma san du βo ko na na]. This long "word" is divided into syllables following the rules above. Note that any final consonant in a word that occurs between vowels begins the following syllable.

Exercise:

Divide the following lines from the chorus of the sailors in the *zarzuela* "La Gran Via", Act 1.

> Cuando los vientos cual furias se agitan,

> cuando las olas se encrespan e irritan.

Zarzuela - A short drama with incidental music, similiar to an operetta or musical comedy. Taken from the Palace of La Zarzuela near Madrid, where festive dramas were presented.

"b, v, d, g" Variations According to Word Positions

These consonants are pronounced differently if they occur at the beginning of a word or if they occur in the middle of a word, even though their position in the syllable is the same. Remember that *b* and *v* are pronounced the same. (See page 258 for a more detailed discussion of the individual sounds.)

When a consonant's position is referred to as "within a word," it can also mean "within a breath phrase", which is like one long word made up of several words run together. See "Breath Phrases" on the previous page.

Note: To produce the fricative *b* [β], put your lips together lightly and blow so that the air flows through your lips. Be sure to voice the sound. You will feel your lips vibrate. Articulating this sound is similar to articulating [b], except that the lips do not completely stop the air flow.

Note: The fricative *g* sound, [ɣ], is articulated the same way as the German ach-laut [x], except that it is voiced. To produce the fricative *g*, [ɣ], raise your tongue as you would for a *k* sound [k], but don't let your tongue completely touch the soft palate. Through the small opening between your soft palate and your tongue, let a stream of air flow. Then voice the sound. You will feel your tongue and soft palate vibrate.

Examples:

be-be	b word initial	[b]
	b between vowels	[β]
ven	v word initial	[b]
uva	v between vowels	[β]
de-do	d word initial	[d]
	d between vowels	[ð]
ga-to	g word initial	[g]
Hu-go	g between vowels	[ɣ]

Exercise:

Look at these lines from the "La Gran Via". Write the IPA symbol for the underlined consonant. Watch out for those sounds that begin a word, but within the phrase occur between vowels:

Ya nuestro barco cual rauda gaviota

Las alas van rompiendo nuestra

suerte en pos. ¡Hip! ¡A bogar! ¡Hip! ¡A bogar!

¡Qué hermosa es esta vida de la mar!

Lack of Aspiration in "p, t, k"

In English, these consonants are pronounced with a puff of air if they occur before a stressed vowel (*Peter, appeal, king*). Spanish has no such aspiration. Pronounce these sounds like the non-aspirated English sounds following an *s*, as in *spill, still,* and *skill*. (See page 258 for a more detailed discussion and more exercises for the individual sounds.)

Exercise:

Practice saying these pairs of words in English to feel the difference in the aspiration/non-aspiration.

peak	speak	till	still	kill	skill
pill	spill	teal	steal	key	ski
punk	spunk	ton	stun	Kate	skate

Exercise:

Now, practice these Spanish words, being careful not to aspirate.

Pablo	[pɑ blo]	taza	[tɑ sɑ]	casa	[kɑ sɑ]
peso	[pe so]	tengo	[teŋ go]	queso	[ke so]
pino	[pi no]	tino	[ti no]	quiso	[ki so]
pongo	[poŋ go]	topo	[to po]	cosa	[ko sɑ]
puso	[pu so]	tuna	[tu nɑ]	cuna	[ku nɑ]

Note: Remember that the [t] is dental (See page 267.)

Exercise:

Practice the *p's* and *t's* from these lines from the " Gran Via".

Y allá en la playa que lejos se divisa
[jɑ jɑ en lɑ plɑ jɑ ke le xo se ði βi sɑ]

pañuelos que se agitan sin cesar
[pɑ ɲwe los ke se ɑ xi tɑn sin se sɑr]

nos llaman con amor
[nos jɑ mɑn ko nɑ mor]

¡Oh! ¡Mágico placer! ¡Oh! ¡Dicha singular!
[o mɑ xi ko plɑ ser o di ʧɑ siŋ gu lɑr]

Note: When a consonant ends a word and the same consonant begins the next word, pronounce both consonants as one.

Note: See page 249 for explanation of vowels across word boundaries.

Assimilation of [s]

The rules for the pronunciation of *s* or *z* are the same. The letters are pronounced as [s] or [z] depending on the sound that follows.

Assimilation - *The alteration of a speech sound influenced by a neighboring sound, which makes it more like the neighboring sound.*

If the next sound is a voiceless sound, the *s* or *z* is also a voiceless [s].

ra<u>s</u>car [r̄as kɑr] ha<u>z</u>tu [as tu]

If the next sound is a voiced sound, the *s* or *z* is pronounced as [z].

ra<u>s</u>gar [r̄az ɣɑr] ha<u>z</u>lo [az lo]

Exercise:
Decide if the underlined *s* should be pronounced as [s] or [z].

má<u>s</u> ango<u>s</u>to	la<u>s</u> mi<u>s</u>ma<u>s</u>
pre<u>s</u>ente	dice<u>s</u>
pe<u>s</u>a<u>s</u>	mu<u>s</u>go
e<u>s</u>te	be<u>s</u>o<u>s</u>
lo<u>s</u> año<u>s</u>	<u>s</u>igno

Exercise:
Remembering that the letter *z* follows the same pronunciation rules as the letter *s*, decide how you would pronounce the following *z*'s.

ca<u>z</u>ar	<u>z</u>apato
ta<u>z</u>a	chori<u>z</u>o
esbo<u>z</u>o	pa<u>z</u>
ve<u>z</u>	<u>z</u>orro
una ve<u>z</u> más	halla<u>z</u>go

Assimilation of [n]

The *n* is pronounced at the same point of articulation as the sound that follows it.

1) *n* pronounced as an alveolar [n]

nena	[ne nɑ]
una taza	[u nɑ tɑ sɑ]
un cielo	[un sje lo]

Alveolar - *Formed by bringing the tip of the tongue near or against the alveoli.*

2) *n* pronounced as a bilabial [m]

un peso	[umː pe so]
unbeso	[umː be so]

Bilabial - *Formed by both lips.*

Note that the sounds following the *n* are bilabial.

inmejorable	[i mːe xo ɾa ble]
inmadurez	[i mːɑ ðu ɾes]

Sp

3) *n* pronounced as [ŋ]

inglés	[iŋ gles]
incubar	[iŋ ku βɑɾ]

Note that the sounds following the *n* are velar

ungato	[uŋ gɑ to]
un caso	[uŋ kɑ so]

(See page 264 for a more detailed discussion of *n* and more exercises.)

Individual Consonants

Unique to Spanish

1) *ll* [ʎ]

The *ll* has two acceptable pronunciations; both are widely used in different parts of the Spanish-speaking world. Both variants are used in parts of Spain and parts of South America. You can pronounce the "elye" as the *ll* in the English word "million"; or you can pronounce it as an English *y* [y].

calle	[kɑ je]	or	[kɑ ʎe]
llamar	[jɑ mɑɾ]	or	[ʎɑ mɑɾ]

(See page 263 for a more detailed discussion and exercises.)

2) *ñ* [ɲ]

The *ñ* is pronounced similar to the *n* in the English word "canyon."

niño   [ni ɲo]   paño   [pɑ ɲo]

(See pages 48 and 264 for a more detailed discussion and exercises.

3) *j* [x]

The [x] is similar to the German sound [x]. Put the back of your tongue close to the roof of your mouth, in the same position that you would use for a [k]. Be sure not to touch the palate. Feel the air rush through the narrow opening.

joven   [xo βen]   enojo [e no xo]

(See page 262 for a more detailed discussion and exercises.)

4) Dental *t* and *d*

In English, these two sounds are alveolar. They are pronounced with the tip of the tongue touching the alveolar ridge. In Spanish, you should pronounce them with the tongue tip touching the back of the teeth.

> tengo [teɲ go] tuna [tu nɑ]

Exercise:

Pronounce the following words.

tengo	[teɲ go]	danza	[dɑn sɑ]
taza	[tɑ sɑ]	desde	[dez ðe]
todo	[to ðo]	dama	[dɑ mɑ]
tuna	[tu nɑ]	duque	[du ke]
tieso	[tje so]	dulce	[dul se]

5) *r* and *rr*

There are two Spanish "r's." The single *r* is pronounced with a flap of the tongue, like the English *t* or *d* that usually occurs between vowels. Pronounce the words "body, Betty, Adam"; feel how your tongue flaps against the aveolar ridge. Now, try the Spanish words "pero, pura, cera".

Exercise:

Pronounce these words.

cerámica	[se ɾɑ mi kɑ]	árbol	[ɑr βol]
brazo	[brɑ so]	otro	[o tro]
fruta	[fru tɑ]	madre	[mɑ ðre]
largo	[lɑr ɣo]	criatura	[krjɑ tu ɾɑ]
verde	[ber ðe]	cortar	[kor tɑr]

There is no comparative sound in American English for the double *rr*. It is pronounced with a trilled *r*. To approximate the sound, flap your tongue tip several times in rapid succession against the tooth ridge.

perro	[pe r̄o]	arroyo	[ɑ r̄o jo]
forro	[fo r̄o]		

In word initial position (even within a breath phrase) a single *r* is pronounced as trilled [r̄]. This is an exception where the spelling of single *r* does not reflect the simple alphabet-sound correspondence of Spanish.

rosa	[r̄o sɑ]	rojo	[r̄o xo]
resto	[r̄es to]		

(See page 265 for a more detailed discussion and exercises.)

Pure Simple Vowels

Note: As in the other languages, [e] and [o] are pronounced without a diphthongal offglide as in English. See page 46 in Italian.

Spanish vowels are never lengthened. The *e, i, o,* and *u* are not longer in a stressed syllable as their English counterparts are.

English	Spanish
ma	ma
me	mi
may	me
low	lo
too	tu

Exercise:

Practice saying the following words. Be careful not to glide the vowels.

masa [ma sa]	mesa [me sa]	misa [mi sa]
moza [mo sa]	musa [mu sa]	

lama [la ma]	lema [le ma]	lima [li ma]
loma [lo ma]	luna [lu na]	

paso [pa so]	pesó [pe so]	pisó [pi so]
pózo [po so]	puso [pu so]	

(See page 252 for a more detailed discussion of the individual vowels and exercises.)

Strong Vowels

Spanish vowels are not weakened in unstressed syllables. Unstressed vowels are not reduced to a *schwa* [ə]. The pronunciation is the same wherever a vowel occurs.

Vowels in unstressed syllables

English	monologue	[ma nə lɔg]
Spanish	monólogo	[mo no lo ɣo]

English	productive	[prə dʌk tɪv]
Spanish	productivo	[pro duk ti βo]

English	legitimate	[lə ʤɪ tɪ mət]
Spanish	legitimo	[le xi ti mo]

Exercise:

Be careful to differentiate between the unstressed vowels in these syllables as you pronounce these pairs.

bueno	[bwe no]	buena	[bwe na]
comieron	[ko mje ron]	comieran	[ko mje ran]
peso	[pe so]	piso	[pi so]

Exercise:

Pronounce these words. Pronounce vowels in the stressed and unstressed syllables the same.

extranjero	[eks tɾaŋ 'xe ɾo]	desgracia	[dez 'ɣɾa sja]
preposición	[pre po si 'sjon]	momento	[mo 'men to]
mañana	[ma 'ɲa na]	francamente	['fɾaŋ ka men te]
estatua	[es 'ta twa]	ahogado	[a o 'ɣa ðo]
ambicioso	[am bi 'sjo so]	inaplicables	[i na pli 'ka bles]

Note that the assimilation of n in extranjero. The letter j is [x] which is velar: so the n becomes velar also. See page 241.

Diphthongs

The vowel closure when pronouncing Spanish diphthongs is much faster than in English and closes more. Because the glides close more, different symbols are used in Spanish:

English	[aɪ]	[ɔɪ]	[aʊ]
Spanish	[ai]	[oi]	[au]

Example:

English		Spanish	
ray	[reɪ]	rey	[r̄ei]
I	[aɪ]	hay	[ai]
boy	[bɔɪ]	voy	[boi]
cow	[kaʊ]	causa	[kau za]

This vowel chart illustrates the tighter closure of the Spanish diphthong [ai] compared to English [aɪ].

Exercise:

Pronounce the following words.

peine	[pei ne]	deuda	[deu ða]
reina	[r̄ei na]	caucho	[kau ʧo]
baile	[bai le]	causa	[kau sa]
naipe	[nai pe]	jaula	[xau la]
Jaime	[xai me]	pauta	[pau ta]

Spanish also has a fourth diphthong eu, but its occurence is rare. Examples: Eugenia, Europa

On-Glide Diphthongs

Spanish has eight diphthongs which have a glide before the vowel. You should be careful not to break these diphthongs into two syllables.

ia	hacia	[a sja]	ua	cuarto	[kwaɾ to]
ie	tierra	[tje r̄a]	ue	cuerda	[kweɾ ða]
io	adiós	[a ðjos]	uo	cuota	[kwo ta]
iu	viuda	[bju ða]	ui	cuidar	[kwi ðaɾ]

Exercise:

As you pronounce the following words, be careful not to break the diphthongs into two syllables.

fuera	[fwe ɾa]	piano	[pja no]
ruana	[r̄wa na]	piojo	[pjo xo]
suave	[swa βe]	patio	[pa tjo]
mueca	[mwe ka]	riego	[r̄je ɣo]
hueso	[we so]	fiel	[fjel]

Stress

There are several aspects of Spanish stress that differ from English stress.

Predictable patterns

Spanish word stress follows simple rules.

Words ending with vowels, or the consonants *n* or *s* are stressed on the next-to-last syllable:

hablo	['a blo]	imagen	[i 'ma ɣen]
esta	['es ta]	visitarnos	[vi zi 'tar nos]

Words ending in other consonants are stressed on the last syllable:

comer	[ko 'mer]	principal	[prin si 'pal]
verdad	[ber 'ðað]	capaz	[ka 'pas]

All exceptions to these two rules carry a written accent:

está	[es 'ta]	imán	[i 'man]
atrás	[at 'ras]	habló	[a 'blo]
rápido	['ra pi do]	impidemelo	[im 'pi ðe me lo]

Vowels in combination with *i* or *u* form diphthongs, unless a written accent is found on the *i* or *u*; in this case, the two vowels occur in separate syllables.

Diphthongs		Separate syllables	
paisano	[paj sa no]	país	[pa is]
tiara	[tja ra]	tía	[ti a]
miope	[mjo pe]	mío	[mi o]
actuacion	[ak twa sjon]	actúa	[ak tu a]

Exercise:

Where would you stress the following words?

limosna	lavar	éstas
pañal	perrito	hable
lesión	estás	animal
lápices	digamelo	periodo
rápido	parar	lentamente

Syllable length

Spanish stressed syllables are louder, but they are not longer. Every Spanish syllable is pronounced in the same amount of time.

English	Spanish
industry	industria
magnificent	magnífico
industrial	industrial

Exercise:

Pronounce the following words. Do not reduce any of the syllables. Remember that the vowels in unstressed syllables do not reduce to [ə].

ho-me-na-je	ex-tra-or-di-na-rio
es-pon-ta-nei-dad	a-gra-da-ble
mo-men-ta-rio	de-sas-tro-so
va-rie-dad	re-co-men-da-ble
ha-bi-ta-ción	psi-co-lo-gí a

Secondary stress

Spanish does not have secondary stress. Long words are not broken up into primary-secondary patterns as they are in English. Words have several weak stresses and one primary stress. Together with similar syllable length, this feature of Spanish stress creates the familiar staccato rythm in this language.

English
ad - min - is - tra- tion
na - tion - al - i - ty
ge - og - ra - phy
ed - u - ca - tion

Spanish
ad - mi - nis - tra - ción
na - cio - na - li - dad
ge - o - gra - fi - a
e - du - ca - ción

Exercise:

Pronounce the following Spanish words. The stress patterns are marked for you.

cla - si - fi - ca - ción
con - ti - nua - ción
cal - cu - la - ción
re - ve - la - ción
con - si - de - ra - ción

i - rre - spon - sa - bi - li - dad
in - com - pa - ti - bi - li - dad
in - ca - pa - ci - dad
ca - ni - ba - lis - mo
sen - ti - men - ta - lis - mo

Cognate words

Many words in Spanish and English have similar Latin roots. Their meanings and spellings are similar; however, watch out for different stress patterns! As in the exercises above, the majority of cognates have different stress patterns.

Exercise:
What are the English cognates for the following words?
Are the stress patterns the same or different?

entusiástico	individúal
examinación	vocabulário
curiosidád	rapidaménte
metabolísmo	departamentál
comunicativo	inevitáble

Stress timing

Spanish rhythm is very different from English rhythm. Whereas English rhythm is determined by the number of stresses, Spanish rhythm is determined by the number of syllables. In other words, the syllable length varies in English according to the stress system, but in Spanish, syllable length stays the same. In poetry, or in songs, the number of syllables gives the "beat".

Rosita, in "Luisa Fernanda", Act 1.

La zurcidora buena [la suɾ si ðo ɾa βwe nɑ]
7 syllables

sabe de sobra [sa βe ðe so βɾɑ]
5 syllables

que a quien mucho le zurce [kea kjen mu ʧo le suɾ se]
7 syllables

poco le cobra [po ko le ko bɾɑ]
5 syllables

Y es que el bolsillo [yes kel bol sɪ ʎo]
5 syllables

también necesitaba [tɑm bje ne se si ta βɑ]
7 syllables

buen zurcidillo [bwen suɾ si ði ʎo]
5 syllables

Guardias, in "La Gran Via", Act 2

Caiga la trampa [kɑi ɣɑ la trɑm pɑ]
5 syllables

con precaucion [kon pɾe kɑu sjon]
4 syllables

que ya tenemos [ke ya te ne mos]
5 syllables

dentru* el raton [den tɾwel ɾa ton]
4 syllables

*u instead of o (adentro) shows a dialect variation

See page 249 for vowel changes across word boundaries.

Due to the strong-weak stress patterns in English, an English speaker will have a tendency to shorten and lengthen syllables when phrasing a musical line, even when the note values are the same. This tendency should not carry over when singing in Spanish. Base the stress pattern on <u>number</u> of syllables when phrasing a musical line in Spanish.

Vowel Changes Across Word Boundries

As Spanish words run together within a breath phrase, several interesting changes occur when two vowels come together at the word boundaries.

Vowel Deletion

Two vowels combine into one vowel. In rapid speech, this vowel is not even lengthened.

aa	tierra arida	[tje r̄a ɾi ða]
ee	aire entró	[ai ɾen tro]
oo	cuatro ojos	[kwa tro xos]

Open vowel + closed vowel

When a more open vowel (i.e. a vowel pronounced with the jaw lower) is followed by a more closed vowel, the first vowel disappears.

a + e	la esposa	[les po sa]
a + o	la hora	[lo ra]
a + i	la isla	[liz la]
a + u	la única	[lu ni ka]
e + i	Me imagino	[mi ma xi no]
o + u	lo único	[lu ni ko]

Exception. This does not usually happen with the combinations *e + u* or *o + i*

le utilizo [le u ti li so]   lo informo [lo in foɾ mo]

Vowel Relaxation

When *e* or *o* come into contact with each other (probably because they both have the same degree of jaw lowering), the first vowel relaxes and almost turns the two vowels into an on-glide diphthong. The two vowels are then part of the same syllable.

e + o	este otro	[es teo tro]
o + e	este o este	[es te oes te]

This also occurs when *e* or *o* comes into contact with *a*.

e + a	este alma	[es teal ma]
	me hablo	[mea blo]
o + a	toto aquello	[to ðoa ke ʎo]
	pudo hacer	[pu ðoa ser]

Vowel deletion and *relaxation* are both very important in singing. Separate vowels combine into one syllable. This allows Spanish rhythm to be maintained.

Notice the following lines from "Luisa Fernanda".

Vidal:

En mi tierra‿extremeña	[en mi tje r̄eks tre me ɲa]
tengo‿un nido de‿amores	[teɲ gu ni ðo ðea mo res]
entre‿encinas bizarras	[en tren si nas βi sa ras]
y castaños y robles	[i kas ta ɲo si r̄o bles]
donde‿el pájaro quiere	[don del pa xa ro kje re]
que‿una pájara venga	[keu na pa xa ra βeŋ ga]
para ser soberana	[pa ra ser so βe ra na]
de mi casa labriega.	[de mi ka sa la brje ɣa]

Exercise:

Divide the following lines into syllables. (From the Chorus in "La Gran Via", Act 1.)
Porque es el caso, que según dicen
doña Municipalidad
va a dar a luz una Gran Via
que de fijo no ha tenido iqual .

Triphthongs

Three vowels together occur only in the Castillian verb forms used with the pronoun *vosotros.* (Note that pronouns in Spanish are often deleted from the sentence. For example, *vosotros cambiais* becomes simply *cambias.*) The three vowels together are pronounced as a glide-vowel-glide, all in the same syllable.

cambiáis	[kam bjais]
estudiéis	[es tu djais]
contiuáis	[kon ti nwais]

Tripthongs also occur with some frequency at word boundaries.

justicia humana	[xus ti sjau ma na]
estatua importante	[es ta twaim por tan te]
negocio importante	[ne ɣo sjoim por tan te]
estudió historia	[es tu djois to rja]

Note: Neither of the glides carries a written accent. If either glide has a written stress, it will belong to a separate syllable.

negocio ímprobo	[ne ɣo sjo im pro βo]
negocio único	[ne ɣo sjo u ni ko]

Dialectical Variations

English dialects differ because of vowel variations. Spanish dialects, on the other hand, differ because of consonant variations. Castillian Spanish and South American Spanish are the two main dialect groups. However, within these main groups, there are several regional dialect groups. The most salient differences are listed below.

		Accepted Pronunciation		
letter	example	Castillian	South American	(Argentina)
z		[θ]	[s]	
	caza	[kaˋθɑ]	[ka sɑ]	
ll		[ʎ]	[j]	[ʒ]
	calle	[ka ʎe]	[ka je]	[ka ʒe]
s (in syllable final)		[s]	[h], silent, or s	
	los rios	[los rios]	[loh ri oh]	
			[lo ri o]	
			[los ri os]	
[s]		[ṣ]*	[s]	

* This sound is called the *apico dorsal fricative.* To produce this sound, curl your tongue tip slightly toward the alveolar ridge as you pronounce the *s.*

You will also hear numerous variations of the consonants (*p, t, k, b, d,* and *g*) in syllable and word final. These variations are not only general dialectical patterns: even within a single dialectical region, an individual's pronunciation of these consonants may vary. The variations are numerous. For simplicity's sake, only the most common variations have been chosen to include in the text. A few examples are given below.

	Variations
o<u>bt</u>ener	[op te ner]
	[o te ner]
	[oβ te ner]
	[ok te ner]
verda<u>d</u>	[ber ðɑt]
	[ber ðɑθ]
	[ber ðɑ]
	[ber ðɑð]

Spanish Vowels in Detail

The letter	
a	The letter *a* in Spanish is always pronounced [ɑ]. It is the same sound as the vowel in the word *father*.

Read aloud:

alma	[ɑl mɑ]	ala	[ɑ lɑ]
Ana	[ɑ nɑ]	mano	[mɑ no]
pasa	[pɑ sɑ]	rosa	[r̄o sɑ]

ay & ai

ay & *ai* occur only in word final or syllable final and is pronounced as the diphthong [ɑi].

Read aloud:

ay	[ɑi]	hay	[ɑi]
laico	[lɑi ko]	baile	[bɑi le]
Jaime	[xɑi me]	Taita	[tɑi tɑ]

Note: This sound is similar to the vowel sounds in the English words *pie, sky*. Notice that your tongue closes as you pronounce the [ɑɪ], gliding upward and towards the front. When you pronounce the Spanish [ɑi], you should glide faster and to a more closed position than in English.

Compare and contrast:

	English		Spanish	
eye	[ɑɪ]		hay	[ɑi]
knife	[nɑɪf]		naipe	[nɑi pe]
tight	[tɑɪt]		taita	[tɑi tɑ]

Remember that if the *i* has a written accent, it is no longer a glide and is pronounced as a separate syllable.

caí	[kɑ í]	maíz	[mɑ ís]	Caín	[kɑ ín]

au

The sound of *au* [ɑu] is similar to the diphthong in the English words *cow, house.* Notice that the jaw closes, gliding upwards and backwards. When you pronounce the Spanish diphthong, you should glide faster and farther to a more closed position than in English.

Compare and contrast:

English		Spanish	
out	[ɑʊt]	auto	[ɑu to]
howl	[hɑʊl]	jaula	[xɑu lɑ]
couch	[kɑʊt]	caucho	[kɑu ʧo]
cow	[kɑʊ]	causa	[kɑu sɑ]

Read aloud:

pauta	[pɑu tɑ]	sauna	[sɑu nɑ]
caucho	[kɑu ʧo]	auto	[ɑu to]

Pronounce the Spanish *e* as [e]. Be careful not to glide it, as you do in English. See page 46 in Italian for singing non-diphthongal [e].

Compare and contrast:

English [eɪ]		Spanish [e]	
day	[deɪ]	de	[de]
May	[meɪ]	me	[me]
say	[seɪ]	sé	[se]
Kay	[keɪ]	que	[ke]
Fay	[feɪ]	fe	[fe]

Read aloud:

eso	[e zo]	era	[e rɑ]
ella	[e ʎɑ]	pero	[pe ɾo]
dice	[di se]	nene	[ne ne]

The letter

e

ei & ey

The letter

e

The Spanish *ey* and *ei* are quite like the English diphthong [eɪ]. As in other Spanish glides, you must raise your jaw faster and close it more than in English.

Compare and contrast:

English [eɪ]		Spanish [ei]	
ray	[r̄eɪ]	reina	[r̄ei nɑ]
pay	[peɪ]	peine	[pei nɑ]

Note: *ey* only occurs in word final.

Read aloud:

rey	[r̄ei]	ley	[lei]
reina	[r̄ei nɑ]	peine	[pei ne]
treinta	[trein tɑ]	peinado	[pei nɑ ðo]

Remember that if the *i* has a written accent, it is no longer a glide and is pronounced as a separate syllable.

rei [r̄e i]

eu

The Spanish diphthong *eu* does not exist in English; however, it is not difficult to pronounce. Put your mouth in the position for [e]; then quickly glide to the position for [u], rounding your lips tightly. Note that this is not a common sound in Spanish.

Read aloud:

deudo [deu ðo] seudo [seu ðo]

The letter

The *i* in Spanish is pronounced as the *y* in *city* is often pronounced: [i]. When you pronounce it, be sure not to lengthen it; there is no glide, as there usually is in English.

Compare and contrast:

English [iː]		Spanish [i]	
me	[miː]	mi	[mi]
tea	[tiː]	ti	[ti]
see	[siː]	si	[si]
bee	[biː]	vi	[bi]
qui	[kiː]	key	[ki]

Read aloud:

informar	[in for mɑɾ]	ira	[i ɾa]
silla	[si ʎa]	comi	[ko mi]

ia, ie, io, & iu

The letter

i

The *i* that precedes another vowel becomes a glide. The two vowels form part of the same syllable. They are not separated into two syllables as they are in English.

Note: Some English speakers add [j].

Compare and contrast:

English	Spanish
piano [pi ja no]	piano [pja no]

Practice the following words. Keep the vowels in the same syllable.

internacional	[in teɾ na sjo nɑl]
atención	[a ten sjon]
conferencia	[kon fe ɾen sja]
desperdicio	[des peɾ ði sjo]
obsequio	[oβ se kjo]
embriaguez	[em bɾja ɣes]

fiar	[fjaɾ]	piojo	[pjo xo]
criar	[kɾjaɾ]	piedad	[pje ðað]

Note: If an accent mark is written over an *i*, the *i* is no longer pronounced as a glide, and the two vowels are pronounced in separate syllables.

río	[ri o]	desafío	[de za fi o]
salía	[za li a]	tenía	[te ni a]

Read aloud:

odiar	[o djaɾ]	historia	[is to ɾja]
criada	[kɾja ða]	cianuro	[sja nu ɾo]
nadie	[na ðje]	diente	[djen te]
alguien	[al gjen]	fiesta	[fjes ta]
miope	[mjo pe]	tardío	[taɾ ði o]
fastidio	[fas ti ðjo]	mafioso	[ma fjo so]
ciudad	[sju ðað]	viuda	[bju ða]

The letter

The Spanish *o* is pronounced the same as the *ow* in the English words *yellow, mello, jello.* The Spanish *o* is never lengthened and there is no glide.

Compare and contrast:

English [oʊ]		Spanish [o]	
no	[oʊ]	no	[no]
cocoa	[ko koʊ]	coco	[ko ko]
dose	[doʊs]	dos	[dos]
low	[loʊ]	lo	[lo]

Read aloud:

olla	[o ʎa]	ocaso	[o ka so]
paño	[pa ɲo]	niño	[ni ɲo]

oi & oy

The *oy* and *oi* in Spanish are similar to the English *oy* as in *toy, boy.* When you pronounce the Spanish, however, you should glide faster and close your jaw more.

Pronounce the similar words.

English [oɪ]		Spanish [oi]	
soy	[soɪ]	soy	[soi]
boy	[boɪ]	voy	[boi]
toy	[toɪ]	hoy	[oi]

Read aloud:

voy	[boi]	hoy	[oi]
boina	[boi na]	coincidir	[koin si ðir]

The letter

The Spanish *u* is similar to the English vowel in the word *food.* However, the English vowel is somewhat longer and is pronounced with a slight glide. When you pronounce the Spanish *u*, make sure you keep it short.

Compare and contrast:

English		Spanish	
too	[tu]	tú	[tu]
taboo	[ta bu]	tabú	[ta βu]
Sue	[su]	su	[su]

Notice that many English words that are spelled with a consonant + *u* are pronounced as the consonant + [ju] as in *cute, beautiful, few, mute.* Spanish words never add a [j] between a consonant and a [u].

Compare and contrast:

English [ju]		Spanish [u]	
funeral	[fju nə rəl]	funeral	[fu ne rɑl]
bureaucracy	[bju rɑ krə sɪ]	burocracia	[bu ro krɑ sjɑ]
music	[mju zɪk]	música	[mu si kɑ]
cube	[kjub]	cubo	[ku βo]
huge	[hjuʤ]	Hugo	[hu ɣo]
municipal	[mju nɪ sɪ pəl]	municipal	[mu ni si pɑl]
occupy	[ɑ kju paɪ]	ocupar	[o ku pɑr]

Read aloud:

una	[u nɑ]	uva	[u βɑ]
puño	[pu ɲo]	ruta	[ru tɑ]

The letter

u

ui & uy

The *uy*, which occurs only in a few words, and the *ui* are pronounced in the same way. There is no equivalent in English. The first vowel is a glide; the second vowel forms the center of the syllable. When you pronounce this vowel combination, put your lips and jaw in the position for [u]; then, quickly move to the position for [i].

Read aloud:

muy	[mwi]	buitre	[bwi tre]
huir	[wir]	cuita	[kwi tɑ]

The *y* in English and Spanish are quite similar. When you pronounce the Spanish *y*, narrow the space between your tongue and the roof of your mouth so that the air hisses slightly.

Read aloud:

yerro	[je ɾo]	yerno	[jer no]
yerba	[jer βɑ]	cayo	[kɑ jo]
yacer	[jɑ ser]	poyo	[po jo]
yaciente	[jɑ sjen te]	yugo	[ju ɣo]
yate	[jɑ te]	yute	[ju te]
yarda	[jɑr ða]	yuglar	[ju ɣlɑr]
yunto	[jun to]	yo	[jo]

The letter

y

Spanish Consonants in Detail

b

The letter *b* in initial position is pronounced the same as the English [b]; however, when the *b* occurs between vowels, you must produce the sound [β]. Remember that this also applies to a *b* between vowels in a phrase, even if that *b* is in syllable initial position in a word. Also, remember that when following an *s*, or an *r*, or when in syllable final the Spanish *b* is pronounced as [β].

buzo	[b]	in syllable initial
mi buzo	[β]	no longer in syllable initial; within the phrase, it occurs between vowels

Decide how you would pronounce the *b*'s in the following phrases.

mi buen abrigo
bueno y barato
baraja blanca
beso baboso
bulto blando

Read aloud:

syllable initial	[b]	beso	[be so]	bomba	[bom ba]
		bruto	[bru to]	brisa	[bri sa]
		bebe	[be βe]	bono	[bo no]
between vowels	[β]	rabano	[ra βa no]		
		soñaba	[so ɲa βa]		
		cantaba	[kan ta βa]		
		hábil	[a βil]		
		lobo	[lo βo]		
following an s-	[β]	es bueno	[ez βwe no]		
following an r-		perturbar	[per tur βar]		
syllable final	[β]	subjectivo	[suβ xe ti βo]		
		obtener	[oβ te ner]		
		obtuso	[oβ tu so]		

c

Pronounce *c* before *a,o,u* as [k].

casar	[ka sar]	caña	[ka na]
cama	[ka ma]	comer	[ko mer]
cosa	[ko sa]	cono	[ko no]
culto	[kul to]	cuñado	[ku ɲo ðo]
cumplir	[kum plir]		

Pronounce *c* before *e, i* as [s].

cerca	[seɾ kɑ]	cerdo	[seɾ ðo]
cera	[se ɾɑ]	cidra	[si ðɾɑ]
ciclo	[si klo]	cimar	[si mɑɾ]

cc

Pronounce *cc* across syllables as [ks].

acción	[ɑk sjon]	ficción	[fik sjon]
acceso	[ɑk seso]	occidente	[ok si ðen te]

Note: Pronounce the Spanish [s] and [k] the same as in English.

Pronounce *ch* as [ʧ].

charla	[ʧɑr lɑ]	achacar	[ɑ ʧɑ kɑr]
chapo	[ʧɑ po]	cuchillo	[ku ʧi ʎo]

Note: Pronounce the Spanish [ʧ] the same as in English.

ch

d

The Spanish [d] is dental; touch the back of the upper teeth when you pronounce it at the beginning of a syllable.

Read aloud:

dar	[dɑr]	decir	[de siɾ]
decena	[de se nɑ]	definir	[de fi niɾ]
don	[don]	domingo	[do miŋ go]
dulce	[dul se]	dormir	[dor miɾ]
doblar	[do blɑr]	dolor	[do loɾ]

Between vowels, following an *s*, or an *r*, or when in syllable final, pronounce the Spanish *d* as [ð]. When you pronounce this sound in English, as in the word *this*, notice that your tongue is between your teeth. When you pronounce this sound in Spanish, however, place the tip of your tongue on the edge of your upper teeth, but do not thrust it out. Remember that these rules apply to *d*'s within phrases also.

[d]   [ð]
<u>d</u>anza   la <u>d</u>anza

Be careful not to carry over the English *d* between vowels, which is pronounced with your tongue flapping against

d

your tooth ridge. If you pronounce the Spanish *d* between vowels as a flap, it will sound like a Spanish *r*, and you will confuse words such as the following:

modo	[mo ðo]	moro	[mo ɾo]
todo	[to ðo]	toro	[to ɾo]
mida	[mi ða]	mira	[mi ɾa]
cada	[ka ða]	cara	[ka ɾa]
lodo	[lo ðo]	loro	[lo ɾo]

Read aloud:

todo	[to ðo]	mitad	[mi tað]
poder	[po ðeɾ]	sed	[seð]
duda	[du ða]	red	[r̄eð]
madura	[ma ðu ɾa]	Usted	[us teð]
adentro	[a ðen tro]	sud	[suð]

Read aloud:

a donde	[a ðon de]
se va de aqui	[se βa ðe a ki]
una duda	[u na ðu ða]
cama doble	[ka ma ðo ble]
casa de arriendo	[ka sa ðe a r̄jen do]
mamá de Pedro	[ma ma ðe pe dro]
la droga	[la dro ɣa]
pega duro	[pe ɣa ðu ɾo]
Rosa duerme	[r̄o sa ðwer me]
Miria dice	[mi rja ði se]

Read aloud:

syllable initial	[d]	denso [den so]	doctor [dok toɾ]
		deporte [de poɾ te]	
between vowels	[ð]	dedo [de ðo]	pido [pi ðo]
		adornar [a ðoɾ naɾ]	
following s-	[ð]	desde [dez ðe]	desden [dez ðen]
following r-		verdad [beɾ ðað]	
syllable final	[ð]	salud [sa luð]	Madrid [ma drið]
		virtud [biɾ tuð]	

The English and Spanish *f*'s are pronounced alike.

Note: The English spelling *ph,* usually pronounced [f], does not exist in Spanish.

forma	[foɾ ma]	fango	[faŋ go]
fiel	[fjel]	función	[fun sjon]

The English and Spanish *g* are pronounced alike, except when the Spanish *g* occurs between vowels or before *e* or *i*. In this case, pronounce the Spanish *g* as [ɣ], or before *e* or *i* as [x]. Many English speakers pronounce the word *sugar* with this [ɣ].

g

[g]	[ɣ]	[x]
gota [go ta]	la gota [la ɣo ta]	gira [xi ɾa]

Read aloud.

before a, o, u.	[g]	gamba [gam ba]	ganso [gan so]
		galgo [gal go]	golpe [gol pe]
		golfo [gol fo]	goma [go ma]
		gusano [gu sa no]	gusto [gus to]
		gutural [gu te ɾal]	

before e, i	[x]	gelatina [xe la ti na]
		gema [xe ma]
		gemelo [xe me lo]
		gimnasia [xim na sja]
		gimotear [xi mo te ar]

between vowels	[ɣ]	soga [so ɣa]	llaga [ʎa ɣa]
		vago [ba ɣo]	daga [da ɣa]
		saga [sa ɣa]	

following s-	[ɣ]	esgrima [ez ɣɾi ma]
		desgastar [dez ɣas tar]

gua, gue, güe, gui, güi

Pronounce *gua* as [ɣwa].

fraguar	[fɾa ɣwar]	guayaba	[gwa ja βa]
guarnir	[gwar nir]		

Pronounce *gue* as [ge].

guerrerero	[ge ῑe ɾo]	guerrilla	[ge ῑi ʎa]

Pronounce *güe* as [gwe].

güepil	[gwe pil]	güelfo	[gwel fo]

Pronounce *gui* as [gi].

guia	[gi a]	guija	[gi xa]	guinda	[gin da]

Pronounce *güi* as [gwi].

lingüistica	[liŋ gwis ti ka]

Read aloud:

la guerra	[la ɣe r̄a]	juego	[xwe ɣo]
aguardar	[a ɣwar ðar]	me gusta	[me ɣus ta]
no hago	[no a ɣo]	es gordo	[ez ɣor ðo]
es grande	[ez ɣran de]	desgracia	[dez ɣra sja]
una gota	[u na ɣo ta]		
no me da la gana	[no me ða la ɣa na]		

h

The *h* in Spanish is silent.

ahogar	[a o gar]	haz	[as]
haya	[a ja]	harto	[ar to]

j

Pronounce the Spanish *j* as [x]. You may have difficulty with this sound at first, as it probably seems "foreign" to you; however, the sound is quite similar to the first sound in the words *Hugh* and *Huron*. Put the back of your tongue near the velum (the soft palate). Feel the air hiss through the small opening. This is how you should pronounce the Spanish *j*.

Read aloud:

justo	[xus to]	juvenil	[xu βe nil]
juzgar	[xuz ɣar]	ajonjoli	[a xon xo li]
arrojar	[a r̄o xar]	bajar	[ba xar]
reja	[r̄e xa]	juego	[xwe ɣo]
jugar	[xu ɣar]	juntar	[xun tar]
jóven	[xo βen]	jaula	[xau la]
adjustar	[a xus tar]	bajo	[ba xo]

k

This letter only appears in words borrowed from other languages. It has the same sound as in English.

karate	[ka ra te]	kilograma	[ki lo gra ma]
kiosco	[kjos ko]	kilometro	[ki lo me tro]

The Spanish *l* has only one sound. Regardless of the position in the word or phrase, it is pronounced the same as the English *l* in the words *like, lake, lisp.* The English "dark l" as in the words *hull, hill, fall* does not occur in Spanish. When you pronounce the Spanish *l*, keep the blade of your tongue flat; do not lower it.

l

Compare and contrast:

English [ɫ]		Spanish [l]	
mill	[mɪɫ]	mil	[mil]
hill	[hɪɫ]	Gil	[xil]
tall	[tɔɫ]	tal	[tɑl]
call	[kɔɫ]	cal	[kɑl]
all	[ɔɫ]	al	[ɑl]
dell	[dɛɫ]	del	[del]
hotel	[hoʊ tɛɫ]	hotel	[o tel]
mall	[mɔɫ]	mal	[mɑl]

Read aloud:

lava	[la βɑ]	lección	[lek sjon]
multa	[mul tɑ]	soltana	[sol tɑ nɑ]
vil	[bil]	febril	[fe βril]

The Spanish "elye" is pronounced in one of several ways throughout the Spanish-speaking world. The two most acceptable variations are [ʎ] and [j]. The first is similar to the pronunciation of the *ll* in the word *million;* the second is just as widespread, especially in Latin America.

ll

Read aloud:

valle	[ba ʎe]	llamaba	[ʎa ma βa]
callar	[ka ʎar]	llama	[ʎa ma]
alli	[a ʎi]	fallo	[fa ʎo]
malla	[ma ʎa]	pollo	[po ʎo]
llano	[ʎa no]	llevar	[ʎe βar]
hallar	[a ʎar]	llave	[ʎa βe]
bolsillo	[bol si ʎo]	llamar	[ʎa mar]

The Spanish *m* is the same as in English.

misa	[mi sa]	amar	[a mar]

m

n

The *n* in most positions is the same as the English *n*, and causes no problems. However, when the *n* occurs before a *bilabial* sound, an [k] or [g], it becomes bilabial like that sound. And when it occurs before a *velar* sound [k] or [g] it becomes velar like that sound. This also happens in English (pronounce that very word: *English*...what happens to the *n*?) but not consistently as it does in Spanish.

syllable initial	[n]	nudo [nu ðo]	inato [i nɑ to]
before m	[m]	inmutar [i mːu tɑɾ]	
		inmortal [i mː or tɑl]	
before [k]	[ŋ]	incautar [iŋ kɑu tɑɾ]	
		inclinar [iŋ kli nɑɾ]	
before g	[ŋ]	inglés [iŋ gles]	
		ingenio [iŋ xe njo]	

How would you pronounce the *n's* in the following words and phrases?

inmejorable	incautar
incantador	comen mejor
denle	comen pan
conmemoracion	conmigo
contento	toman vino

ñ

The Spanish ñ is pronounced the same as the *ny* in the English word *canyon*. You should not have any problems with this sound.

Read aloud:

niño	[ni ɲo]	puño	[pu ɲo]
ñapa	[ɲɑ pɑ]	paño	[pɑ ɲo]
reñir	[re ɲir]	baño	[bɑ ɲo]

p

The Spanish *p* is pronounced the same as the English *p* in the words *spill, speak spank*. There is no aspiration, regardless of where the *p* occurs.

Read aloud:

pena	[pe nɑ]	apelar	[a pe lɑɾ]
óptimo	[op ti mo]	apitutde	[ɑp ti tuð]

Read aloud:

English [p]	Spanish [p]
paper	papel
Paul	Paul
Pessimism	Pesimismo

The Spanish *q* is pronounced as [ke] or [ki], depending on the spelling. The [k] sound in the word *quien* [kjen] is the same as in English.

que *syllable initial* [ke]
    que [ke]   quebrar [ke brɑr]
    quejar [ke xɑr]   quechua [ke ʧwɑ]

qui *syllable initial* [ki]
    quicio [ki sjo]   quiebra [kje βrɑ]
    quien [kjen]

q

Spanish has two *r* sounds. The first sound, [ɾ] is called a flap. When you pronounce it, flap the tip of your tongue against your tooth ridge once. The sound is similar to the English *t* or *d* between vowels, as in the words *Betty, city, reader, feeder*. Notice that this [ɾ] is always spelled with a single *r*.

The second *r* sound is called a trill. There is no comparable sound in English. When you pronounce it, flap the tip of your tongue against the tooth ridge several times. Notice that this [r̄] can be spelled either with a single *r* or a double *rr*, depending on the position in the word.

r

Note: The IPA symbol for *tapped r* is [ɾ] and for *trilled r* is [r̄].

word initial	[r̄]	religión	[r̄e li xjon]	remo	[r̄e mo]
		rito	[r̄i to]	resulta	[r̄e sul tɑ]
syllable initial	[ɾ]	pared	[pɑ red]	mira	[mi ɾo]
		virar	[bi rɑr]	orar	[o rɑr]
		pájaro	[pɑ xɑ ɾo]		
syllable final	[r̄] *or* [ɾ]				
		subir	[su βiɾ]	teñir	[te ɲir]
		venir	[be nir]	hablar	[ɑ βlɑr]
after an n, s	[r̄]	enredar	[en r̄e ðɑr]	Israel	[is r̄a el]
the letters rr	[r̄]	barra	[bɑ r̄ɑ]	hierro	[je r̄o]
		cierro	[sje r̄o]	enterrar	[en te r̄ɑr]

rr

Decide how to pronounce the r-sounds in the following words. Are they flaps, trills, or either?

ce<u>rr</u>ado	toma<u>r</u>
sub<u>r</u>aya<u>r</u>	ot<u>r</u>o
<u>r</u>oto	<u>r</u>oba<u>r</u>
en<u>r</u>ojar	en<u>r</u>iquece<u>r</u>
al<u>r</u>ededo<u>r</u>	b<u>r</u>isa

Contrast the two *r*'s

	[r]		[r̄]
pero	[pe ɾo]	perro	[pe r̄o]
caro	[kɑ ɾo]	carro	[kɑ r̄o]
vara	[bɑ ɾa]	barro	[bɑ r̄o]
cero	[se ɾo]	cerro	[se r̄o]
fiero	[fje ɾo]	fierro	[fje r̄o]
amara	[ɑ mɑ ɾa]	amarra	[ɑ mɑ r̄a]

Do not confuse *t* and *d* between vowels with the *r*. Compare the following pairs. They are NOT pronounced alike.

todo	[to ðo]	toro	[to ɾo]
cada	[kɑ ða]	cara	[kɑ ɾa]
moto	[mo to]	moro	[mo ɾo]
meta	[me tɑ]	mera	[me ɾa]
mida	[mi ða]	mira	[mi ɾa]
seda	[se ða]	cera	[se ɾa]

S

The [s] and the [z] in Spanish and English are pronounced in the same way; the only problem you might have is in deciding which to pronounce in which position.

Note: The same rules apply to the letter z. (See page 268)

syllable initial	[s]	sin	[sin]	sobar	[so βaɾ]
		sur	[suɾ]		

syllable final	[s]	casas	[kɑ sɑs]	asfaltar	[as fɑl tɑɾ]

between vowels	[s]	caso	[kɑ so]	piso	[pi so]

before voiced consonants [z]

	esbirro	[ez bi r̄o]	rasgar	[r̄az ɣaɾ]
	desbocar	[dez βo kaɾ]	isla	[iz lɑ]

Decide how to pronounce the *s*'s in the following words or phrases.

mesclar	disgusto
es de	esposo
las vacas	los niños
es mío	está
tienes pecas	tienes becas

Note: All plurals in Spanish are pronounced [s]; plurals never have a [z] sound as they do after voiced sounds in English (*boys, chairs, doors*).

Compare and contrast:

Careful with the following cognates! Don't fall into the trap of pronouncing them as you would their English counterparts!

[z] English	[s] Spanish
president	presidente
present	presente
visit	visitar
rose	rosa
plaza	plaza
museum	museo

The Spanish *t* is dental. When you pronounce it, put the tip of your tongue against the back of your upper teeth. It is never aspirated, as it is before a stressed vowel in English.

ten	[ten]	tinta	[tin tɑ]
taza	[tɑ sɑ]	Atlántico	[ɑt lɑn ti ko]
ritmo	[r̄it mo]		

Compare and contrast:

[t] English	[t] Spanish
two	tu
tea	ti
tan	tan
tuna	tuna
tall	tal

t

The *v* follows the same rules as the *b*. There is no difference in pronunciation between the two. You may hear speakers using the [v] for reasons of social prestige, but they are not consistent and the use is confined to a few common words. The words "tuvo" and "tubo" are pronounced alike. (See the discussion for the letter *b*, page 258)

syllable initial	[b]	verde	[ber ðe]
		verificar	[be ɾi fi kɑɾ]
following s- following r-	[β]	desvanecer	[dez βɑ ne ser]
		intervalo	[in ter βɑ lo]
between vowels	[β]	vive	[bi βe]
		cavar	[kɑ βɑɾ]

W

This letter does not belong to the Spanish alphabet. It occurs only in a few borrowed words. When this letter does appear, it is pronounced the same as the English *w*.

syllable initial	[w]	Whisky ['wɪ skɪ]

X

Only a few words begin with *x*. Most words with this sound [x] are written with a *j*.

word initial	[x]	xearquía	[xe ɑr ki ɑ]
syllable initial	[ks]	próximo	[prok si mo]
		exámen	[ek sɑ men]
		experiencia	[eks pe ɾjen sjɑ]

Z

The pronunciation of the *z* is the most distinctive feature that distinguishes the Castillian and Latin American dialects. When singing songs from Spain, use the sound [θ], which is the same as the English *th* in the words *thin, think, thank*. When singing Latin American songs, use the same rules for the letter *s*. In Latin America, the letters *s* and *z* are pronounced in the same way. (See the letter *s* for a detailed discussion.)

		Latin American		Castillian
syllable initial	[s]	zambuco [sɑm bu ko]	[θ]	[θɑm bu ko]
		zarzuela [sɑr swe lɑ]	[θ]	[θɑr θwe lɑ]
word final	[s]	paz	[pɑs]	[θ] [pɑθ]
		haz	[ɑs]	[θ] [ɑθ]
final before voiced sound				
	[z]	paz de	[pɑz ðe]	[θ] [pɑθ ðe]
		juzgar	[xuz ɣɑr]	[θ] [xuθ ɣɑr]

Decide how to pronounce the following *z*'s in both the Latin American and Castillian dialects.

chori<u>z</u>o	pla<u>z</u>uela
ra<u>z</u>ón	a<u>z</u>ul
influen<u>z</u>a	a<u>z</u>úcar
cerve<u>z</u>a	<u>z</u>abullir
<u>z</u>alamería	re<u>z</u>no

English

Kenyon, John and Knott, Thomas. *A Pronouncing Dictionary of American English* Merriam-Webster, Springfield, Mass. 1953.

Lessac, Arthur. *The Use and Training of the Human Voice* Drama Book Publishers, New York 1967.

Marshall, Madeleine. *The Singer's Manual of English Diction* G. Schirmer, Inc., New York 1953.

Uris, Dorothy. *To Sing in English* Boosey and Hawks, New York and London 1971.

Wall, Joan. *International Phonetic Alphabet for Singers* Pst...Inc., Dallas1989.

Italian

Agard, Frederick and Di Pietro, Robert. *The Sounds of English and Italian* The University of Chicago Press, Chicago, 1965.
The Grammatical Structures of English and Italian The University of Chicago Press, Chicago 1965.

Coffin, Berton; Errolle, Ralph; Singer, Werner; and DeLattre, Pierre. *Phonetic Readings of Songs and Arias* Pruett Press, Inc., Boulder, Colorado 1964.

Colorni, Evelina. *Singers' Italian* G. Schirmer, Inc., New York 1970.

Errolle, Ralph. *Italian Diction for Singers Third Edition* Pruett Press, Boulder, Colorado 1963.

Hall, Robert A. *Descriptive Italian Grammer* Cornell University Press and Linguistic Society of America, Ithaca, N.Y. 1948.

Hoare, Alfred. *A Short Italian Dictionary* Cambridge University Press, Cambridge, Mass. 1967.

Love, Catherine E. *Collins Italian-English Dictionary* Berkley Books, New York, 1982.

Melzi, Robert C. *The Bantam New College Dictionary Series* Bantam Books, New York 1980.

Moriarty, John. *Diction* E. C. Schirmer Music Co., Boston, Massachusetts 1975.

Rebora, Piero. *Cassell's Italian Dictionary* Macmillan Publishing, New York 1981.

Wise, Claude. *Applied Phonetics* Prentice-Hall, Inc., Englewood Cliffs, NJ 1957.

Bibliography

Latin

De Angelis, Michael and Nicola A. Montani. *The Correct Pronciation of Latin According to Roman Usage* St. Gregory Guild, Inc., Philadelphia 1937.
(This pamphlet contains translations and pronunciations for many sacred texts.)

Diamond, Wilfrid. *Liturgical Latin.* Benziger Bros. Inc., New York 1941.
A dictionary of Liturgical Latin Bruce Publishing Co., New York 1961.

Hines, Robert S. *Singer's Manual of Latin Diction and Phonetics* Schirmer Books, New York 1975.
(This book contains IPA transcriptions and translations of many sacred texts.)

Liber usualis Edited by the Benedictines of Solesmes Desclee and Co., Tournai, Belgium 1947.

Moriarty, John. *Diction* E. C. Schirmer Music Co., Boston, Mass 1975.

Simpson, D. P. *Cassell's Latin and English Dictionary* Collier Books, Macmillan Publishing Co., New York 1987.

Traupman, John C. *The New Collegiate Latin and English Dictionary* Bantam Books, Inc., New York, 1966.

Trusler, Ivan. *The Choral Director's Latin* University Press of America, Lanham, MD 1987.

German

Fischer, Kammersangerin Lore. Personal voice study and observation of German Lied Master Classes. Stuttgart & Munich West Germany and Weimar, East Germany, 1969 - 1989.

Grebe, Paul, ed. *Duden Rechtschreibung der deutschen Sprachen und der Fremdworter* Bibliographisches Institut AG, Mannheim 1958.

Hey, Julius. *Der kleine Hey: Die Kunst des Sprechens* Newly edited by Fritz Reusch. B. Schott's Sohne, Mainz 1956.

Langenscheidt's Taschenworterbuch Deutch-English English Deutcsh

Mangold, Max, ed. *Duden Aussspracheworterbuch* Duden Volume 6. Bibliographisches Institut, Mannheim 1974.

Messinger, Heinz. *Langenscheidts Handworterbuch* Deutsch- English Barnes & Noble, Inc., New York 1961.

Moulton, William G. *The Sounds of English and German The Contrastive Structure Series,* Charles A. Ferguson, general editor The University of Chicago Press, Chicago 1962.

Sheil, Richard. *A Manual of Foreign Language Dictions for Singers* Fourth edition Edacra Press, Fredonia, N.Y. 1986.

Siebs, Theodor. *Deutsche Hochsprache Buhnenaussprache* Walter De Gruyter & Co., Berlin 1958.

French

Bernac, Pierre. *The Interpretation of French Song* Praeger Publishers, New York 1970.

Coffin, Berton; Errolle, Ralph; Singer, Werner; and DeLattre, Pierre. *Phonetic Readings of Songs and Arias* Pruett Press, Inc., Boulder, Colorado 1964.

Cox, Richard G. *The Singer's Manual of German and French Diction* G. Schirmer, New York 1970.

Girard, Denis. *Cassell's French Dictionary* Macmillan Publishing Co., New York 1981.

Grubb, Thomas. *Singing in French* Schirmer Books, New York 1979.

Mansion, J. E. *Harrap's Modern College French and English Dictionary* Charles Scribners' Sons, New York 1972.
> This dictionary contains transcriptions of words using the International Phonetic Alphabet.

Moriarty, John. *Diction* E. C. Schirmer Music Co., Boston, Massachusetts 1975.

Sheil, Richard F. *A Manual of Foreign Language Dictions for Singers* Palladian Co., Arcade, N.Y. 1979.

Steiner, Roger J. *The Bantam New College French and English Dictionary* Bantam Books, New York 1972.
> This dictionary contains transcriptions of words using the International Phonetic Alphabet.

Wall, Joan. *The International Phonetic Alphabet for Singers* Pst, Inc., Dallas 1989.
> This book is a manual that teaches the symbols of the International Phonetic Alphabet.

Warnant, Leon. *Dictionnarire de la pronunciation francaise* Editions J. Duculot, Gembloux 1968.
> This is a pronouncing dictionary and contains no definitions and indicates both conversational and stage diction as well as names of important people and places.

Spanish

Alarcos Llorach, Emilio. *Fonologia Espanola* Editorial Gredos, Madrid 1976.

Cressey, William. *Spanish Phonology and Morphology: A Generative View* Georgetown University Press, Washington, D.C. 1978.

Dalbor, John B. *Spanish Pronunciation: Theory and Practise* Holt, Rinehart, and Winston, New York 1980.

Finch, Diane F. and Ortiz, Hector. *A Course in English Phonetics for Spanish Speakers* Heinemann Educational Books, London 1982.

Nash, Roje. *Comparing English and Spanish: Patterns in Phonology and Orthography* Regents Publishing Co., New York 1977.

Stockwell, Robert P. and Bowen, J. Donald. *The Sounds of English and Spanish* The University of Chicago Press, Chicago, 1970.

About the Authors

Joan Wall is Professor of voice at Texas Woman's University, where she has taught diction courses for over twenty years. Ms. Wall is an active member of NATS, presents seminars and workshops, and has had a celebrated international performing career, singing as a principal performer with the Metropolitan Opera, the Deutche Oper Berlin, and in concerts, operas, and recitals throughout the United States. She has sung under the direction of such conductors as Leinsdorf, Mitropoulos, Goldovsky, Wallenstein, Morel, Cleva, Brusilow, and Hindemith. Ms. Wall is also the author of <u>Anyone Can Sing</u> and <u>International Phonetic Alphabet for Singers</u>.

Robert Caldwell has taught voice and performance at Texas Women's University and currently conducts master classes and seminars throughout the U. S. on performance. He maintains a private consulting practice for professionals for a wide variety of performance situations. He is the author of <u>The Performer Prepares</u> and <u>MusiKeys Sightreading Primer,</u> and edited the <u>International Alphabet for Singers</u>.

Tracy Gavilanes is Professor of Linguistics at the Pontificia Universidad Catolica del Ecuador, where she has taught phonetics and linguistics for the last fifteen years. She has also taught Linguistics at Georgetown University in Washington, D. C. Ms. Gavilanes is an active speaker throughout South America on topics of Bilingual Education. She founded the Fulbright commission in Ecuador, and works as an Acedemic Specialist for Scott Foresman International Division (Linguistics). Her publications include <u>English Phonology for Teachers</u>, PUCE, Quito, 1989 and <u>Manual of Corrective Phonetics</u>, PUCE, Quito, 1989.

Sheila Allen, Associate Professor of Voice and Coordinator of Vocal Studies at Texas Christian University, has taught voice, diction, and vocal literature at T. C. U., S.U.N.Y. Fredonia, and Washington State University. She has studied the German language and repertoire as a Fulbright scholar to Stuttgart, during summer seminars in Weimar, and most recently, in Munich on a grant from T.C. U. specifically geared to the improvement of the teaching of German diction. Her performance activities include recitals and appearances as soloist in contemporary, operatic, and orchestral repertoire in the United States and Europe. She has sung under the direction of such conductors as Sergiu Comissiona, Helmut Rilling, Walter Hendl, Howard Hanson, Lucas Foss, and Simyon Bychkov, and recorded for C.R.I., the Public Broadcasting System, and Deutschlandfunk. Dr. Allen holds degrees from the Oberlin Conservatory and the Eastman School of Music.

International Phonetic Alphabet for Singers
A manual for English and foreign language diction
Joan Wall
ISBN: 1-8777 61-50-8   18.95

UNIQUE ARTICULATION WORKBOOK FOR SINGERS

IPA for Singers in the companion volume to this reference. Diction for Singers. It is an articulation drill workbook designed to lead the reader to a complete and thorough awareness of using their articulators. Because the IPA is used extensively in diction and vocal pedagogy, Ms. Wall used this alphabet as a basis for identifying and defining sounds of language.

"While teaching singers about vowel modification, it became clear that they needed a much fuller grasp of how they produced their sounds. To take advantage of the plethora of tools for singers, which all depend on the IPA, they needed an awareness of how to adjust their articulators with far more precision than usual. The IPA offers the best basis for developing that precision. It also enables them to take advantage of phonetic spellings of foreign language arias and songs " says Ms. Wall.

After introducing the IPA, Ms. Wall covers the forward vowels, back vowels, central vowels, diphthongs, stop plosive, fricatives, nasals, lateral, and glide consonants. Each section focuses on the specific sound, how to produce it in the vocal tract, how to avoid the common problems with that sound, how to hear that sound. Drill exercises follow, which include distinguishing the sound from other closely related sounds, writing the symbols, transcribing the symbols from known and unknown words, and singing the sounds. Copious notes fill the margins to clarify individual points and answer sheets for the exercises are included in the appendix. The exercises can be accomplished quickly, while at the same time, drilling the base distinctions of awareness every singer needs.

The entire book is written so that the singer can lead themselves through it, and, because of its effectiveness for singing teachers, it has been widely adopted as an auxiliary text — both for diction courses and for studio lessons.

"I am writing this letter to tell you how excited I am to be using your new book International Phonetic Alphabet for Singers. I was first turned on to English Diction by Dorothy Uris whom I have known for twenty-five years and for whom I did much research for her book To Sing in English. Over the years I have valued this book and her inspiration to me while at the same time bemoaning its clumsiness and verbosity. Therefore I had set out to streamline it and add many practical notes from my own experience. How exciting to see so many of my own thoughts and drills mirrored in your new book! It is as if you have saved me the trouble of re-writing To Sing in English. Congratulations!"

Lyndon Poston-Smith
Southwestern Baptist Theological Seminary

"IPA for Singers is a wonderful new addition to the literature for singers, conductors, and teachers. It's well organized, clear, and full of excellent examples, which makes the IPA a useful tool and wipes away the mystery many people feel in regard to this century old tool for languages. I heartily recommend this book to all who want to improve their knowledge and skills with singing diction."

Dr. Leonard Van Camp
Southern Illinois University

The Performer Prepares

ISBN: 1-877761-25-7 16.95

NEW BOOK TEACHES PERFORMANCE TECHNIQUE

Music educators know the frustration of bringing a student to his or her technical peak only to hear it subverted in a less-than-peak performance. Performer of all types often anguish over their inability to convey their artistry effectively to audiences. For the last decade, performance consultant Robert Caldwell has been helping music educators and performer develop and master performance skills that bring peak results over and over. As a private consultant, Caldwell has demonstrated his techniques to thousands of educator and performers nationwide.

Caldwell explains that his pragmatic approach to improving performance gets results because he doesn't prescribe rigid, arbitrary quick-fixes that may or may not suit a particular performer. Rather, the strategies provide performers of all kinds with the tools needed for individually crafting a program that leads to powerful performances—performances tailored to fit each artist. Educators can adapt Caldwell's techniques for each student, helping all to achieve his or her best.

Trained as a pianist and vocalist, Caldwell maintains a private consultancy and holds master classes while lecturing extensively at such institutions as the University of Texas at Austin, the University of Arkansas at Little Rock, and Texas Women's University. The Author holds a bachelor's degree in piano performance and a graduate degree in vocal pedagogy. His is also the author of MusiKeys Sightreading Primer, an innovative approach to sightreading. In addition, Caldwell has edited and co-authored two works for singers, the former a manual aiding vocalists in using the International Phonetic Alphabet, and the latter a reference for foreign-language diction for singers.

The nuts-and-bolts nature of Caldwell's program is based on his conviction that performance charisma is not an innate quality, but rather a set of skills that can be learned and perfected. The astonishing results Caldwell can point to place him in the vanguard of performance study and his strategies are in line with the current theory on personal development. But Caldwell stresses that the process he outlines in The Performer Prepares involves the performer not in theoretical speculation but in challenging exercises that can lead to real change and continuing improvement.

APPROACH EMPHASIZES WORK, NOT SHORTCUTS

Just as there is no substitute for wood-shedding a difficult passage of music, Caldwell contends there is no getting around the work needed to attain a top-notch performance. Performance work —in addition to technical and interpretive work—is essential, Caldwell explains in the opening chapter of The Performer Prepares: it's a practical and necessary element that must be developed beforehand in order to fully exploit the performer's artistry onstage. After introducing the reader to the concept of performance work, the author goes on to described the conditions that signal readiness to perform and guarantee peak results. "The performer's job description could read, 'build a congruent, compelling, and potent internal state and take it into the performance,'" Caldwell writes. Next the author outlines specific techniques for getting at what will achieve that all-important internal state, dealing with such considerations as conflicts and commitment, action and outcome, possibility and physiology, objections, stage fright, and audience connection. Chapter VIII, an annotated transcript from one of the author's master classes, shows Caldwell's strategies in action. The final chapter is devoted to artistic evolution, providing guidance for continued development over a lifetime of performance.

"The art of performance is the art of pulling yourself together for the time on stage. It all begins with you, so you might as well pay attention to what you want, your objections, and what you need to solve them. You might as well approach the subject with an attitude of skill, rather than talent. You will accomplish more, " Caldwell explains.

"You performances will work when you develop what you want in music.Your desires will include states of mind, emotions, attitudes, skill acquisition, career achievements... Maybe you don't know what kind of performer you want to be. Maybe you don't know what music to select or how to respond to the person in charge of the concert or audition...This is your performance work—to shine a bright light on every aspect of the performance, to address every one of your concerns, and to tailor each one into something you genuinely desire so that, in the end, everything about the performance fits you like a glove, Then, complete commitment will naturally follow, the music will hit its peak, and you will deliver a powerful performance."

Designed as a tool that will be reached for again and again, The Performer Prepares offers quick scanning via the information included in its wide margin. Effective graphics serve as worksheets for use with the techniques. Extensive indexing allows easy access for future review of the material. The book and companion tape are available from Pst..Inc.

"I think the book The Performer Prepares can and should be of definite help to many musicians who either aspire to perform or having started to appear on stage need help, be it of psychological or just simply practical nature.

I don't know of another book of its kind. It is well researched, well-meant, and deserves recognition and a lot of attention. "
Vladimir Ashkenazy

"he Performer Prepares is an exciting, insightful book which shows performers how to attain 'inspired performance.' Musicians who are interested in self-mastery can reach expanded levels of performance by using the practical, convincing, and encouraging suggestions offered by Robert Caldwell."
Joan Wall

Pst...Inc. Order Form **1-800-284-7043**

Title	Price	Qty	Amt
The Performer Prepares	16.95		
Diction for Singers	29.95		
International Phonetic Alphabet for Singers	18.95		
The Performer Prepares, Master Class Video Tape	39.95		
The Overtones of Bel Canto	35.00		
Phonetic Readings of Songs and Arias	22.50		
Word-By-Word Translation of Songs and Arias: German and French	32.50		
Word-By-Word Translation of Songs and Arias: Italian	32.50		
Pronunciation Dictionary of American English	12.95		
Repertoire for the Solo Voice	89.50		
The Structure of Singing	35.00		
Great Singers on Singing	12.95		
Master Class with Maria Callas	25.00		
Sherril Milnes at Julliard, video tape	42.50		
The Science of the Singing Voice	32.50		
Singer's Repertoire, Volume I	19.50		
Singer's Repertoire, Volume II	19.50		
Singer's Repertoire, Volume III	19.50		
Singer's Repertoire, Volume IV	19.50		
Singer's Repertoire, The Whole Set	62.50		
The Science of Vocal Pedagogy	22.95		
The Unabashed Self Promoter's Guide	34.00		
Phonetic Readings of Brahms Lieder	25.00		
Sounds of Singing	32.50		
Getting it Together	18.50		
The Performing Artists Handbook	10.95		
Through the Jingle Jungle	22.95		
An Interpretive Guide to Operatic Arias	27.50		
Large, Wall Mount IPA Symbols (laminated)	30.00		
	SUBTOTAL		
	SHIPPING (2.50, plus .50 for each additional book)		
	TAX (8% if Texas Resident)		
	TOTAL		

Name _____

Address _____

City, St. Zip _____

Phone _____

Enclose check with order and mail to:
Pst...Inc   P.O. Box 800208   Dallas, Tx. 75380